Lucky Girl: Growing up
Italian-American in Appalachia

Lucky Girl: Growing up Italian-American in Appalachia

A MEMOIR

Jane DiVita Woody

ISBN: 1977666280
ISBN 13: 9781977666284
Library of Congress Control Number: 2017915562
CreateSpace Independent Publishing Platform
North Charleston, South Carolina

In Memory of My Parents
Benny (Liborio) and Josephine Maruca DiVita

Contents

Acknowledgments   ix

Introduction   xi

Chapter 1   Love and Marriage   1

Chapter 2   My Dad's Car Accident   19

Chapter 3   The First Family: Three Brothers   30

Chapter 4   The Second Family: Three More Brothers   43

Chapter 5   Tomboy-Girlie Girl   62

Chapter 6   Family and Food   77

Chapter 7   Our Town: Location, Location, Location   93

Chapter 8   In the Name of the Father   111

Chapter 9   School: My Sanctuary   123

Chapter 10 Two Women   135

Chapter 11 The Box Office   152

Chapter 12 Dad and Alcohol   163

Chapter 13 Across the Tracks: College Miracle and Magic   175

Chapter 14 Leaving Home: Stage One   187

Chapter 15 Leaving Home: Stage Two   195

Chapter 16 My Mother, Myself   210

Chapter 17 Hello, Daughter   220

Notes   225

Acknowledgments

I AM GRATEFUL TO READERS who reviewed my work in various stages. Valuable suggestions for early pieces came from Instructor James McKean and fellow students Rosemarie Iwassa, Lee Black, Joe Jobbits, and Rick Thomas, in the 2015 memoir workshop at the University of Iowa Summer Writing Festival. For reading early versions of the first three chapters, I thank my friend and former colleague, Robin Russel, and Instructor David Phillip Mullins and students in his 2016 graduate prose workshop at Creighton University (Quentin Chirdon, Meredith Spears, Chris Hamel, Marta Fiedler, Meghan Townley, Arnulfo Hermes, and Jim McFarland). Robin Stratton of Big Table Publishing also offered helpful suggestions.

Thank you, my dear brothers, Ed, Bob, Phil, and Richard, for reading the complete manuscript, answering my endless questions, verifying accuracy, and offering ideas and new information. I am grateful to my cousin Charlie for his encouragement and some old photos. To my daughter Jennifer Woody, your close reading and honest responses sparked many improvements. My sons Bob and Matt will read the book here for the first time as I did not want my manuscript to add to the demands of their current lives.

I am also indebted to the many family members, friends, and neighbors mentioned in my memoir. They helped to nurture me as I grew up. Finally, to the best editor, proofreader, and soulmate, husband Robert Woody, my deepest thanks for your skills, encouragement, and love.

Introduction

THE STROKE THAT KILLED MY mother was her third. The second one had left her confined to a wheel chair in a nursing home, unable to speak except for gibberish sounds, instead of the messages her functioning mind intended. She was eighty-one.

The date was April 1, 1994, Good Friday. I was home alone, no classes to teach that day when Frank, my oldest brother, phoned, his call leaving me in a state of shock, heart pounding, barely able to stifle and fight off tears and keep listening. The funeral was set for several days later, allowing me, her only daughter, and three out-of-town sons, to arrive in Montgomery, West Virginia, where she had lived nearly all her married life. My husband Bob and I would travel from Omaha, Ed and Pat from Los Angeles, Gene and Kathleen from Houston, and Bob and Arlene from Grand Rapids, Michigan. Our three West Virginia brothers lived much closer to Mother: Frank in the same town and Phil and Richard about thirty miles away.

Frank must have told me more details about the funeral arrangements, but I only remember that I needed to make plane reservations and bring an outfit for the funeral director to dress her in.

Unable to reach my husband at the university, I immediately went into high gear on my own. I made the flight arrangements, then took off for TJ Maxx to buy the dress. That didn't take long: appearing as if by magic, a lovely pink two-piece light-weight summery suit with long sleeves, size eight. But once back home paralysis and stupor claimed my body and brain. I drew a blank for my own clothes to take—stuck, unable to think or decide. I called my daughter Jennifer, then twenty-nine and working as a school psychologist in the city. She listened to my quivering voice and realized that I needed someone to take care of me. She would bring me a long dark multi-print skirt of hers to wear for the funeral and shop to get me a black blazer to go with it.

Getting there—the flight, the car rental, the twenty-five-mile drive to my hometown—I don't recall any of it. The next distinct memory, the evening visitation at the funeral home. Mother's body was so tiny. I should have gotten a size two dress, but the undertaker had pinned it back to fit. More feelings of failure struck: should I have known how the body shrinks? I knew nothing about death and funerals. Suddenly I remembered twenty-one years ago when my father died. On arriving home then and seeing my mother sitting on the couch, I had hidden my shock when she had cried out, moaning, "Oh, Jane, he's gone, gone." Of course, I went to hug her but remained startled, maybe embarrassed, by her uncontrolled expression of grief.

My mother's funeral service and luncheon reception for guests went off perfectly, just as she had planned: a Catholic Mass of Christian Burial, ending with everyone singing her favorite, a Protestant hymn, "Amazing Grace."

The next day we seven siblings talked and shared about our lives, glad to be together, even if for the sad occasion of our mother's funeral. We were comfortable with each other, reminiscing but no highly personal or intimate conversations. I was convinced they had all been closer to Mother than me, had more memories than I did of her recent years. I rationalized why so few visits back to see her: I had a demanding career, not to mention a husband and three children approaching "young adulthood" with ups and downs.

Later that day a major task lay before us: go to Mother's house and make decisions about her "things." We descended on her Fourth Avenue home, the house we had built for her after Dad died, all us contributing money and the local brothers adding their sweat labor. Everyone ready to jump in and take care of the business at hand, just as our family had trained us to do. The mood seemed almost lighthearted. If we were having sad or complicated feelings about Mother's death, these remained private, unspoken.

At some point we entered her bedroom and looked in the closet and chest of drawers, everything neatly organized. Besides holding a few clothing items, the drawers yielded several large yellow mailing envelopes stuffed with papers. Also, several small notebooks and writing pads appeared in full view. Most surprising, a small yellowed packet of letters tied with a thin, tattered red ribbon. Someone untied this and discovered five love letters our father had written to our mother before their wedding. At this point our search stopped. Almost disbelieving what we saw, we began passing the letters around. Holding them gently, our sense of surprise gave way to a trickle of tears. We read them out loud for each other, enchanted by our father's tender words of love and passion, all handwritten in his broken English using phonetic spelling. Reluctantly we put aside the letters and kept searching.

The more we rummaged drawers and purses and small boxes in the closet the more we discovered what felt like a hidden treasure. So many papers. We saw Mother's handwriting gracing pages of notebook paper, large and small writing pads, the backs of bank deposit slips, greeting cards, and all manner of paper scraps. The pieces were dated, so she must have been writing a diary of some sort. Who was this mother? Someone we didn't know.

We began to talk in bits and pieces about her diary entries, then shouting with each new discovery. Only gradually did we sense that all of this was her legacy. The conversation turned to mish-mash, everyone talking at once: "I can't believe she did all this." "I had no idea." "She wrote about us and everything that was going on in her life." "Who knew?" "She dared to reveal herself—I couldn't do that." At some point we realized that we needed to collect and deal with all of it later. I volunteered: I would keep, safeguard, organize it, type everything and keep everyone posted on my progress.

And I did. The dated entries began in 1965 and ended in 1991. They documented Mother's visits to her adult children out of state as well as accounts of her daily activities at home, with her West Virginia sons and their families and other friends and relatives. Four years later, I had all entries in chronological order and had typed them into computer files, everything laid out for printing. I had added copies of our father's love letters and a few family photos and documents. I gave a title: "Memoirs of Josephine Mary Maruca DiVita" and had Kinko's print copies with a spiral binding. Now we had a printed book, her gift to her descendants—all finished and ready for exploring her world. (When I quote from her Memoirs here, I cite the page number in the text.)

That compilation of my mother's Memoirs should have pushed me to act on my own long-standing intention to write about my growing up—my childhood with my parents and brothers. Through the years, with a vague notion of writing our family's history, I had scribbled notes and stored them away in folders in my filing cabinet. I imagined telling the story of seven siblings growing up, from the 1930s to the 1970s, in a large Italian-American family in a small town in Appalachia. I was proud of my family: I wanted to say, "Look what we accomplished." I wanted to capture the truth of a family both ordinary and special. But the only truth—I hadn't written a line, and my notes remained secreted away in their hiding place. Then in 2014, all that changed when I retired from my university professorship. But was it too late, too long ago, to remember and write about our lives?

I began my memoir, struck by its several transformations. First, it would be a kind of family history, a legacy for us seven siblings and our children and their offspring. I wanted to honor our parents and how they encouraged and supported their children's achievements. Yet my mother's oft-spoken warning against pride haunted me: "I don't brag about my children, I will let others do that." Then my vision of the memoir changed. It would have to be my story, my experiences and character, the so-called historical facts emanating strictly from my perceptions, my truth.

So much to tell, so many influences making me the person I was and became. I trace the diverse and colorful threads that made up the fabric of my life, then and now. I thought I knew the exact bolt of cloth from which I was cut. Maybe I started thinking more deeply about my character and identity as I took a new look at my mother's Memoirs. Could I do what she had done and write honestly about myself and my life? I thought no. I had always kept my feelings to myself, guarded my privacy, kept my own counsel. Whatever you call it—that was the real me. How did I come to be this way? As I allowed more questions about myself, it seemed high time to admit that I didn't have all the answers.

I started: scrambling, unearthing the old notes and furiously scribbling new ones on any handy scrap of paper—just like my mother. This project became my *raison d'etre*, and I feared I wouldn't finish it (although my health was and remains good). I had to move fast and consistently even as the clutter in my messy office swelled to near chaos levels.

I have aimed for accuracy in my recollections and corroborated details as needed with notes taken through the years, information from my brothers, and documents from family and the Internet. The memoir contains imagined, recreated situations and events—most that I witnessed and vividly recalled, some that I recalled but without details, and others that I heard about as a child or adult. The truth flows from my understanding of the characters. In a few cases initials replace actual names.

It has taken much energy to manage my ever-shifting emotions and keep writing, as so many feelings pushed against my usually well-defended psyche. Regret and guilt penetrated, especially for my silence and negligence. Why didn't I ask my parents about their lives when I had the chance? Why didn't I realize their sadness as four of their children left, moving to distant states? Why didn't I look deeper into my own personality all those years that I provided therapy for others and taught graduate students about human behavior?

Excuses abound. More and more I see myself as a puzzle with missing pieces. Is it now too late to find the lost pieces of my character and fill in the whole puzzle? What picture will appear as I write, and will I be able to accept what I see?

CHAPTER 1

Love and Marriage

Jo and Benny
sitting in a tree
K-I-S-S-I-N-G.
First comes love,
then comes marriage,
then comes baby
in a baby carriage.

OF COURSE, JO WAS SCARED. Why wouldn't she be? She had just awakened, the morning of her wedding day: exactly sixteen and a half years old. A few days ago, her mother had sent her to her godmother to learn the facts of life and marriage—that was the Italian tradition. Afterwards, Jo worried: she understood yet didn't. All she knew for sure was that she was very much in love with Benny, who this morning was still asleep in the room her brothers shared.

It was love at first sight. Benny had been working around Adrian, West Virginia. Somehow on his road construction job, he got acquainted with Jo's older brother, Sandy, who invited him, a fellow Italian, to come to his house for dinner. Expecting them, Jo and her younger sister, Betty, spotted the two men walking down the railroad tracks toward the Maruca home. Surprising even herself, she said to Betty, "I hope he ain't married." So, who was Benny, her husband-to-be and my future father?

I see this handsome twenty-eight-year-old man traveling in central rural West Virginia in 1928, with a road construction crew that worked long hours. This terrain so different from his Kanawha Valley home. Here he felt a sense of freedom: the expanse of gently rolling hills and green meadows dimmed memories of his years in the coal mines, left him feeling happy with his job of driving a dump truck. The men stayed in boarding houses and ate whatever was served. But Benny, with love on his mind not food, somehow found paper to write letters, and tiny post offices to mail them, to sixteen-year old Josephine, my future mother. Soon after their first meeting in July they became engaged.

His love letters began in August—in his own cursive handwriting and using his immigrant's phonetic spelling of English. Although Mother had told me stories about meeting my father and her disappointment with their wedding picture, she had never mentioned love letters. There were only five, all written on small unlined tablet paper, placed in envelopes addressed to "Miss Josephine Maruca, Adrian, w va," and dated from August 16 through October 28, 1928. The greetings included: "Dearest Josephine," "My Loving Joe," "Dear Sweethart." We knew our father could read and write in English, and surmised that he had taught himself, but such intimate expressions of love came as a surprise.

With only a fifth-grade Sicilian education, thirteen-year old Benny had come to America in 1913, with his mother and three siblings. Francesco, husband and father of the children, had arranged their travel and awaited their arrival in southcentral West Virginia, where Ellis Island agents had sent him to work in the coal mines. There the rugged mountains, rivers, valleys alive with green, so different from their town of Valguarnera, Sicily, where the low, brown, dry foothills meant grinding poverty.

The letters revealed a man undaunted by the distances separating him from Jo, allowing only short, unpredictable visits. Consumed with thoughts of his fiancé, he reassured her with words that showed a heart overflowing with love, passion, tenderness, and high hopes for their future together. The summary remarks and brief excerpts below reveal a man disclosing his soul.

August 16-28: He wrote that there was trouble with one of the trucks, he was trying for another job, and he couldn't see her for ten days.

"Joe I love you and I can[t] forget you Im thinging about you all time . . . I will send you my best love and kisses."

August 30-28: "I wish wee were married so you can stay whit me all time but it won't be long know Just about six weeks."

Sept 10-28: He told her he couldn't sleep, staying awake "about three hour Just wearing about you becase I love you an I can[t] do without you."

Sept 28-28: He wrote that he may not come to see her until they finish a work job. "Joe I no that you love me but I love you Just as much and I allway wil. You the onley girl that I care from now on becase I love you with all my heart." Under the flap of the envelope he added: "I am goin save Some money to by close for our Baybe."

Oct 7-28: He explained he didn't come to see her because he had no way to get there and he was nearly done where he was working. He apologized: "Joe. I hope you dint get mad about that little Joke about Baby. . . . Joe I hate to hear that you have a bad cold but I hope you get better. I give you my best love . . . ."

The wedding was set for November 4, at the Catholic Church in Clarksburg, West Virginia, about fifty miles from Jo's home. Benny took charge of all arrangements, including her wedding dress.

Last night Jo was thrilled when Benny arrived and handed her several boxes. He had selected and brought her entire wedding outfit. She took her mother's hand, moving her to the back bedroom to open the packages. Under white tissue paper, all white silk. Lifting only the dress slightly, almost afraid, never had she seen such beautiful things. "Bella, bella," her mother said and left the room. Jo stifled tears, knowing her mother was sick again, didn't have a nice dress, and wouldn't be attending the wedding.

Jo slightly nudged Betty sleeping beside her. "I need to get dressed. I want to be ready. I don't know how long the drive to Clarksburg will take. Benny made all the arrangements."

Opening the box, Betty, though just eleven, took charge. "Start with the underclothes and slip and then the silk stockings." Hands shaking, Jo lovingly picked up one item at a time, holding each to her cheek, feeling its softness. She smiled and asked for help with the stockings. Then Betty held up the knee-length dress, white silk, flapper style, with beading along three horizontal rows of pointed scallops on the front. She said, "I can't believe Benny picked out such a beautiful dress. It looks so expensive."

When Jo was ready and looking in the tiny face mirror, she heard voices and movement in the rest of the house. "I'll hold the veil and gloves in the car and put them on when we're there. Papa and Benny should be ready by now. I wish Mommie could come too."

Jo worried that she didn't know the others who would be at the church. Benny's brother, Tony, and his wife Catherine would stand up for them, and a couple other of Benny's friends would also attend. She was thankful his parents weren't coming—she would meet them soon enough. After the wedding they would drive to Montgomery, three hours away, where they would live, only a mile away from his parents in Smithers.

"How do I look? I wish we had a big mirror."

Betty looked her over and said, "You're beautiful." And she was—a slim five-feet four inches, with the Maruca high cheek bones, fair skin, and abundant raven hair cut in short bob; she wished her lips were fuller.

As she entered the front room and saw Benny, he gave her a big smile. He too was all dressed up—a new dark single-breasted suit and white shirt, brightened with a stylish red polka-dot bow tie. Her father Alphonso, wearing his only old dark suit, white shirt, no tie, stood, uncomfortable, but ready by the door. On leaving the house he took the front passenger seat beside Benny in the driver's seat. Jo, in the back, quiet, carefully held her veil and gloves on her lap. Thinking of leaving her family, especially her mother, she fought back tears. Always worrying, about everything—that was her nature. Once on the road, she relaxed a bit as Benny spoke in Italian to her father about the car, the traffic, and the towns they passed. Then remembering his love letters, she told herself that everything would be okay.

Never had Jo seen such a beautiful church: on the wall behind the altar, a wooden cross depicted Jesus crucified, and life-size statues stood on pedestals on either side. She somehow knew the one on the left was the Virgin Mary and guessed the other must be Joseph. With no Catholic church in their remote rural area, she and Betty had been attending, with their mother's blessing, a nearby small Protestant church, its structure and style simple and unadorned.

Benny introduced Jo to Tony and Catherine and the three others who were in the wedding party. Everyone was friendly, and Jo tried to talk a little, but she had never been around young people all dressed up for a social event. When it was almost time to line up with her father for the procession, she put on the long gloves and then struggled by herself with the veil, not thinking to ask help from Catherine, her attendant. The service, the words spoken, all seemed to float above her consciousness like a dream. She felt herself awakening at the end as Benny guided her out down the aisle. Then the wedding pictures. Jo felt the top of the veil slipping slightly down toward her forehead, but in her nervous state, didn't to try to fix it, just worried how it would look. Too late, the photographer was finished.

They left, driving first to take her father back home, say final goodbyes to her family, and then on to Montgomery. Jo had never been out of the Adrian area, so her eyes widened with the changing terrain as they drove south. "Benny, this looks so different, not rolling hills like home, these big mountains, so many trees." Then she was struck by the beauty of the evergreens and the remnants of fall colors on mostly bare branches.

"Just wait till you see what it's like in Montgomery," he said. Driving on the valley road next to the river, he told her they were almost there. Looking on the opposite side, Jo felt the nearness of the car to the looming mountain, the craggy tan rocks at eye level and trees above.

Benny explained, "See how they built the road, cutting out the bottom and top of the mountain. Heavy rain can bring rock slides down on the highway." He knew the geography of his home area: he was accustomed to the Kanawha River, the valley, and the mountains ranging from 2,000 to 3500 feet in height. But without schooling, he didn't know that his state sat in the middle of the Appalachian Plateau, didn't know this land's ancient history. "The area of West Virginia was part of a shallow sea throughout most of the Paleozoic Era. It was mildly disturbed by tectonic developments that raised mountains to its east, along the continental edge, but mainly it accepted sediments from those mountains from Cambrian time (more than 500 million years ago) into the Permian (about 270 million years ago)."[1]

What Benny did know and feel was fatigue from the long day and long drive, but this had not dimmed anticipation of his wedding night with his beloved. As the evening shadows descended Jo felt a sense of being closed in. She missed her familiar home and worried about living in this new place. But she said nothing.

They arrived in Montgomery at the small furnished apartment Benny had rented on the second floor of a house on Sixth Avenue. Their first home—they would share it with Mary, Benny's younger sister, and her new husband. At age eighteen, she had incurred her father's wrath by running away and marrying her cousin.

The next day Benny and Jo drove the one mile across the Kanawha River to Smithers so that his parents, Francesco and Filippa, could meet the bride. As they parked in the backyard, Benny described how he had helped his father build this house, proudly pointing out the maroon-colored, smooth cinderblock exterior of the foundation and the painted white wood frame siding above. He said, "So much nicer than our old coal company house." Approaching the kitchen door, they saw Filippa coming out, her husband behind her. Greetings were in Italian, and Jo was thankful that they easily understood each other. Filippa gave her a hug, but Francesco remained standing stiffly with a stern expression, although he accepted Jo's required kiss of respect. Jo saw their clothes as much nicer than anything her parents owned, but maybe they were dressed up for the occasion. Her father-in-law, wearing dress pants and a white dress shirt, appeared a couple of inches shorter than Benny. Jo barely noticed his short, grey-black hair and clipped mustache before looking to Filippa for rescue her from his dark piercing eyes on her face.

Shorter than Jo, with a thick middle left from ten pregnancies, Filippa wore a nice dress along with navy blue fabric house slippers with the sides cut out to prevent pain from bunions. She guided Jo into the living room to meet Benny's younger siblings. Katie, eleven, greeted her with a big smile and a hug, while Charlie, nine, and Jimmy, six, shyly said hello in English, planted a fleeting kiss on her cheek, and quickly ran out the front door. After snacks and drinks were set out, others arrived. Jo already knew Tony and wife Catherine from the wedding. Then she met two other younger brothers: Joe, twenty, and Frank, fourteen.

Everyone was speaking in Italian all at once. Jo heard her father-in-law's voice grow louder as his sons arrived and quickly understood his swearing complaints. For Tony and Joe, why didn't they bring wine and food? For Frank, why was he late? Tony and Joe answered back in Italian as if used to their father's angry criticism, but he continued reciting their past failures. Jo gave up on making small talk with the women and retreated behind Benny, shocked at the loud, angry voices, so different from her quiet humble family. Another worry: could she and Benny really have a happy life?

Weeks later Benny was pressured to move. Francesco said they should live in one of his properties (former coal company houses) just around the corner from his house—better to pay a father rent than a stranger. Tony and Catherine were already living in the family compound. So Benny and Jo rented a house there. Sister Mary and her husband followed suit—after a Catholic wedding, she was allowed to rejoin the family. The unpainted, weathered wood frame houses sat close together, not side by side, but clustered behind each other and a stone's throw from Francesco's house. Only a few steps on the dirt landscape to go back and forth to any house.

After one month Jo was pregnant, only gradually figuring out her condition as she struggled with nausea and vomiting. Explanations and reassurance came from her mother-in-law and sisters-in-law, Catherine and Mary, who were also in their first pregnancies. Jo knew she had a lot to learn and welcomed their advice. But she was different. While she listened to their talk and worries, she was naturally shy and quiet and wouldn't talk private stuff about husbands like they did. She depended on Benny: he comforted and reassured her about the pregnancy and her fear of Francesco's drinking, yelling, and railing against everyone.

Jo gave birth at home to the first male grandchild; the Italian tradition demanded he bear the name of the paternal grandfather. Francesco became his name but he was called Frankie. When he was born with light, almost blond hair, the in-laws whispered and criticized, saying he didn't look like Benny. Jo was shocked and hurt but let it pass. As a growing infant, Frankie willingly sat on the lap of his grandfather, "Big Poppy," who sometimes chewed up food and then put it in the baby's mouth. Disapproving of this for her baby, Jo remained silent to keep the peace. The grandparents lived by the customs of the old country.

Still, there were some pleasant times. She truly liked her sisters-in-law as they learned from each other about babies. Her mother-in-law also helped, but she had to care for her own three young children. And she could be bossy, warning the daughters-in-law with superstitions like the evil eye and folk tales about women who were unfaithful to husbands. When she was present they all spoke Italian; Jo mostly liked her company and was always respectful.

All the married families were expected every Sunday at the parents' home. The scene always the same: Francesco dominated with rants. He would sit at the kitchen table, sometimes placing his pistol in the middle. Benny and Tony were expected to bring him wine and whiskey, which they did despite Prohibition. Jo had learned that, after arriving and politely greeting Francesco, she should stand quietly and listen for a few minutes. This day he was angry that his teenage son Frank was not at home. Then he complained that Joe, his twenty-year old son, had not given any of his job earnings to his father for two weeks. And on and on it went. Jo had also learned to escape his tirades by settling in the living room where the "women folk" talked. Later they prepared and served the meal, first to the men, then the children, and lastly themselves.

It was at the rented house in Smithers where Benny and Jo's first six babies arrived. And where two of them died. The birth order: Frank (1929), Alphonso I (1931; died 1935), Eugene (1933), Edward (1935), Jane (1936), Alphonso II (1939; died 1940).

After the death of their four-year old Alphonso I at the local hospital, a dark cloud of grief shrouded the household. Still three young children required care: six-year old Frankie, Gene a toddler, and eight-month old Eddie. Even in the depths of sorrow, Jo and Benny went on living.

Now, a spontaneous scene sparks my imagination. Gene was almost three, and Eddie, an infant not yet walking. Within four months of burying their little boy, my mother was pregnant again—with me. Did her milk dry up with the anguish of her child's death, ending breast feeding for baby Eddie, leaving her vulnerable to this pregnancy? Several weeks in a row, feeling nauseous, she knows she is carrying another baby. She sits on a kitchen chair, with her body rocking Eddie, Gene tugging at her dress—all while I am tucked away snugly in her womb. Sadness envelopes her soul, but just as quickly she looks at her baby, hugs him tighter. Fighting back tears, she finds joy in Eddie's broad smiling face, and soothes her toddler, stroking his back. She prays, asking God for strength to endure the pain and to believe once again in the future. As I dwell within her, am I absorbing her conflicting feelings:

stifling sadness, allowing glimmers of hope and reason? Is her character flowing into my fetal brain?

After four boys, I arrived: a girl. What a surprise! Thrilled and happy, so from time to time, they put aside the unrelenting sorrow from the death of their little boy a year ago. Then they had to name me.

Benny worried, but said, "Our first girl. You know we have to name her for Mommie."

Jo, in bed cuddling my swaddled newborn body, sat up and said, "I don't see why. Tony and Catherine have a Phyllis and Mary and Benny also named their second daughter Phyllis after Filippa. Our little girl should have a name of her own."

Knowing she was right, still he said, "It's expected. I'm the oldest son, so I have to honor my mother. We will never hear the end of it if we don't."

In her heart she knew it was true: they would have to endure more criticism from Benny's parents and other family. She spoke up, holding her ground. "Okay, we will name her Phyllis Jane, but we will call her Jane." Benny agreed, relieved to let go that worry. Only my namesake grandmother, "Big Mommie," would call me by my full name, sounding it with her broken English as "Phyllisa-Jane."

The household was busier than usual but my parents were thankful that I was a healthy, easy baby. Frankie, age seven, happily held me occasionally so his mother could do housework and cooking. Since I was always physically active as a child and youth, I guess that I was walking before turning one-year old, wanting to get down and play rather than nurse. Now I wonder again if my mother ended breast feeding for me early, although people said it would keep you from getting pregnant. Four months after my second birthday, she was pregnant again yet could not speak of her mixed feelings and sense of weariness. Still, she carried on. The four children brightened her spirits, although sometimes when the sisters-in-law talked, she expressed frustrations, especially sharing with Mary, who also had a large family and was pregnant again.

Of course, as a three-year old, I have no memory of the birth in November 1939, of the new baby, another boy. He was named Alphonso II, to honor Jo's father. Once again, my parents relived a nightmare as he became sick with meningitis, the same illness that killed their little boy. The doctor offered no hope. The gods again struck our family: giving life and taking it away. The baby died at five months old.

As I write, I see my mother barely able to function, stricken by the loss of a second beloved child, but there was more pain. Benny arrived home one evening, just three days after the funeral. Jo was in the kitchen crying, then moved toward him, grabbing the front of his shirt with both hands. "Do you know what they're saying, your family?"

"What is it? What's going on?" His face shocked, ashen at her anger.

Wiping her tears with a dish cloth, she yelled. "Catherine told me what she heard."

"Jo, what are you talking about?" he asked again.

She took his hand. "They're blaming us for the baby's death."

"What did they say? Who said this?" His face fierce, yet a string of swearing remained stuck in his throat.

"They're blaming me for giving the baby my father's name. They said it was bad luck, giving him his dead brother's name. Benny, I can't stand this. Your parents are so cruel. Everyone in the family is repeating and whispering about this."

Calming himself and wrapping her in his arms, he said, "I'll talk to Mommie, but we just have to ignore this. They're old country and superstitious. We can't change them."

Three brief memories, images only, remain from my early life in Smithers, probably after the baby's death, when I am around three and a half years old. Still, they are vivid after all these years.

I am on the porch of our shabby, weathered, wood frame house. The yard and the narrow street in front are all dirt. My parents and I are watching a dog called Skippy run around (Is he ours? He's not in our lives later.)

In the second image my mother is in the kitchen fixing cornflakes with "canned" milk for ten-year old Frankie, who sits at a small table. She may be saying that there is no fresh milk, or he may prefer this kind of milk.

In the final image, next to our house sits a small plain concrete block building, a non-denominational "Protestant" church with outdoor concrete steps going down to the back-basement entrance. Several of us little cousins, two boys and two girls around three or four years old (we all live in Big Poppy's family home place), stand huddled, hidden away on the bottom step, some with pants down, apparently showing genitals, I remain outside the inner circle, feeling that this is a bad thing to do.

These memories, so intense at such a young age—do they foreshadow aspects of my future character? Maybe they will lead me to new discoveries about myself as I continue my story.

In 1940, my parents' Smithers saga came to an end. I believe they knew they had to escape that house of death, but they would never forget their lost children. I imagine them talking, making plans to move. Coming home from work at nine in the evening, Benny saw Jo setting his supper on the table. She asked, "What did you find out today?"

"I looked at a good place. It's a small apartment building in Montgomery. There's a large apartment on the second floor that faces the street, and in the back, two more with one bedroom."

"Which would we live in?"

"In the big one, of course. We need three bedrooms. I think we should buy the building."

"But we can't afford that."

"Well, I think I can get a bank loan. Then we pay it off from renting the smaller apartments. They gave me a loan to buy the two cars to set up the taxi business. The folks in the coal camps and hollers need a way to get back and forth to town, so we're making good money."

"Oh, Benny, can we? Can we really leave this place?"

"We will. Poppy will raise hell, but he does that anyway. It's only a mile away from them. Just two blocks to get to the taxi stand and the school is almost next door."

I believe the move gave my mother a new lease on life. Her desperation clearly appeared in her diaries (which I compiled and named "Memoirs"). In one entry she looked back in time and reminisced about my father's family (p. 62):

> I won't say any more about the elder DiVita family. It was a nightmare for me when I came into . . . a family environment like that. I just sometime (still do) wonder how I survived living there about 15 years and still have a sane mind (Smithers, that is).

In the new home she escaped Big Poppy's rants and the in-laws' daily scrutiny and squabbles. The sense of independence and relief allowed her to cope with recurring grief and care for her four living children.

The earliest memory I have of the new apartment home in Montgomery haunts me. It's the only visit from Big Mommie that I recall, so it may have been soon after we moved and she was there to help with cleaning and setting up the household. Suddenly she was confronting my mother and me in the kitchen, angrily waving a pair of my flour sack panties (which I had soiled and hidden behind the couch), calling out in Italian "Cacata." My face burning with shame, but I also felt hurt from being treated unfairly—I knew that I had been sick and couldn't help this accident. But I said nothing. That scene may have set the stage for my lifelong need to be in control and be perfect.

Once in our new home, with my father spending long hours at his taxi business, my mother was totally in charge of the household. Every morning she got my brothers off to school, just four houses away: Frankie in the fifth grade, Gene in the third, and Eddie in the first. I wanted to go with them but had to wait two more years to begin first grade. In summers, she allowed us to play outdoors, charging Eddie to watch over me and be back home for lunch and then for supper before Dad arrived. We kids soon had friends at school and in the neighborhood. And our parents also embraced the town. Mother met neighbors on both sides of our apartment and made a new best friend,

Mildred, whose husband was a state trooper. My father too added more acquaintances from people who owned or worked in the businesses in town, and he enjoyed getting to know his regular taxi customers.

We began to see the grandparents and kin in Smithers only on Sundays. And since Big Poppy's tirades continued to darken those excursions, no one looked forward to these visits. As years passed we kids even became bold enough to complain, "Do we have to go?" Yes, we always went, but, sadly, ended up avoiding both grandparents. Later as other family members departed from Big Poppy's compound, we had many pleasant gatherings at our different homes with uncles, aunts and cousins. Belonging to this large extended family, we hardly realized the absence of grandparents—especially since we had never felt love or pampering from them. As a result, our family became even more close-knit, self-directed, self-reliant.

Thinking of my parents' early years of marriage and family life, I now sense how this period influenced the course of my own life. Their personal histories and personalities spurred them on to early and later life-changing decisions that created an interesting family structure.

First, their love, courtship, and quick decision to marry. These actions flowed from their heritage: poor Italian immigrant families that asked little of life except to be able to work and have a better life than the one left behind. For his first job my father worked alongside his father in a Kanawha Valley coal mine, probably starting as a youth of fourteen or fifteen. At age eighteen, he reported "miner" as occupation on his 1918 draft registration. But no one in the family knows how much longer he worked in the mines, if he had other jobs, or when he began working as a laborer doing road construction. Clearly, he was employed at that job in August 1928, when he began writing to his fiancé.

After their marriage, again we lack information about his employment. Hard times were definitely underway. Between 1929 and World War II the coal industry greatly declined due to liquidation by many companies and mechanization to cut costs. "There were many days in 1932 and during the Depression when 80%-95% of the miners in dozens of coal towns across the U.S. were out of work—and even then, you were not guaranteed a full week's worth as jobs were often rationed."[2] Without coal production, many other job opportunities would have gone down the drain. How my father earned a living during this time when his family was growing is unknown. He was in the taxi business in 1942, and probably as early as 1940, when the move to Montgomery took place. But what of the intervening years?

I believe my father was proud to have a job driving a dump truck for road construction and saw it as a step up from the mines. Plus, more good luck, working in central West Virginia allowed him to meet his future bride, a young woman who was, like him, from an immigrant Italian family. Now I wonder if his driving experience birthed the idea to start the taxi and moving business.

The mines had also provided employment for my mother's father, Alphonso Maruca. He had been able to move his family out of the coal camp to a small house with land for a garden, near a tiny crossroads called Adrian. After he and his wife and daughter had emigrated from Calabria, Italy, in the mid-1900s, they initially spent time in the New York City area where he worked as a longshoreman. They ended up in rural central West Virginia and had eight more children, including my mother. From their shared immigrant family history, both of my parents had known hardship, so they were eager to work toward making a good life while still showing respect for and loyalty to family.

When it comes to personal characteristics, my parents' opposite personalities were mostly complementary in their early life together. During the courtship, they saw what they liked in each other and let themselves quickly fall in love, trusting the marriage would bring happiness. My father, as his love letters suggested and I witnessed, was affectionate (especially with young children), caring, easy going, humorous, enterprising, and mostly confident. From brief snippets I heard growing up, before marriage he had several women "chasing after him." But he was waiting for the right one: he found her in the virginal sixteen-year old Josephine.

In temperament, Mother was quiet, respectful, devoted to family, unassuming in demeanor though quite pretty, and given to worry and anxiety (before marriage she already had a snake phobia, stemming from the real childhood trauma of being chased by her brothers with a dead snake nailed to a stick).

These two partners must have seen each other as perfect mates. For her, my father was the experienced, confident older man who captured her heart with tender passion. For him, she was the lovely innocent Italian girl he had been waiting for. Aware of Benny's strong old country views of women, she likely did not tell him that she had been smart and competent in school and had wanted to become a teacher.

Their personalities blended smoothly after marriage while they lived in the DiVita family home place. But as the babies arrived and two children died, grief left them both weakened to manage life under the in-laws' domination. I think Mother began to assert herself and pushed my father to leave that place of sadness and turmoil. I believe they made the decision together to move yet barely realized how life-changing it would be for them and our family.

The move to Montgomery, just a mile away from the in-laws, took place in 1940, and created a family structure primed for ambition. By then, the town, population about 3,000, was a booming commercial center for the area's coal mining industry. It had paved streets and sidewalks, numerous retail and service businesses, schools, a hospital, and a state college. Smithers, the town left behind, was a "Little Italy" where Italian immigrants were dominant:

". . . Significant clusters of Italians were . . . drawn to southern West Virginia. . . .. [T]he Fayette County communities of Boomer, Harewood, Longacre, and Smithers constituted the greatest single concentration of Italians in the state. . . .. The great majority of Italian immigrants were employed in the coal industry as pick-and-shovel miners."[3]

Montgomery, on the other hand, was more of a "mini-melting pot" with only a few immigrants from each of several ethnic groups: Irish, Italian, Lebanese, Jewish, Syrian, Hungarian, Scots-Irish, Blacks, and English (the town's founders). Most of the residents were at the same lower middle-class status.

Once away from the in-laws, my parents no longer spoke Italian on a daily basis and were freed from the scrutiny, advice, and criticism from elders. The sense of relief energized them to pursue their own individual interests and ambitions. They could make new friends and take full charge of their children. They could openly laud education and set this expectation for their offspring, and they never feared or envied, as some Italian immigrants, their children's achievements. Despite early family tragedies, they kept their simple but optimistic dreams and hoped Montgomery would afford a decent living, a good life, and an even better future for their children.

Although the move loosened ties to our Italian heritage, my parents never consciously distanced from or rejected their culture. For obvious reasons, we children had never had a close, loving relationship with the grandparents, so that remained the same. And I believe my parents, with their strong wish to fit into American society, did not look back and had never intended to teach us to speak Italian.

As their elders before them had left an entire homeland for a much longer journey, my parents also took the risk of leaving the Smithers DiVita family compound. That decision, a new life in Montgomery, created ever expanding effects, as a pebble thrown in a pond sends ripples far and wide. It was the difference that created unique influences on our family. And these made me the person I was and am.

The new home may have eased the sorrowful memories of their dead sons, but they never forgot these children. My mother often mentioned their names in some passing conversation, only briefly, but always adding a blessing spoken in Italian. We kids knew that moment of sadness demanded our respect. She distinguished between the two boys, using the name Baby Alphonso for the infant who died. No stories about them or tears from her, just moments of remembrance. In fact, they already existed in my young mind. At five or six, I had a fantasy: on drives to visit relatives, seeing the carved rocks on the mountain running alongside the road, I imagined our two brothers buried in caves behind the rocks.

Years later in our second home, each of us kids separately discovered, but never spoke of, the green trunk in an upstairs bedroom closet that harbored precious mementos of our brothers' brief lives. We silently looked and touched them: a knit sweater set, booties, a couple of simple toys, a pair of worn leather shoes. There also, a dead-baby photograph of our infant brother: unbeknownst to Mother, this had been taken by our uncle who worked at the mortuary and its existence caused my mother unspeakable anguish. A wall in our parents' bedroom held a large, dark oval-framed formal photograph of four-year old Alphonso I standing in a white and bluish colored romper suit. His stomach appeared distended, his expression dour. Was he already seriously ill?

Why didn't we ask questions about our brothers who had died? Fear of our own feelings? Fear of causing sadness for our parents? Although we didn't realize it at the time, those heart-rending deaths shaped much their overly cautious care of us—they did not intend to lose another child.

One more discovery. All my life I knew my mother's birthday to be May 2. Now I have learned differently. Years ago at a family reunion in West Virginia, my brother Gene told youngest brother Richard a story while they were viewing the grave markers of our dead brothers. Mother's actual birthday was May 1. But since this was the date of Baby Alphonso's death in 1940, she decided she could not ever celebrate her birthday on that date and moved it to May 2. So she had her day of remembering her lost child, but also allowed a birthday celebration for her living children.

My parents' marriage, their personalities, the family tragedies, the distancing from grandparents, a new welcoming town—the memories and stories swirl around me. Am I entirely different from my parents? Which of my long-held notions about my history and myself will survive? For the first time, I seriously search for the missing and mixed up pieces of my personality puzzle and promise to take a hard look at the image that emerges. In the next chapter, and the next, and. . . .

CHAPTER 2

My Dad's Car Accident

ONE DAY I DIDN'T KNOW, the next day I knew—a terrible thing. My dad had been badly hurt in an automobile accident involving one of his taxi cabs. I had just turned seven, the fall of 1943. No one, not my mother or three older brothers, specifically told me about this. Maybe I became aware, overhearing talk among family, gradually absorbing bits and pieces of information. He was in the local hospital, his condition serious. But I don't remember feeling scared or worried, and no one told me everything would be okay. Gradually I would learn more. But later, my emotions came alive when a painful, puzzling feeling took up permanent residence in my psyche. That was the dawning of my sense of me as a person. Only in writing this memoir have I realized the impact of this accident on me and on our family.

We were living in Montgomery, the first family home that I clearly re-member—an upstairs apartment; the lower basement, sidewalk level housed a distribution center for mining equipment. Before this place we had lived in Smithers, which had imprinted on my three-year old mind only a couple of images. But the apartment I remember and liked a lot. A dark blue flowered wool rug covered much of the hardwood floor in the living room, which featured a couch in front of the spacious front window and on the opposite wall a large Philco wood radio, a hassock in front where my dad would sit while dialing for programs. A six-foot wide opening led to the kitchen, and between these two rooms on the floor, a large furnace register. The linoleum kitchen held a square white metal table near the middle—large enough to seat our family of six—and to the left a free-standing white metal kitchen cabinet next to the sink. Off to the left rear of the kitchen, the bathroom, and at the right rear, the door to the bedroom shared by my three older brothers. My parents' bedroom opened off the living room, and mine, very small and without a door, adjoined theirs. Outside, twelve concrete steps led up to the fenced stoop; from there stretched a clothesline on a pulley for hanging the wash.

Once I was aware of the accident and that Dad was in the hospital, life went on as usual for me. I went to school every day just like my older brothers. Then one Sunday morning as I left my bedroom heading for the kitchen, I stopped, hanging back as I overheard my mother in the kitchen talking to my fourteen-year old brother.

"Frankie, it's awful, what I found out yesterday at the hospital."

"What happened? Has anything changed?"

"No, he's still in a coma, after a week. But the janitor told me something else. The night they brought your dad in, they left him in the hallway on the gurney. No one was helping him, like they thought he was dead or dying."

Frankie, holding back tears, "But someone helped, right? He's going to be okay?"

"I just don't know. They don't tell me much about the coma or what his chances are."

I didn't know the meaning of coma, and I didn't ask, but I must have believed he would get better.

Several weeks later my curiosity uncovered new details about Dad's condition. I was standing in the kitchen, my mother busy at the table. Something smelled good.

"What are you doing?" I asked.

"I'm fixing some special food to take to your dad at the hospital. His mouth is wired together. He can only take in food through a big glass straw."

"What are you making for him?" I said, wondering how she is doing this and about the metal contraption on the table.

"I've made vegetable beef soup, and I put it through this food grinder, then into these glass jars. He says he needs something that has taste in it. So I fix it and take jars of thick homemade soup to the hospital for him to eat with the straw." Now I knew a little more and assumed this a sign that he was getting better.

He remained in the hospital but Mother seemed calm and in charge. She didn't tell me more, like she had talked to Frankie. Because of my young age, she must have shielded me from her worries. Looking back, however, I wonder if she continued to share details and worries with Frankie and possibly Gene, age eleven. Wouldn't they have been upset? She likely also protected Eddie, almost nine. Bobby was six months old.

Why did I not cry or feel scared about my dad's condition? Where were my feelings? Just months before my bursting heart had greeted the arrival of my new baby brother. One evening Eddie and I were sent to an aunt and uncle to stay overnight. When we got back the next morning, what a surprise—a tiny bundle in a blue blanket! Before long, from time to time, Mother put me, excited and proud, on a kitchen chair to hold him.

Recently I asked my older brother Ed and youngest brother Richard for their recollections of our father's accident. They provided details; some but not all, were familiar to me, probably from talk I heard later in life.

The accident had happened during the evening on U. S. Route 60, several miles outside of Montgomery. R. G., one of Dad's taxi drivers, a young man, was to deliver sandwiches to a nearby plant. A passenger sat in the front right seat, my father in the back seat with the food. He didn't need to go, but R. G. asked him to come along, saying he would drop him off at home on the way back. A tractor trailer was parked on the edge of the highway. R. G. apparently didn't see it, hit the back of the trailer, and somehow the back end of the cab, where Dad sat, swerved, slamming into the rear of the trailer.

My brother Richard said that many years later our father had told him the story of being left to die on a gurney in the hospital corridor. There were other details new to me. Dad recounted the outcome of a lawsuit against the trucking company: how the court initially awarded my father a judgment for $3,500, and how the verdict was later reversed on appeal; excerpts below show the case description and the Court's final decision (Supreme Court of Appeals of West Virginia. 129 W. Va. 267 [W. Va. 1946]).

> This action was instituted by Benny Divita to recover damages for personal injuries resulting from a highway collision between an automobile owned by plaintiff and *269269 driven by his employee, in which he was riding and a motor truck owned by defendant, Atlantic Trucking Company. To a judgment of the Circuit Court of Fayette County, entered on a jury verdict in favor of plaintiff in the amount of thirty-five hundred dollars, defendant, Atlantic Trucking Company, prosecutes this writ of error. . ..
> Supreme Court of Appeals of West Virginia
> Decided November 12, 1946.
> Judgment reversed; verdict set aside. . ..

I believe that, during the period after the move to Montgomery, Dad's business was growing and he was making a decent living. He worked long hours at the taxi stand: answering phone calls, coordinating pick-ups, maintaining the two or three cabs he had, and making sure the drivers turned in all the fares. Without his constant presence, drivers could steal from the business. He tried to hire trustworthy drivers and he treated them as friends, some almost like family. The cabs were just cars, not like those in cities. They didn't have any light on top, but might have had "Divita Taxi" painted on the side and the phone number "305."

By 1943, when the accident happened, we had five children in our family. As the next youngest and the only girl, I lived in a more restricted world than my older brothers. At home I played or helped Mother with small chores, I made the two-minute walk down our street to school, and I loved being outdoors, usually with a girlfriend or Eddie. We often parked ourselves on the concrete steps to our apartment, watched the trains, counted coal and refrigerated cars, and memorized the initials for the various railroad lines. The two oldest brothers began serving as altar boys at the Catholic Church in town, and once our baby brother was old enough for Dad to watch, Mother took Eddie and me to church.

Weeks must have passed but still no one told me more about my father. One afternoon it dawned on me that he had been gone a long time when my mother said, "I'm going to take you and Eddie to see your father in the hospital." We were excited. Maybe we walked the four blocks or went in a cab (we never had a family car). Once there, we kids were not allowed to go in. Mother took charge placing us at the edge of the sidewalk about ten feet from the main hospital entrance.

"I want both of you to stand right here while I go up to his room," she said.

I asked, "Will we be okay here by ourselves?"

"Of course. Just wait about two minutes. Then look up to those windows on the third floor," she answered, pointing her finger to the area. Soon, when we looked up, our father was standing at a window, and we could see his face, though blurred by the window screen. He waved; smiling, we strained to get a better look and swung our arms and hands back and forth, for about a minute.

"He looks different," I said to Eddie.

"He looks better. I got to go in last week with Mom. He still had bandages wrapped around his head and face." When Mother came to get us, we started the walk home, Eddie and I running and skipping ahead, then returning to her again and again.

The day my father came home left a memory that has always haunted me. I was excited about his return. In our living room, bright winter sunshine streamed through the large front window. I didn't see other family members. Maybe a Sunday morning, with my older brothers at church and Mother in the back bedroom with the baby. My father would have come in a taxi and climbed alone the twelve steps to our apartment. He appeared in the doorway, a big smile on his face and his arms opened to me.

But I immediately ran away, into the kitchen, but not to any person as no one else was there. Why did I run away? For a moment I wondered who he was—didn't recognize him as "Daddy." Yet he didn't look much different, no visible scars. Maybe his face and whole body looked thinner. No one was there to react to my behavior—no reprimand, no comforting. My fright was short-lived, and soon I was sitting on his lap.

Immediately after his return—no memories of whether he had to rest and recuperate or went immediately back to work. But off and on, I overheard adult talk about the accident, worries about the hospital bill, a lawsuit, insurance issues—all beyond my understanding. Hushed voices hinted that alcohol was involved: the driver or my dad or both. I sense now that my father's surviving the accident and its aftermath was a critical turning point in my life and that of our family.

As a youth and adult, sad to say, I never asked either of my parents or my two oldest brothers about Dad's accident. Now that my writing has forced me to seek others' memories, I sense the accident's effects and meaning for all of us.

First, my father. Some family members now believe that he had been drinking, although he was not driving. If true, I have more questions than answers and some guesses. Was his later lifelong problem with alcohol abuse already in full swing? Was his drinking at this point a way to dim memories of his sons' deaths? Was it simply a custom of Italian hospitality that got out of hand? Was his drinking a diversion from the long hours he had to spend at his business, where being boss gave him the freedom to drink even on the job? Or, did the abuse of alcohol arise later, from the accident itself, the brush with death leaving new traumatic memories to drown out? Or could he have used alcohol to relieve lingering physical pain or diminished brain functioning from the extensive injuries? He later developed diabetes: someone once mentioned that the accident may have injured his pancreas. After the accident Dad's usual personality seemed mostly the same. Still easy going in temperament, humorous, hard-working, and over-protective with his children, he continued to enjoy movies, get-togethers with family and friends. The one undisputed certainty: excessive drinking later became his modus operandi.

I now wonder about the effect of my father's accident and its aftermath on his taxi and moving business. In 1943, when it happened, the town was in a commercial boom period. With the country gearing up for the war, coal production had increased to meet energy needs for military preparations. Many town residents, and especially miners employed in the surrounding areas and "hollers," did not own a car, relied on taxi transportation to get to Montgomery for shopping and services, and had the money for cab fare. Instead of reaping the benefits of this growth period, for many months my father's accident left him injured, hospitalized, and unable to manage the business. It's possible that his only competition, the Marsico Taxi Company, a mile away in Smithers, picked up the slack and gained some of Dad's regular customers who never returned. Adding to the likely financial hardship, the law suit against the trucking company went on for three years. Initially, Dad's judgment to receive $3,500 was reversed on appeal, resulting in no compensation for injuries and hospital expenses. Yet he faced expenses for attorneys and a likely increase in insurance rates for the cabs. The accident may have struck the first blow, an assault on the financial integrity of the business.

My mother met the grave challenges of the accident and its aftermath much as she had survived the deaths of two sons—she carried on despite her anguish. With my father's long hospitalization, she prepared special foods to aid his healing and at the same time cared for her five children. She shielded Eddie and me from worry about our father's precarious condition, and with little money kept the household running. I would learn later of her inner turmoil only as I began writing my memoir and re-discovered a passage in her diaries. There, decades after the accident, as she reminisces, she admits the anger and resentment she bore with silence at the time and her worries about the loss of income and uncertain fate of the business. I had forgotten the 1975 entry quoted below in which she recalled the accident (p. 62).

February 26, 1975
[She mentions her marriage into the DiVita family and how different they were from her "quiet, humble and peaceful home and family."] . . .

Enough of that. I want to think about happier times with my husband and children. And we did have many of them. For many years. Then came the terrible car accident, which your father nearly lost his life and business. There I was with six children and Bobby, my seventh one, was only six months old. [She is counting the two sons who died in early childhood. Bobby would have been her fifth living child at the time.] No help from no one, no concern from any members of the family if we had food to eat or not. Tony [Dad's next younger brother] was supposed to take care of his taxi business while he was on duty as a city policeman. But he was more concerned about his own self. So when he would bring me some money, it would just go for food. The business existed on my husband's reputation. And all the rest God took care of. After six long weeks your father came out of the coma. And how hard he fought from then on to live. He became aware of our condition. So after two months, they let him come home. Not that he was well. But at least he would be able to watch his business. He was over one year getting well. But thank God, he did. And we survived.

This account revealed my mother's true character: she could bury painful feelings of being abandoned or wronged yet still meet life's demands. After my father's recovery, again, her stoic face exposed no grudges or hurt feelings. She continued to think the best of people, put the past in the past, accepted personal disappointments, and tolerated the foibles of others. Even when her diaries reluctantly disclosed painful feelings, her next sentence would give others the benefit of the doubt.

When I think about my two oldest brothers amid our father's accident and hospitalization, I imagine its lasting impact on them. Frank especially, at fourteen, would have known of his uncertain condition and helped Mother in any way needed. Just recently Beverly, Frank's oldest daughter now middle aged, recounted advice that her father had given her as a teenager: "Because you are the oldest, you have to be the most responsible and help your family. That's what I have tried to do all my life."

Throughout my childhood I often saw Frank and Gene return from grocery shopping, carry in the bags, and put things away. Maybe this was an ongoing responsibility or a new one while our father remained hospitalized for two months. Of course, they also continued meeting the family expectation to do well in school. About this time Frank may have started his job as a projectionist at the local movie theatres, Gene following suit a couple of years later as usher. With their example, Eddie, by age thirteen, also went to work as an usher, and eventually I too worked at the theatres as a cashier. We all gave some of our small earnings to Mother (a time-honored Italian tradition). For my two oldest brothers, the car accident simply further secured their tether of responsibility and loyalty to family.

And then there's me. Through the years, my reaction of running away from my father on his return home has troubled me. Initially, I disputed my thought that I had simply forgotten him, thinking I would have been old enough to remember. Then I accepted that I was shocked as his appearance had really changed. I believe the accident and this period unleashed a new consciousness of my emotional life and that of others. My running away left me feeling guilty—seeing from his expression that I had hurt his feelings. This strong emotion seared the memory in my brain. I am now glad to own the guilt. At least I was feeling something.

After Dad was back, I remember feeling close to him, wanting more time together but rarely expressing this. As talk of war and drafting men for service increased, fearing he would be called, I had a secret plan to hide him in a closet so they couldn't take him. When I was around eight years old, Mother sometimes allowed me to walk the two blocks alone to his taxi stand just to visit with him. On one occasion I stopped there, grubby from playing outside. He pulled a white handkerchief from his pants pocket, spit on it, and cleaned off my messy face; then he opened the desk drawer and gave me a piece of hard candy. Another time, after supper, I must have been clinging to him as he tried to leave the house.

"Daddy, don't go. Stay home with us."

"Janie-Lou, you know, I got to go back to work."

"Please!"

"I'll tell you what. Come with me." He called to Mother that he was taking me for a ride. He put me in the back seat of the cab parked in front of our apartment. The gray fabric felt soft and warm on my legs, and as he started the car I pushed my face close against the window, wanting to see everything. A trip around the block and back home—such happiness!

During this time, along with new awareness of my feelings, I believe much of my core personality was emerging. I remember nights of feeling scared or sad, unable to go sleep, and then reminding myself of a birthday party coming up or something fun happening the next day. It seemed I was learning to manage on my own and keep a positive outlook on life.

In the next few years I recall vivid details of our family and a growing sense of myself as a person. The war was ongoing and brought changes. Two of my dad's younger brothers served in the Army overseas; the wife of one lived with us for a few months, shared my bed, and was like a wonderful big sister to me. I also felt close to my parents, often going with them to movies or visits with their friends. I think they took me because oldest brother Frank had enough to do looking after the younger brothers. As I got older my father and I also shared a few activities alone, such as a movie now and then, maybe to give my mother a break. And once, when I was thirteen, after my persistent begging, he took me to Charleston with him to see wrestling. I hated it!

Now as I wonder if my running away from my father has a deeper meaning for my life, I am uncertain. His car accident occurred around the time that I began to sense who I was, the person who lived in my skin. A year later, by age eight, I had hatched a private dream: I would leave this town, go on my own someday, and be in charge of my life. Where did this notion come from? It took up residence in my psyche long before the start of Dad's extreme overprotection and strictness during my teenage years, which gave way to my confused feelings for him: love, alienation, disappointment. Was my running away a psychological foreshadowing, symbolic of my later need to escape his control while keeping his love?

Over the long haul, the accident and my father's survival shaped the future of our entire family. I count it a miracle that someone at the hospital finally paid attention as he lay dying. Without him, our family would have been destitute. Without a provider, what would have become of my widowed mother with five children ranging in age from six months to fourteen years? What would have become of me—without him and his intense protection? I might have abandoned my dream, stayed in Montgomery, entered a marriage at sixteen or eighteen and become a very different person from who I am. Although our family would face other hardships and crises in the future, what luck that he survived and remained in our lives for many years to come.

CHAPTER 3

The First Family: Three Brothers

WHAT IF I HAD NOT had all these brothers? If the three oldest had been sisters and me just the fourth girl? I cannot imagine it. The person I was and became would not exist.

I grew up in two families, but both shared the same biological parents. My three older brothers with me as youngest and only girl I call the "first family." The next chapter tells the story of the "second family" in which my three younger brothers came on the scene. My straddling in the middle of all these boys gave a unique shape and color to my life.

When I think of my older brothers, the images mostly capture our younger years at our apartment home at 124 ½ Fourth Avenue in Montgomery, where we lived after leaving Smithers.

Saturday morning, October 6, 1945, I shuffled myself, still in pajamas, to the kitchen. My oldest brother Frank, now sixteen, in charge. Why was he cooking at the stove? Eddie and Gene were already sitting at the table.

"Okay, look here what I've got for you—pancakes," Frank said. We were all excited and they smelled so good. "Janie, you're the littlest, so you get the first one. Sit down. Here it comes."

I didn't say anything, just put on the margarine and syrup and started eating. He then passed plates with pancakes to Gene and Eddie.

"Can I have some milk?" I asked. "Where's Mom?"

Gene was smiling a big-brother knowing smile. "You don't get to know, you're too little."

"No, I'm not. I'm going to be nine in two weeks."

Frank gave Gene a stern look, "Don't tease her. That's Dad at the door. He'll tell you." He walked in with a big smile on his face and said, "You have a new baby brother. Now, you get to guess what we named him."

Eddie and I jumped in, giggling, "We don't know. You tell us."

I'll give you a clue," Dad said, "the initials P. R."

Gene spoke first, "Peter," as if bored with the game.

Then Frank, "Tell us. We'll never get it."

"Well, it's Philip Ray. Your mother and the baby are at the hospital. They'll come home in a couple of days."

Hearing toddler sounds, Dad went to the bedroom and got Bobby, now two and a half years old, tossed him in the air a couple of times, put him in the playpen, and told Frank to feed him some pancakes and milk, "Your Aunt Catherine is coming in about an hour to help take care of everyone. I need to get some sleep, and then I have to go to the taxi stand." The excitement was over and we got dressed to go out to play.

My oldest brother Frank, besides knowing how to take care of us, was special in other ways. He played trumpet in the high school band and performed in plays. In the evenings he walked around the kitchen, holding the script, saying his lines out loud, memorizing. I think the play was about a detective, but I didn't know what his role was. Dad was proud of Frank's trumpet playing and gave him tips on how to elevate his horn like Harry James (from the movies). It was this oldest brother who bought the record player for the family and listened to his favorites, Sinatra, the Kay Kaiser Band.

As Frank continued in high school and later, I heard: "he's popular" and "girls chase after him." His job as projectionist for the town's two theatres brought him in contact with the owner's twenty-six-year-old "playboy" son, who invited my brother to some of his parties. After these events Frank often told Mother about the foods served: delicacies like kibbe, stuffed grape leaves. Rumor had it that a twenty-two-year-old woman from the party group had a crush on Frank. If my parents were concerned about his social life, I was not aware of it, but one day he had the law laid down for him. He was probably a freshman in college when he sauntered into the kitchen modeling his new college, letter-type sweater and said, "Don't I look sexy?" To which Mother said, "Don't you ever use that word again in this house!" A message for all of us kids!

Then Gene, the second oldest, a little smart-alecky, but mostly full of gags and all-around goofiness. Once he came in the kitchen holding a medicine bottle and started a performance.

"Oops, almost forgot to take my medicine. Let's see, it says 'shake before using.'" Then Gene jumped and jiggled his arms and legs in all directions." Eddie and I laughed, his perfect audience always. Other times he teased us, "I have something none of you have."

"No, you don't. What is it?" we argued. Then he flipped up the back of his shirt showing us the deep scar under the lowest rib.

"See, I have a scar. You could almost put a penny in it." We knew the scar was from surgery he had as a young child but didn't know why it was done.

When I was around nine years old, once Gene scared me to death but then another time he came to my rescue. We were at a county park on a rare family picnic. I was on an open board swing and Gene started pushing me higher and higher till the swing was wobbling. I screamed and screamed for him to stop and he finally did. I was really mad at him. But he could also be nice. One evening I was sitting at the kitchen table trying to do fourth-grade homework but totally befuddled with the assignment to write a story. Hiding tears as he moved toward me, "I can't do it, I don't know how to write a story."

"Just make up something, something about dinosaurs from the past," he said. His words helped me try, and I managed to finish something, but I felt terribly stupid.

Gene too was active in school and very smart. For a while he was on the junior high basketball team. As a sophomore he had rheumatic fever, missed a lot of school, and had to sleep downstairs in a twin bed placed in the dining room. Even so he made a big splash in high school. He was in the National Honor Society and was named valedictorian of his graduating class of about one hundred. This really got my parents' attention. The school also selected him as its representative to West Virginia "Boys State," a week-long camp about government. But somewhere along the line I heard Mother's usual caveat to keep us humble, "I don't brag on my children. I'll let others do that." Still no hiding her pride as one day I overheard her say with disdain that some people in our town had criticized these awards going to an Italian boy.

I looked up to my two oldest brothers and their accomplishments and wanted to be like them, and I guess Eddie did too. He was my buddy—only fifteen months older than me. We spent a lot of time together: skating on the sidewalk, watching trains go by, playing marbles. Indoors we enjoyed monopoly, comic books, a few toys, playing cards, and radio programs ("Only the Shadow knows!"). We didn't get television until 1950, when Eddie and I were in high school and Frank and Gene were in college. Our next-door neighbor gave us their old black and white when they got a color TV.

One summer day, I was nine and Eddie, eleven, I brought the mail in and started yelling, "Eddie, where's Eddie? "It's here. It's in the mail. Here's your letter."

Mother said, "He's outside somewhere, maybe in the back field playing ball."

"But, it's here, his letter from the art place, where he sent in the drawing. I'll go find him."

After running to two different weed-covered empty lots behind our apartment, I saw him. "Your letter came. You have to come home and open it." He knew exactly what I was talking about, so we both ran.

When we got there, Mother handed him the letter, "You open it."

He did, just tearing at it. "Look what it says. My drawing was very good. They say I have artistic talent and could be an artist. I'm going to show it to Dad."

Mother just smiled but I was jumping up and down. For months, Eddie and I had seen magazine ads with a sketch labeled "Draw This—You Could Be An Artist." He had drawn several of the printed pictures, and we kids always thought they were great. Finally, he sent one in, and this letter had evaluated his work. Eddie's artistic skill impressed me the most, although he too was smart in school. Admitting that I didn't have an ounce of artistic ability—all I could draw were stick people—I was proud of him.

As he got older, Eddie spent less time with me and more time with boys his age, playing ball, riding friends' bikes, sledding, and even sneaking off with Gene to a special, safer part of the river to play—these violations mostly undetected by Dad. (Those two brothers actually learned to swim, while Frank avoided water his entire life, and for me three sets of adult swim lessons left me able to paddle only while holding my breath.) When he was a sophomore, Eddie made the high school football team, unbeknownst to Mother and Dad, and desperately wanted to play. Fearing that team obligations would prevent him from keeping his job as an usher at the theatres, he talked to his brother Gene, who advised, "Go for it." Instead, Eddie, gave up his dream, decided to keep the job and keep contributing much of his small earnings to the family.

From age eight, I had a private dream of leaving my home town. Where it came from I don't know, but the achievements of my two older brothers surely nourished my plan. I believed I could be like them, become somebody, gain recognition. It was a realistic dream, never a fantasy, never like becoming famous or a movie star. I suspect that my brothers also had their own private future dreams. Maybe our dad inspired our vague ambitions. On every trip to Charleston, when we drove by the Governor's Mansion, he said, "You could be living there someday." And more often we heard his message, "Get your education; no one can take that away from you. I never had the chance but you do." (I bet Dad had heard the stereotypes, when he arrived in America, that Southern Italians were ignorant, uneducated, unwelcome.) Both Brother Ed and I recalled Dad's respect for lawyers, often mentioning the names of several in town as well as that of Clarence Darrow. Dad may have hoped these remarks would stir a son toward the legal profession. Mother was also on the same wave length for education and saw school as all important. She helped us with homework, putting this above chores. She ordered the *Funk & Wagnalls Encyclopedia* for us and liked to learn for herself from books and magazines.

I realized I had talents too. After all, I got straight A's in school, the standardized tests the teachers give every other year showed me three or four years above grade level, and one year I went to the county-wide spelling bee. My parents' belief in education and achievement included me as well as the brothers. No one ever said, "You can't do that because you're a girl."

But we knew not to get too self-centered in our future aspirations—responsibilities kept us grounded in everyday life. The two oldest brothers were altar boys and went to church regularly; Mother and I went only when Dad could watch the two little ones. He was back at work, having survived the terrible auto accident that almost took his life. Frank and Gene also contributed to the family, doing the grocery shopping and having jobs at the movie theatres. As the two youngest, Eddie and I had small chores like drying the dishes.

We kids mostly got along. One day when Gene and Ed were scuffling in the living room floor, getting a little too rough with each other, Mother, openly upset, quickly pulled them apart, "Don't you ever do that again! There will be no fighting in this family." Sometimes Gene and Eddie teased me, putting a fist right in front of my face, and pretending to punch me, but faking it, pulling back and laughing. I would say, "Stop that. Don't you realize you could hit me and ruin my nose?"

Then they called me "Banana Nose."

I answered back, "No, you're Banana Nose." But I never cried or tattled.

Our parents required respect for elders, following family rules, and staying out of trouble. Dad loomed as a figure larger than life, more powerful perhaps because he was away from us for long hours running his taxi business. We knew the rules and pretty much automatically followed them. No one reminded us to do homework. I don't remember any preaching or even discipline or punishment for any of us (but I could be wrong).

Dad got mad mostly when we got hurt. We knew the forbidden activities, presumably for their danger to life and limb. No going near the river, no sledding, no swimming (even at the city pool), no bicycles, no getting into any kind of trouble. This was just our dad, what our family was like. If one of us got out of line, we gave the warning: "Just wait till Dad gets home. You're going to be in trouble." As we got older we might bristle at his over-protectiveness, but say nothing. For the record, some of the boys broke his rules, only occasionally getting caught. My transgressions were few and far between.

Mostly, we kids didn't get too full of ourselves. Not consciously thinking it through, we knew we were part of a big family. Change was a given. For one thing, babies kept arriving, so not one of us was the center of our parent's universe, at least not for long. Nothing like a new baby to deflate the fantasies of childhood egotism.

Here's the record. With the first six children born, on average, every twenty-one months, we learned to share Mother's attention. Arrival in this order: Frank, Alphonso I, Gene, Ed, Jane, Alphonso II. Brother Alphonso I died at age four, before I was born. I was three when the second Baby Alphonso was born and survived only five months. Within a few months, we moved to the apartment in Montgomery, and I became the youngest in the family—for another two years. My older brothers had to adjust to me, a sister who often tagged along with her parents while Frank cared for the younger boys. (Later as adults, the older brothers said I was "spoiled." I always denied this. But, from the over-protectiveness of my parents, I did get time alone with them—visiting their friends or going to movies, mainly musicals, which Dad loved.)

I too had to adapt when, without warning, my status as the six-year old youngest in the family changed with the birth of baby brother "Bobby Jim." Sometimes I felt neglected—what my older brothers may have felt at times. On occasion when I was put to bed (in my room that adjoined my parents' bedroom) while others were still up, I intentionally coughed until my mother came in. Her brief presence comforted me. And I was thrilled with the rare special occasion when Dad, after supper, took me for a quick ride around the block in one of his taxicabs. Now, I wonder if the boys too had any treasured moments of closeness with Mother or Dad. Did they ever feel overlooked but just ignored their hurt, moved on, and grew up fast as expected in our large family?

Still more scary changes—parents are people, get sick, and have problems. My brothers and I accepted less personal attention without tears or terrors. We got through Dad's terrible car accident. Then within a year, Mother was gone, maybe a few weeks, to a tuberculosis sanatorium, about forty miles away in Beckley. Once Dad took a couple of us kids to visit her; on the drive we pestered him to stop and get us some food, which didn't happen. (The actual visit and the place remain vague, though I think we sat outdoors at a picnic table. Given Mother's absence, someone must have taken care of us, but I have no memory of this period. Maybe it was Aunt Alline, who lived with us for a time while her husband, Uncle Charlie, was in the Army.) When Mother returned she carefully explained that she had bronchiectasis, a chronic condition of scarred lung tissue, emphasizing that she did not have tuberculosis; she must have known of the terrible stigma attached to that disease.

Amidst these changes and family crises my three older brothers and I carried on as usual, doing homework, playing, and staying out of trouble. When Bobby came on the scene, he was a rowdy baby and toddler. Ever amazed, Dad said, "He can make that playpen walk." And he did! We giggled as Bobby stood inside, shaking the rails of the playpen, getting the wheels to scoot across the rug on the living room floor. When he was two and three years old, we had to watch him closely in the winter to prevent his falling on the large floor furnace register between the living room and kitchen. One time he landed on it and someone grabbed him but not before he got slight burn stripes on the calf of his leg.

Two years later another baby brother arrived, and though he was not rambunctious like Bobby, Philip took center stage for a while. We were used to that by then, old enough to realize how much care a baby needs—no big deal to share our parents' attention. So we became more independent, more involved in the larger world. I imagine we all unconsciously expected that marriage and having a family would be part of our own future lives—nothing to fear or run away from.

I was aware of my parents' views on how their two oldest sons should make their way in the world. Dad wanted Frank to be a doctor (M.D.), and Mother's heart was set on Gene's becoming a priest. Their preferences for the first two sons did not work out.

Frank started college in our home town at West Virginia Institute of Technology (Tech). Here's what I think happened, maybe not all at once: Frank got lackluster grades the first semester, realized that becoming a doctor was not for him, and decided to major in music education. Although Dad had been proud of Frank's trumpet playing in high school, he was disappointed with his oldest son's new decision.

Frank completed the bachelor's degree and took a first high school teaching job in a small town, Rupert, West Virginia. Right before that he married Betty Young, a student in nurses' training at the local hospital. My parents thought he was too young, but he made his own decision. They and I traveled a couple of times to Rupert to see Frank's band's concerts. After one year, during the Korean conflict, Frank volunteered for the Air Force (serving in the unit's military band) instead of waiting to be drafted. Throughout his life, his wife's ongoing mental illness meant recurring crises and her incapacitation. Because of Betty's serious health problems, after two years Frank received a hardship discharge from the military; he brought his family back to Montgomery and lived many years with our parents. They helped care for Betty and the children, and Frank helped Dad with his declining taxi business. There my oldest brother achieved a successful business career, owning an auto dealership, and twice elected mayor of the city. Though proud of Frank's success, our parents, more than anything, felt blessed to have him and his family nearby.

I never heard how Mother took the news that Gene was not going to become a priest. I doubt Dad was ever keen on this idea, maybe thinking he should be a lawyer instead. I heard that Gene became interested in medicine when Mother had a serious bout with pneumonia and he got to know our family doctor. At Tech, Gene followed the pre-med curriculum. Dad must have been heartened by this decision, but I don't have a clue if Mother was disappointed. Gene was successful: he completed the medical degree through the joint program at West Virginia University and the Medical College of Virginia, did an internship at Methodist Hospital in Houston, engaged in general medical practice there for several years, then completed a residency in Psychiatry, and enjoyed a long private practice in Psychiatry in Houston, Texas.

Our parents were proud of Gene's success, but were surprised, maybe disappointed, when he got married, right before finishing the M. D., to Peggy Arthur, a nurse he had met during medical school. Later when Gene decided to go into Psychiatry, Dad was not impressed, saying this specialty was not medicine but something akin to voodoo; "psychshit" he called it. With Gene in Houston, my parents missed him tremendously, hurt by the physical distance but also by his emotional distancing from family. They may have expected that, with his profession, he would have helped more with their ongoing financial problems. But later they made several trips to his Texas home, often staying for weeks at a time, and renewing feelings of love with this son and his growing family.

Of course, Ed and I always assumed we would attend college at Tech, but as we got older Mother and Dad never tried to influence our future careers. In a sense we were "home free." In fact, Ed has reported, as an older adult, that

Mother was not "pushy" with him about school work and grades as she was with Gene. In his next breath Ed retracted this feeling of neglect by saying that Mother responded differently to the innate qualities in each of her children. By the time Ed and I enrolled in college, our parents had more immediate concerns: three younger children, the declining taxi business, and worries about their two married sons. So Ed and I independently selected majors and planned our adult careers. Only once, during high school, did my dad ever hint about a vocation for me, off-handedly remarking that I could become a "stenographer." I didn't respond and nothing further was ever said about this or my college career.

Ed had both scientific and artistic talents and completed a degree in Engineering Physics at Tech. At graduation he sought a position in the aeronautical industry, which, of course, meant he would leave home. I was impressed when he proudly told me about the several companies that he applied to. By this time Mother and Dad knew he'd be moving, but their pride in his job did not allay their sense of loss with another child leaving. He went to work for Martin Aircraft Industries in Baltimore. In 1958, Ed was drafted into the Army and completed basic training; however, his service requirement was decreased due to his employer's involvement in defense work.

Within two years Ed was engaged; my parents and I attended his wedding, a Catholic Mass, joining his life with Patricia Kelly, a recent immigrant from Ireland. At this point my parents no longer questioned whether this son was old enough to marry or his decision about his career, and they were very happy with his choice of a Catholic bride. Although Ed moved next to California, eventually working at the Jet Propulsion Laboratory, and my parents saw the West Coast as another world, acceptance was their only choice. They made several visits there through the years, greatly enjoyed their grandchildren, and even experienced an earthquake. Clearly, their children's wanderlust had expanded their world.

When I entered Tech, I chose to major in English. To my parents this meant that I was preparing to be a teacher. Beyond that, what I studied and my plans for a career I held very close to my heart and became more private about my life dream, if that was even possible, having never shared much of anything about myself with anybody. But the real story of my college career comes in a later chapter, "Across the Tracks: College Miracle and Magic."

The first family, my three older brothers and myself, probably experienced our parents at their best, as compared to their later years. Dad was still the respected authority for his wife and children, and Mother could give her full attention to us, although we shared her with the new brothers as they came along. In our childhood and early teen years we still sensed our parents' optimism, ambition, and close, loving relationship. This family atmosphere left us feeling secure and free to imagine our own future dreams. Much of that family tone and mood changed in later years and affected the lives of our three youngest brothers as shown in the next chapter.

Now I can say that my older brothers, with their distinct personalities and abilities, captured my heart in special ways. I appreciate what they gave and still give to me (my memories of Frank and Gene, who have died, remain a gift). Realizing my past reticence, I try now to express my deep feelings of affection and thanks that went unspoken for too long.

Frank was forever and always my big brother. When I lived with him and Betty for two years for my first two teaching jobs, he continued to look out for me, showing fatherly concern once when I went on a blind double date, but also treating me as an equal teaching colleague. From his and Betty's early marriage and later, I was part of their life, felt close and connected, and remained so with him even after his divorce from Betty and her death. In later life, he shared his feelings more than I ever could. I listened and kept in touch by frequent phone calls, yet never expressing straightforwardly my sorrow that his last years were so painful due to health problems and family conflicts.

After Frank and Betty returned to the family home, I lived as well with Gene and wife Peggy the one year I taught in Houston; there I got beyond my experience of him as the teasing brother. They welcomed me to their home and transported me to several plays and cultural events I would otherwise have missed. Many years later he too got divorced but never explained reasons for this decision, and I never asked. Afterwards and during his remarriage, we talked openly of concerns and frustrations with our adult children. In late life Gene and I also connected with our shared interest in writing and literature. He gave me a precious gift, a five- volume set of James Joyce's works; he remembered that early on I had sent him a copy of *Portrait of the Artist as a Young Man*. I am grateful that in our frequent phone calls I could show love and concern as he faced the numerous illnesses that took his life.

Once we were adults, Ed reached out to me much more than I did to him, and I am sorry that I was not more responsive. I regret that I did not find a way to comfort him and Pat in person when their nineteen-year old daughter Cathy lost her life in a car accident. But he and I have since become open about all aspects of our lives—work, families, infirmities, our writing projects, and especially his continuing art work. I appreciate our current long phone conversations about anything and everything, even at times our political differences.

Writing about life with my older brothers has revealed their tremendous influence on my identity and allowed discovery of some of my personal failures. I should have talked more with them: shared my childhood dreams and asked about theirs. Maybe that's asking too much for all of us growing up in that era—we were just kids, and ours was not a talkative family, especially when it came to personal stuff. But as an adult, I could have and should have done better—to stay in touch and to have honest, open conversations, not just superficial obligatory contacts. This project, my memoir, has uncovered my distancing, remoteness, and excessive reticence with my brothers. Why has it taken so long to get past all that when my heart was always filled with love and respect? Now I know I have much more to learn about myself and my view of the world in which I grew up. On to my second family.

CHAPTER 4

The Second Family:
Three More Brothers

So, THREE YOUNGER BROTHERS PUSHED their way into my world. Who was my favorite? I can no more answer that question than any good mother could. It's not an excuse to say that their differences—in temperament, personality, even looks—kept me engrossed with each one individually but also with them as a cohort. They left me feeling love, fascination, annoyance, worry, pride. My actions more than my words captured my intense attachment.

For me, the era of the second family began in summer 1948, when I was eleven, with the move to our home at 618 Third Avenue in Montgomery. There I started adolescence and took on a part-time mothering role. My repertoire expanded as I practiced on three younger brothers: becoming adept at caring for others and worrying about their well-being and happiness, while still at front and center stage, following the script of academic achievement as key to my life dream.

Although I portray here the personalities of my three younger brothers and my relationship with them, the story is more complex: the household comprised both the first and second families intermingling and in a new home to boot. Anticipating the move went on for months. Five blocks from our apartment, at the west end of town, our future house had two stories, four bedrooms, one bath and a second toilet in the tiny laundry room. It was being remodeled by workers that Dad had hired. Our parents permitted us to stop by after school to watch but warned us to stay out of the way. Dad was proud of the new solid plastered walls with a swirl finish and archway openings from the living room to the dining room to the kitchen.

Financing for the house purchase probably came from a loan. I often heard Mother's worrying remarks about paying off bank notes and other loans. Owning property, however, validated my father's success in being a good provider for his family. I think the plan was that rent from the apartment we were vacating and the two smaller units in the building would help cover the loan payments.

The house gave us much more room and felt new from the remodeling. It sat close to the sidewalk, with six feet of lawn in front of a wide porch. Outside, the original wood siding, painted white, looked nice enough, until Dad had it replaced with a type of siding pretending to look like red brick. The entrance door opened to the living room. Off to the right with an open archway was a large room that became our parents' bedroom. To the left was the stairway to the second floor. The living room opened to the dining room, which opened to a large kitchen. The white plaster in all rooms remained unpainted.

The floors in these downstairs rooms were covered in a light blue linoleum except our parents' bedroom, which had a dark varnished wood floor. A large four-burner gas stove was situated to the left of the dining room archway by the kitchen. In the living room a smaller gas burner stove sat on the floor alongside the stairway. In summers, one of the dining room windows held a large fan that drew out hot air, doing a fair job of cooling the house.

Upstairs the three bedrooms had dark varnished wood floors, no rugs. I got the smallest room, Bob and Phil got the other small bedroom, and the three older brothers shared the largest bedroom with two double beds and a gas burner stove. In winter, the hit and miss heating system often left me scorching my legs in front of stoves, twisting and turning as needed.

The backyard, about twenty by forty feet, featured mostly dirt, not grass; to the far-left side four clothes lines were strung between metal T-posts. A paved alley adjoined the backyard. The house was nice, as good as or even better than many of our friends had, but appreciation of our good fortune didn't overcome our disdain for the fake brick siding.

The furniture in the new house looked good—mostly a combination of the few pieces we had in the apartment along with some additions. Within a few months of moving we acquired a dining room set, nicer than anything I had ever seen. Dad apparently took this set in lieu of payment from a moving job he did. The dark walnut finish looked classy: a big table even without the leaves, a long buffet with three drawers, a glass-fronted china cabinet, and six matching chairs. My parents' light walnut bedroom set also may have come from Dad's moving business—a double bed and headboard with short posts, a chifforobe, and a low vanity with mirror with three drawers on each side. But the living room couch, my bed, and the brothers' beds were the same that we had in the apartment. Later purchases for the living room included a wood telephone stand with a seat, a large picture of a rural scene hanging over the couch, and an up-holstered easy chair. We had a lot to be proud of in our new home.

With the move, here's what the household looked like. My three older brothers already had jobs. Since age fifteen Frank had worked at the two lo-cal theatres, the Kayton and the Avalon, as a projectionist. Gene began as an usher and became a lobby manager. Eddie was also an usher and had other small paid jobs that used his artistic talents, such as creating wooden signs for a couple of county parks.

But school was more important than jobs. Frank was a freshman in col-lege. In high school Gene was a junior and Ed, a freshman. I was in seventh grade. The two younger brothers, Bobby, five, and Phil, three, still too young for school. The three oldest boys were in and out managing their own job and school schedules. Except Gene—he often had trouble getting up for high school and later for early morning college classes. From the bottom of the stairs, Dad would yell at him, "Get down here! You're going to be late." I would get myself up, grab something for breakfast, and walk the four blocks to our same grade school but to the second-floor housing junior high classes.

Life in our family mostly resembled a revolving door, an image that will fit as we children came of age in subsequent years. Yes, we were still at home, but there was a lot of exiting and entering. We set off to school or college classes, maybe back for a quick lunch, then off again to our jobs, then back for bedtime. Since the younger brothers needed Mother's care, we older ones made our own meals, at odd hours if needed. Until the demise of the taxi business in the late 1950s, Dad was gone all day, often no longer present for the evening meal, although we still had family suppers together when most of us could gather at the kitchen table. Mother was the anchor we took for granted: running the household, cleaning, doing laundry, and cooking. This coming and going meant that we older ones tuned into our individual lives and paid less attention to the younger brothers. (We didn't know it, but we were practicing for the real future departure, leaving home and family for jobs and independent lives.)

Although my older brothers were often gone from home, I still saw them in certain moments that made an impression on me. Frank and Gene routinely had friends coming by to pick them up for some event or activity. I knew Gene's three best friends, Louie, Leroy, and "Brown" from church, and Frank's good friend, Jimmy, occasionally stopped by. When I answered the front door to let them in, I sometimes became aware of a stare or gaze from one of these guys older than me. Feeling flattered by this attention, but also a little embarrassed, I didn't show interest, just scurried out of the room, letting a brother know that a friend was waiting.

Frank got married when I was fourteen, his wedding being the first one I ever attended. Of course, we had all come to know and love Betty over the two years they were dating. While Dad thought that his twenty-one-year-old son was too young to marry, he was truly angry that our priest, Father Doyle, would not allow their wedding in our church, but would perform only a brief ceremony in the rectory, since Betty was not a Catholic. Two years later Betty lived with us for several months while Frank completed Air Force basic training in North Carolina.

I remember a worrisome situation with Gene when the day arrived for Betty to join Frank and live on the base. Since her train was to leave at two a.m. in the morning, most of the family stayed up late that night to say goodbye, and Gene would drive her the three blocks to the town's depot. Since our house faced the railroad tracks, we watched out the front window as the train came by and slowed for the stop. What I recall most is that I stayed awake, aware that Gene didn't return right away. Everyone else in the household had gone to bed. After over an hour of worrying, unable to imagine where Gene could be at this hour, I finally fell asleep. Since he was home the next morning, he must have returned later, but I never asked him about it and no one else even noticed.

Once in the new house, I saw a lot of my two little brothers. At twelve and even into high school, I helped with them but didn't feel this as a demand from my mother. They hung out in their backyard playground where the grass never grew, so they were often grubby. Sometimes I supervised the baths of these two youngsters, turned their grimy little bodies into sweetness, and got them ready for bed. In the next few years, their rowdiness increased, playing cowboys, roughhousing, running through the house, making messes.

At that stage, I became more attuned to social status and our family's lack of it, so I took on the role of trying to "civilize" these boys. When I explained table manners, they just laughed at me. But I also felt love: helped them write letters to Santa, selected and ordered clothes and Christmas presents from the Sears Catalog (cap pistols), and once they were in school, assisted with homework. In other words, I felt motherly and wanted them to have a good childhood. After I left home, I bought them a used bike.

Although my brothers' friends often stopped by, my girlfriends rarely came to the house. I probably unconsciously kept them at bay to avoid their judgment on our household and its loud, crowded, often messy appearance. Sometimes when the younger brothers got in trouble with Mother and hid, I took her side: helped chase them down, unearthing secret hiding places upstairs and down, under beds and in closets. Of course, I still loved them as little brothers but also sympathized with my overburdened mother.

About one year after our move, we got our last baby in the family. This time, I was twelve during Mother's pregnancy at age thirty-seven. I obviously knew about her condition; however, she did not talk to me about it, except on one occasion. She blurted out that she was upset about being pregnant again—this intimate revelation leaving me speechless. At that moment, she must have felt terribly alone and helpless, and I was not able to respond. What could I say?

Richard was born at home, during the night when I was asleep and assumed that all the kids in the family were in bed, but I don't know if that was true for the older brothers. They often arrived home late from work and started studying and filling the house with their cigarette smoke. When we woke up on the morning of July 8, 1949, our baby brother Richard was there, and Mother's friend Sarah was in charge; she had attended the birth, along with Dad and our elderly family doctor. Having a new baby in the family seemed okay to me. (But only now do I wonder about my older brothers' reactions. Frank was in college and had a girlfriend, Gene about to be a senior in high school. We knew not to talk about our feelings or serious, personal stuff. We were primed not to complain, not brood about things, at least not too much.)

With the new arrival, I helped as asked. I was not afraid of babies. I fixed and gave bottles, changed diapers, and helped with baths. Here's one memory, probably a few months after Richard's birth. It was night time, around ten p.m. Mother called up to my room asking me to warm a bottle for the baby. I came downstairs barefoot and in pajamas to the kitchen and stood by the stove, the bottle heating in a pan of water. Suddenly something on the top of my bare toes. Looking down, I saw a mouse scurrying away. A bit of a shock, but I just finished the bottle, wiped it off, squirted a bit on my arm to test it, and took it to my mother waiting in her downstairs bedroom with the baby. Maybe I told her about the mouse, maybe not.

There was a baby bed for Richard, but I don't remember having one at the apartment for either Bobby or Phil, although we definitely had the wooden playpen there. I guess now that those two younger brothers, like all of us who came before them, slept in bed with our parents as infants and toddlers. If so, could this body closeness and comfort be part of our sense of security, not needing our parents' constant reassurance? But I could be wrong on the memory of no baby bed.

I felt close and affectionate with my three younger brothers and fascinated by their unique personalities, but our experiences together decreased as I devoted time to high school and college studies and my job. When I started high school, they were seven, five, and one. Four years later when I started college, Bob was eleven, Phil, nine, and Richard, five. So for my three years of college, me still living at home, these boys were in junior high and elementary school. This meant I saw first-hand much of their childhood growing up years. Since I was not present when they were teenagers, I came to know that stage of their lives second-hand, from my brief visits back home and Mother's letters and phone conversations.

A sad truth about large families—on leaving home the older ones forgo experience with their younger siblings and can feel detached and vice-versa. I feel fortunate to know many of my younger brothers' personal stories from living with them. Others I have learned from time together at family and sibling reunions over the past two decades and from interviewing them for this memoir. So I know whereof I speak as I look at the growing-up years of Bob, Phil, and Richard. During my life I was convinced that all of us siblings had similar experiences in our family, but now as I write, many surprising differences emerge.

Bobby Jim (aka Bob), as he grew up, showed talent as a comedian and at ten or eleven began entertaining us kids with his impersonations of certain people in our town (but not in front of Mother and Dad). Compared to the first family siblings, he sometimes displayed a rebellious side in high school and tested the limits. He didn't obsess over homework. He had a ducktail hairstyle. He liked to wear his Levis drooping, without a belt. His appearance did not sit well with Dad, who told him to get a belt on before leaving for school and took him from time to time to a barber for a sensible haircut. At last, a nonconformist in the family!

Other arguments arose between Dad and Bob when he wanted to be a volunteer member in the town's official fire department. Dad objected, saying that was too dangerous. Bob tried to explain that he could learn from this experience and even asked his father to call the fire chief for more information. Still Dad said no. But Bob did not back down and went on to participate, the argument apparently fizzling out. In college, he played drums with a rock band, rode with the group for out-of-town gigs, and made some money from this job. No objections from Dad.

Phil moved into high school age as a more serious-minded youth, a bit of a worrier, always conscientious. He cared about his appearance but favored a more preppy style. He too wore Levis, but he also had Mother "peg" his black khakis in the style of the day. He seemed able to strategize with our parents. Instead of asking permission to play football, he told Mother the coach wanted him to try out; she didn't object. A good student and athlete, Phil had outgrown some of his childhood anxiety, became captain of the football team and was voted Homecoming King in his senior year. As he realized the family's ever more dire financial condition, he made no waves, didn't add any stress for his parents with adolescent antics.

The younger brothers followed the family tradition of going to work to earn money, but they got much more experience than their older brothers doing physical labor. Bob and Phil moved up the ranks of part-time jobs. From paper routes and grass cutting, they were hired by Brother Frank's auto dealership for jobs such a washing cars, getting tools and materials for the mechanics, moving cars around the lot as needed. Dad routinely counted on help from these boys, sending them to the apartment building he owned to clean messes left by tenants and paint the three units. When the family home needed plumbing repairs or other projects, the younger brothers worked alongside their father. They did the digging and burrowing work to upgrade the house's foundation and install venting for a gas furnace. They also painted at rental properties owned by their brother Frank. My younger brothers learned early on to muscle through hard work, no complaints allowed.

After high school, Bob, Phil, and eventually Richard, started college at Tech, with the two youngest joining the Sigma Phi Epsilon (the same group their older brothers had belonged to when it had a different name); the new version had a house, only a few doors away from our home. Bob (ever the rebel?) did not join; instead, as a reporter for the college newspaper, his assignment was to cover the Greek organizations, which sometimes complained about his reporting of their activities. Phil and Richard liked hanging out at the frat house as an easy escape from the increasing chaos at home; they also enjoyed the parties, which sometimes got them in trouble with Dad. Bob and

Phil, although two years apart in age, graduated the same year. (Bob had left Tech after his freshman year to work a full-time job but returned the next year.) Phil earned a degree in industrial management, Bob, in history and social studies.

When Bob explained his desire to do further study in art, Dad was unhappy with this plan, saying a job painting houses would be a better career. Bob, however, was able to follow his dream, mainly because of happenstance. Since Phil planned to start graduate work for the Master of Business Administration at West Virginia University, the two brothers arranged to attend at the same time and share housing, allowing Bob to start the Master's in art education. Fortunately, they both got assistantships with the University and independently financed their studies—though just barely. Overall, Bob, probably more than anyone in our family, seemed able to assert and stick to his goals in the face of Dad's disapproval. Thus, two more brothers exited the revolving door, leaving the family home to start their independent lives.

Richard was an active little boy, often drifting into escapades that got him hurt. When he learned how to pound nails, he filled up the back-porch floor with nails. Stepping on a roofing nail with his bare foot prompted a visit to the hospital emergency room. When he had recurring tonsillitis and the doctor recommended some type of radiation for his tonsils, my parents took him to Charleston on multiple occasions for this treatment.

At around four years old, Richard was also curious and had a mind of his own. Once, still in his hammering stage, he heard me telling the family about the set of Melmac plastic dishes that I had ordered from the Sears Catalog. (Always concerned about our family's lack of social status, I was proud for us to have a matching set of everyday dishes.)

"Look at this. They are guaranteed to be unbreakable," I said, setting the table. Later that evening, Richard came in, holding pieces of a broken dinner plate and announced, "See, I broke it, just hit it once with the hammer." Dad went into hysterics with laughter.

Unlike his older siblings, Richard was not afraid to ask questions of our parents and so unearthed new information for all of us. When he questioned

Mother about our dead brothers, she told him both had died from meningitis. He also learned more than I ever knew about Dad's car accident in 1943, and the failed lawsuit that denied Dad compensation for his injuries and hospital costs. Maybe being the youngest, Richard was part of a new generation that spoke more openly with parents.

During the time frame when our father no longer had the taxi business and spent more time at home, Richard became his helper on house projects. Even as a ten-year old, he spoke his mind—"mouthy" is what my parents called it—and argued with Dad about how best to approach repair and home improvement tasks. It's possible that of all the children in the family Richard got the most time and meaningful conversations with our father. As he moved into adolescence and teen years, like his siblings, he always had part-time jobs (a paper route, cutting grass, bagging groceries at the A & P grocery store). By the time he was in high school, he didn't bother asking his parent's permission, he just played on the football team. Near graduation, he raised the issue of college with Dad.

"I think I would like to go away to school."

With a deadpan expression, Dad replied, "That's okay. I don't care where you go as long as it's Tech." Nothing like Dad's wry humor to put this boy in his place!

Of course he enrolled at Tech and did well in his studies while keeping part-time jobs. But this youngest one in the family also liked fun and was not above shenanigans. He especially enjoyed the fraternity parties and recounted a funny story. He returned home one night from a frat party by eleven-thirty p.m., thereby not getting locked out of our home. But he wanted to go back. Around one a.m., from an upstairs window at the back of the house, he got on the roof and dropped down six or seven feet to the ground. Knowing he would have to get back in the same way, he stacked up a few cinder blocks in the back yard just under the window to allow him later to reach the roof and pull himself up. At the end of the party, he easily got back inside, planning to get up early the next morning, before Dad to remove the cinder blocks. Awaking suddenly and realizing he had overslept, he hurried downstairs, hoping to move the evidence. Too late, in the kitchen he faced his father, who said, "Looks like someone tried to break into the house last night." Poor Richard! Speechless, he had been caught, put on notice, and reminded of one of Dad's favorite sayings, "No matter what you do, I will always find out about it." In 1971, the end of an era, Richard, the last child in the family, received a bachelor's degree in industrial management from Tech.

Earlier I mentioned how the first family readily adapted to newly arriving babies; the younger brothers learned a similar lesson. A sobering experience for them occurred after I had left—Frank and his family moved into the family home due to his wife's mental illness. This living arrangement lasted for several years and kept Mother busy helping Betty. This period also coincided with Dad's declining income from the taxi business and an increase in his drinking. Combining both families' resources was necessary and mutually beneficial—Frank oversaw management of the last days of Dad's business and contributed financially toward family needs, and Mother helped Betty in caring for the five grandchildren.

Only now do I realize that my younger brothers had to navigate this complex family structure. With two generations living in the same household, they likely witnessed increased conflict between our parents, such as about Dad's drinking and discipline of the grandchildren. Bob, Phil, and Richard endured the frustrating reality of mental illness. They adjusted to the daily needs of three nieces and twin nephews as these youngsters grew from toddlers to adolescents. They also absorbed their mother's stress as she worried and schemed to make ends meet. When Phil, after paying freshman college tuition from his small job savings, asked if she could give him $35 to join the fraternity, she told him, "No, I can't. You should write to your brother Gene and ask him." Gene sent him the money. Telling this story, Phil conscientiously remembered he never paid back the money.

At this point the family was somehow getting welfare food commodities—powdered milk and cardboard cartons of cheese (probably not officially). The younger brothers cringed as they saw their father buy beer with the little money available, their respect for him draining away with his every swig. Dad's pattern of drinking led to his own numbing, not to anger, argument, or violence. Typically, when arriving home intoxicated, he would sit at the table, often dozing off without eating the food Mother placed before him. Once sobered up a bit, in the middle of night, he would join his wife in bed. Then the next day, back to his usual self, as if nothing had happened, until the next binge.

In this complicated, troubled second family, a possible upside: my younger brothers escaped some of our parents' previous strictness. Since they had to grow up fast, become responsible for themselves, and help with Frank's children, I now wonder if they resented the loss of Mother and Dad's attention, even while gaining some freedom. Phil recounted little parental oversight of his risky boyhood escapades: tampering with razor blades on one occasion and a firecracker at another time—both of which landed him in the emergency room. These boys got drivers' licenses early and drove for their part-time jobs—apparently without parental concerns for safety. Phil made trips to Charleston to pick up parts for Frank's auto dealership. Richard drove a flower shop van to make deliveries. Bob got rides with band members to play jobs in various locations miles away from Montgomery.

The younger brothers also managed to get permission for special travel events: a senior trip, out-of-town sports events, a spring break trip with friends—gaining more privileges than their older brothers ever enjoyed. On the sly they had some close calls from running around with a couple of cousins who had cars. What happened to parental strictness? Dad's increased drinking likely dulled worries about his young sons. And our parents were preoccupied with Frank's children, were getting older, were worn out with family problems and demands, were occasionally out of town visiting their older children, and were likely facing the changing culture of the 1960s. As with the rest of us, the younger brothers had jobs, gave money to Mother, and saved their earnings for clothes, school, and personal needs.

Both Phil and Richard played on the high school football team for several years, yet their parents never attended a single game. These sons probably did not expect them to go, knew not to ask, and ignored hurt feelings, if any arose, about their absence. My parents may not have really wanted these boys to play sports, or they worried about injuries, or they didn't think it was important to attend school events. Or they may have been overwhelmed with the endless demands of family life. I know they went to my dance recital when I was eight years old, but my memory is fuzzy on whether either one attended my high school graduation. Surely, my mother did—I was class salutatorian! As kids, we may have felt secure in our parents' love, not needing their constant attention, not prone to feeling ignored. That era, the 1950s and 1960s, did not place children at the center of their parents' universe with the right to make demands.

Like their older siblings, my younger brothers had ambitions, perhaps even amplified by the desire to escape the family chaos. With goals beyond degrees from Tech, they pursued additional studies that led to successful professional careers. After receiving the Master's degree in art education, Bob gained a teaching position at the Kendall School of Art and Design in Grand Rapids, Michigan (later Kendall University). With the Master's in Business Administration, Phil eventually held the post of comptroller with the West Virginia State Police for many years and later manager of a non-profit healthcare association. Following the Tech degree in accounting, Richard completed additional graduate courses, worked as a financial officer in several auto dealerships, and became a Certified Public Accountant.

After college, two of the younger brothers faced the draft before getting their careers underway. Phil received an educational deferment while in graduate school; over a year later when he was drafted, his boss appealed on his behalf, and Phil received a job deferment based on being employed in a State agency focused on crime reduction programs. Richard volunteered for the Army National Guard to fulfill his military obligation. While in basic training at Fort Polk, Louisiana, he used his furloughs to visit Gene and Peggy in Houston, allowing these two brothers, sixteen years apart in age, to get to know each other.

I remain amazed at growing up with these six brothers. My memories have produced new insights about their experiences in our family and new appreciation of how they helped shape me as a person. No doubt, my first and

second families struck the veneer of my genetic makeup, sculpting and forming the finishing touches for my character and identity. Writing about them
has helped me better accept my life then and now—warts and all. Just like
me, they had private experiences, that I know nothing about, that added pa-
tina to their personalities. Later as adults they have talked more openly about
their childhood memories. Let's just say the boys in the family broke a few of
Dad's rules.

Still, we had much in common. Our ordinary, simple lives revolved
around school, family, jobs, and church. Although we breathed deeply the
family atmosphere of seriousness about life, we also enjoyed fun, friends, and
activities in school and the community. When we felt deprived because of
our large family, limited financial resources, and life in a very small town, we
rarely wasted time on self-pity. Without much awareness of the larger world,
we were comfortable in our home town, glad for the shops and businesses, two
movie theatres, and the college. Vaguely aware of other immigrant families,
we felt accepted—no different from other kids.

Even so, my brothers and I also all had some private and public moments
of shame that branded us as not quite good enough. (Mine are scattered
throughout these chapters.) In college Frank had a girlfriend until her mother,
a professor at Tech, put an end to the relationship. Same with Gene: when
he was about to leave for medical school, his girlfriend's mother pushed her
daughter toward a young man from a local prominent professional family;
she soon married him. I recently heard from Ed that as a child and youth, he
thought of himself "as a hillbilly, not knowing why and with the same remorse
as Blacks feel about the N-word, I didn't want anyone to call me one, except
myself." And even Richard, the youngest, reported that in the 1960s, he felt
the stigma of being Catholic and Italian: having been refused by two different girls for dates, he later learned from a friend that their parents were not
impressed by his pedigree.

Just like me, but for different reasons, my brothers had little time to sample the fruits of teen life, such as hanging out, dating, or getting a car. Our
lives centered on doing well in school, having a job, and helping the family.
There was no family car or even the option of saving for a first "junker."

Brother Bob told me that he always wished he had a car but knew that wasn't going to happen until he was on his own. There was never enough money, bills went unpaid, and the boys always gave some of their meager earnings to Mother. (And I sent money home from my teaching jobs until I was married.)

The boys were lucky to have friends, guys they ran around with, who had cars. These friends could drive them to special events, such as proms; all of us got to attend a couple of these, mostly as a rite of passage not with a regular dating partner. Although Frank and Gene each had a girlfriend (for a brief period), my guess is that if they needed a car they arranged a double-date, counting on buddies who had a car. For the younger brothers, having a steady girlfriend came after leaving home. Richard, the youngest, was the only one to have a car while still at home: when he was a sophomore at Tech, he bought it on credit for $400, to get back and forth to a job loading freight for a trucking company in Belle, twenty miles away.

Getting subtle or overt reminders—not good enough, whether due to social status, lack of money, Italian heritage, or personal qualities—spurred dreams of proving our worth and value, not only to ourselves but to the larger world. Through the years, Frank, consciously comparing himself to Gene, revealed his sense of not being smart and later lambasted some of his own life decisions. More than once in our private conversations he labeled himself "a dumb shit." Gene had an embarrassing problem in childhood and teen years—bedwetting. My parents had no ideas for a solution, but never punished or harassed, just reminded him to try to wake up. During his first year of medical school at WVU, he sought help, and the problem was quickly remedied with some physical or surgical procedure. In recent years, Brother Ed has shared that he wished Mother had encouraged his school work and achievements, as she did with Gene.

Although ever loyal to the family, the younger brothers also felt moments of shame as friends and townspeople knew they lived crowded in a home with two families. My brothers early on let Frank's children decide what shows to have on the television. Then the task of getting a picture on the television. I can imagine a brother's embarrassment when Dad routinely called them to adjust the TV antenna. Sending one of the boys to the roof, visible to passersby, he would yell through an open window, back and forth, until a decent picture was secured. Phil said that, when he and Bob finished at Tech and decided to go to graduate school, he knew his leaving home was long overdue, that he had lacked the courage to do it sooner.

We appreciated the good, decent, and stable family life that we had: our parents were present day in and day out, Mother running the household and Dad working to provide for us. Yet at times we felt burdened by our own and our family's limitations. Not surprisingly, we desired independence, recognition, and success. But the private dreams we nurtured were always realistic, the primary pathway being higher education. What unbelievably good luck to have a state college in our home town! Without this—no academic degrees for us—we would never have made the lives we did. The college treasure chest offered new knowledge, a vision of the wider world, and a gateway to careers. But our personal dreams were also buoyed by lessons learned from our parents: work hard and be responsible, good citizens, and loyal toward family.

Another insight, my gender. Being the only girl in the family, has influenced me more than I ever imagined. When I was young, I played with and competed with the older brothers, was an unabashed tomboy, and later emulated their high school and college achievements. As a teen, with the younger brothers, I naturally fell into a mothering role. All the boys, whether in the first or second family, had more freedom and independence than I had. In their teens, they could come and go without much parental concern—whether out with friends or going to and from work, including late at night. Not so with me. I accepted Dad's over-protectiveness, though with private feelings of humiliation. As theatre cashier (even during college), getting off work some evenings at 9:30 p.m., I wasn't allowed to walk the three blocks home or be escorted by an usher. I had to call one of Dad's cabs.

Was I simply too cowardly to speak up for myself, too readily submissive with Mother and Dad? Yes, but maybe not just me. My older brothers were aware of Dad's strictness with me yet did not question this. At our siblings' reunions in the past fifteen years, oldest brother Frank, in hysterics, would recount the incident when I was fourteen and asked Dad about going on a date, and describe Dad's "third degree" interrogation of me about this boy. Although a witness at the time, Frank wisely kept to himself any brotherly sentiments of support for me.

From writing this memoir, a strange thought sometimes hovers over my psyche—I should be thankful for the existence I had. Uncharacteristically letting my imagination run wild: What a piece of luck that I got to be conceived and born as the only girl in this family! In nine pregnancies, eight were boys—not good odds. Maybe I made it in by the skin of my teeth. Once, when I was around eight or nine, I told my mother that I must have been adopted since I was the only girl. Although I was just being cute, seeking attention, her look of shock said I had crossed a line. Coming back to my innate highly rational personality, I am grateful for my unique position among all these brothers—a cornerstone of my developing identity.

Now I wonder about my adult relationships with my younger brothers and begin to sense my failures. I admit to a strong element of *hubris*, constricted emotions, an excessive sense of privacy, and difficulty accessing and expressing deep feelings. Regret haunts me that I never tried to break out of my shell of isolation to tell them openly how lucky and thankful I feel to have them as brothers. But then we all copied our parents' way of being in the world—the demands of life forcing feelings to the back burner. We all may have had an unconscious motive for holding back emotions: the fear of being engulfed in each other's current problems, of being drawn back into the familiar complicated family life we grew up in. I now own up to that fear.

Recently, we have all tried to break out of the pattern of denying feelings and have become more transparent with each other. No longer satisfied with obligatory visits, we seek and enjoy opportunities to spend time together and share aspects of our lives—good and bad. Retirement readily allows for travel, and we take the extra step of making time for each other. Now for my thanks that are much overdue.

Bob is the brother with whom I have had the most contacts through the years—this because we lived for a while in the Grand Rapids area where he and Arlene still live. They took care of our two children when I gave birth to our third child, Matthew. Arlene, the ultimate caregiver, spreads warmth and fun by her very presence. We see them regularly since we travel to Michigan, my husband's home state, at least once a year, and they too have visited our homes in different locations. In the past and currently, we enjoy family celebrations and meals together, talk about our work, hear about my brother's art projects and Arlene's quilting jaunts, and share about our lives and families— not just the good but also worries, failures, disappointments,

Phil and Richard gave a great deal of care and assistance to Mother for many years after Dad died. It's impossible to imagine their constant attention to her. I never thanked them even though I was benefiting from their efforts. I took for granted the comfort and companionship that they provided her, something I felt distance and my work schedule prevented me from doing. Brother Frank showed this same devotion as he too continued to live near her. All three brothers took her places and included her in their family lives and events. For this, I should have thanked them repeatedly. I am glad that I insisted that Mother come to my home for several long visits. Although she didn't like to travel, she came, and my family and I were able to show her our love.

Writing about life with my brothers has revealed much about myself. I should have trusted them with my feelings and shared my childhood dreams and asked about theirs. As an adult, I should have stayed more in touch, made more effort to have honest, open conversations. My memoir has brought us closer: they have welcomed and responded to my many phone calls and emails as I searched out their stories of our lives together and apart. An unexpected new gift from them: I am more in touch with my heart and better able to share that part of me.

Another discovery: I believe my parents never imagined that any of us would leave home or move to distant locations for careers and dreams. With a large family, they had no time to contemplate this future happening, instead unconsciously envisioning their adult children happily living within their purview. Only now, myself in this stage of life, do I understand my parents' sense of loss when, one by one, their children departed into independent lives.

CHAPTER 5

Tomboy-Girlie Girl

I AM FIVE OR SIX as I sit outside our apartment on the concrete ledge below in front of the basement business that sells small mining equipment. I am trying to burn a small piece of string with a match. Suddenly my dad is heading down the steps, "What the hell are you doing? You'll burn down the house." Towering over my trembling body, he swiftly removes his belt. But he doesn't strike me. I'm thinking there's no danger of fire because the string is on concrete. Wisely, I keep my mouth shut about that.

Summertime. Six years old, I've just finished first grade, which I loved. I couldn't wait to get outside and run around with my brothers. We had a new baby in the family, Bobby, just two months old, so Mother was busy, glad to get us out of the house. Right after lunch we stomped down the concrete steps of the apartment, and looked for something to do.

"Let's play marbles," Eddie said. "I'll go back and get them." He was in charge, kept them under his bed, safe in an empty Campbell's soup can. He was my best buddy, just fifteen months older than me but two grades ahead; his January birthday meant he got to enter first grade four months before turning six.

Gene slouched behind, "I don't want to. You can't play that good. It's boring." He always thought he was better than us—just because he was ten and so smart in school. But we were smart too.

Eddie got back. "I fixed up the ground yesterday in Mrs. Young's yard. It's all clear and good hard dirt." So we scattered to our next-door neighbor's house. In a minute, Eddie, kneeling, drew a circle in the dirt, arranged a bunch of marbles. Gene just ignored us, moved on toward the house, sat on the front porch steps, and started yelling at us.

"See this bannister. I jump off all the time. Bet you two can't do it." Eddie, up in a minute, ran toward him, leaving the marbles.

Standing in front of Gene, he said, "Show me. Do it. That's five feet high."

Gene climbed the four steps to the porch, easily getting up, standing on the bannister, "Just watch me." Making a smooth landing, quickly up on his feet, he said, "Don't be a scaredy cat. All you have to do is jump." Then Eddie ran up the steps, lifted one leg over the bannister, pulled himself up, stood on top, and jumped, another smooth landing.

"I can do it too. It's easy," I quickly said. While they watched, I got to the porch, struggled to get onto the bannister, but made it and stood up. "Here I go."

I landed on my feet, but my right knee had pushed up hitting against my jaw. It hurt, a lot. What happened? I tasted blood inside my mouth, spit it out, and hid my hot tears. They looked really scared as I spit out more blood. When Gene said, "C'mon, we got to get you home," we all ran, headed up our steps, inside to find Mother.

They both blurted out, "Janie got hurt. We were just playing. Look inside her mouth."

As soon as Mother saw where the teeth had cut inside my jaw, she called Dad at the taxi stand, and he was home in three minutes. Looking at me, then inside my mouth, he said, "What the hell? What did you do?" He looked mad; we were all even more scared now. Then he said, "Put some toilet paper on it. We'll go to the doctor." So he led me to the cab and off we went. We were quickly at a doctor's office in town—I don't remember his name. I had to keep my mouth open as his fingers in my mouth pushed a needle with black thread through the flesh. I could feel the piercing and threading sensations but it wasn't exactly painful. Dad had me back home, probably within an hour, and drove off to work.

Although my parents were upset, I don't recall any warnings about being a roughneck, any punishment, or any restrictions of my play. I must have gone back for removal of stitches but don't recall that either. After a while we learned that Dad always got mad when we got hurt: Eddie sliced his thumb working on a model airplane, and he got banged up hooking on the back of a car while on a friend's sled. Be we also knew that his anger quickly passed and life went on as usual.

Maybe I was rowdy, ever ready for physical pastimes. Mother reprimanded me once for constantly doing cartwheels in the living room, saying, "You're just too active." Criticism also came from our next-door neighbors, an older couple. Mrs. Mosseau warned my mother about my high activity level, that my hair was always in my eyes, and that this would make me blind. She once asked my mother, "Is Janie hard of hearing? She's always yelling." There's more. Because they never saw me on the front steps playing with dolls, the Mosseaus gave me a doll one Christmas, my only one (I don't remember ever playing with it). I vaguely recall that Mother once asked me, "Why can't you play with dolls like your cousin Mary Ann?" Since no one else criticized me for being wild, I didn't give it a thought. Maybe I didn't play with dolls because I had a real baby brother to play with. And maybe it was a good thing that my mother was so busy, leaving me free to roam outdoors with my brothers, try whatever games and tricks they did.

A favorite hangout, the school playground was just four houses from our apartment. I loved going there, especially in summers. There, for several weeks, a few teenagers supervised and organized games for the younger kids. Dodge ball was the most fun, but I sampled everything: slide, swings and, a set of gray metal tubular horizontal bars, which left me feeling a failure. You could climb up the three bars on either end, and then one hand at time grab the cross bars and "walk the ten bars" swinging from one bar to the next till reaching the end. More than once all I could manage was to swing for two or three bars and then just drop down. One summer, maybe I was eight and Eddie ten years old, we were at the playground and he was easily walking the bars.

I complained, "Why can't I do that?" I showed him and had to drop after reaching the third bar.

He said, "You just have to keep practicing. Get your arms strong and get some callouses on your hands. You're skinny so you should be able to move your body along." After that I kept going to the playground by myself.

A couple of weeks later when we were together and he had forgotten all about it, I said, "Here I go. Just watch me." I got all the way across.

Then he was smiling, "Hurrah! I told you. You did it." I could always count on him, full of energy, enthusiasm, my best buddy.

In grade school recess, I played hard, whatever the game. Later in junior high and high school, I never missed gym, liked our blue cotton gym jump suit, and learned volley ball and basketball with gusto. During this time I admired my gym teachers and imagined becoming one myself. In junior high, no sports programs for girls, but Miss Roeser organized an informal basketball team and took us to play against the girls in a couple of nearby schools. In high school, again no girls' teams, just gym. I never missed a class, never begged off when having my period.

Dad's rules for all of us were strict—no bikes, no swimming, no playing near the river. I know the boys broke the rules at times and mostly escaped detection. But the one time I rode a bike I got caught—I was probably eleven. On a Sunday visit with Uncle Joe and his family, I got on my cousin's "boy" bike and took off down the asphalt street in front of their house, amazed I could ride on my first try. Then I crashed and got hurt. Gravel pierced my knee leaving a small triangle-shaped cut loosening the top layer of skin but not much blood. Again, Dad did a little cussing but got me to the doctor. This time no stitching, he just cut off the skin flap and cleaned out the gravel. Still have the shiny gray triangle scar.

In my younger years, when not at the school playground, I trailed along in the neighborhood mainly with Eddie and girlfriend Gigi—endless games of jacks, tag, roller skating, races, jump rope, hopscotch. Occasionally in the empty lot behind our apartment, a sawhorse turned up along with an old two by four, and we would struggle with the makeshift seesaw. In the house Eddie and I did head stands and tried walking on our hands. We also had moments of patriotism for the war effort: saving foil gum wrappers and gathering scrap metal.

Since my parents also saw my "feminine" interests (not that they knew this label), I doubt they were ever seriously worried about my tomboy activities. Besides, plenty of experiences with my mother gave me a strong dose of the traditional role of wife, mother, and homemaker. And although I never played "dress-up," I liked pretty clothes yet don't recall as a child asking for specific items. I loved a white furry muff for keeping hands warm that my parents must have bought for me. When I was around six, Mother took me to get a "shop" perm: the Shirley Temple curls looked wonderful to me. Except the next day, the frizzy mop head surrounding my face brought on a few rare tears. But without any follow-up memories of this, I must have managed my feelings about my hair.

One Halloween was thrilling when a neighbor teenage girl, Dorothy, dressed me as a gypsy. I loved my looks, a colorful long skirt, make-up, and jewelry—this the only Halloween costume I remember, other than later get-ups trying to look like a hobo. Then my transformation for the prom at the end of eighth-grade. I was invited by one of the "cute" boys. I wore a pretty white dotted Swiss dress with a sweetheart neckline and a waist peplum (did my mother make this?). Richard, my escort, arrived with his mother, who drove us to and from the school. We somehow knew how to dance and mingled with other junior high kids amidst the crepe paper streamers decorating our basement gym. The evening was perfect.

When I was eight, word got out that two sisters from a dance studio in Charleston, would offer tap dance lessons in Montgomery. I signed up, along with Gigi, and other girls I knew. Lessons took place once a week at the town's Woman's Club about six blocks away; we could walk there together after school.

Everything about the dance lessons was fun and exciting for me--learning basic tap steps and working on the group routines for the recital. We must have been exposed to some so-called acrobatic moves. It turned out I was quite good at these—cartwheels, backbends, splits—so the teachers decided I would do an acrobatic routine for the recital. The sketches of the costumes to be made for us were enchanting; mine was a set of satiny red shorts and a sleeveless cream-colored top. To the sound of soft slow piano music, my routine took about two minutes, the performance ending with my final back bend over so far that I picked up a stemmed rose on the floor with my teeth. What a surprise, all the applause! My parents were so proud.

I don't have clear memories of dance lessons the next year or the recital. Some of the older girls had professional-looking black patent leather tap shoes that tied together with a ribbon, but Gigi and I had the shoe repair shop put taps on our brown oxfords. I must have asked for real tap shoes. Later a pair arrived in the mail from my mother's sister Betty, who lived in New York. They were much too big, but I stuffed cotton in the toes and practiced my tap steps outside on the sidewalk. A final vivid memory of this era—I heard the dance teachers criticize people for showing grief at Roosevelt's death in 1945. How mean, I thought. They ended the lessons in our town, so my dance career was short-lived.

The skill that I developed in acrobatics gave me a sense of power in my body. I felt strong as I worked to control and perfect my movements. But I also pursued silly tricks. Somewhere along the line, the term "double-jointed" caught my fancy, and I would proudly show my family how I could bend my thumbs backward to touch my wrist. Another performance—scrunching my bare toes back to the soles of both feet and walking on the bent toes as if in ballet toe shoes (which I always wanted but never had). Being healthy may also have boosted my trust in my body. As a young child, I heard my mother say the doctor thought I had asthma but would grow out of it. Maybe her one smelly mustard plaster treatment on my chest fixed that problem. Other than chicken pox, measles, and mumps, I was rarely sick and aimed for perfect school attendance.

I gradually showed a typical feminine interest in clothes and began noticing what other girls were wearing. Mother on her own bought my dresses (probably from the town's G. C. Murphy's "dime" store or the Sears catalog), usually a cotton print with a belt tying in the back. I wished my dresses would fit tighter in the waist, and I really disliked my brown leather oxfords, wanting nicer shoes. From about ten or eleven I was allowed to go alone to buy things at a children's clothing shop owned or managed by Mrs. Farha. Clothes for sale were piled in stacks all around the tiny, one-room space, no more than a cubbyhole. On greeting me in her heavily accented English, she would start pulling out and recommending things in my size.

Mother taught me some "homemaker" skills not required of my brothers, although they had chores. One day she instructed me on how to iron Dad's white long-sleeved dress shirts. At age nine or ten, I already knew how to handle the iron, but she conveyed that ironing shirts was special, a right way to do it.

There we were, standing at the ironing board in the kitchen. She set out a white shirt tightly rolled after having been sprinkled so it was damp throughout. Then she began the step-by-step directions, explaining slowly as she moved the shirt around and guided me how to iron it.

1. Start with the back yoke on the inside, stretch it around the narrow end of the ironing board, and press. Keep your fingers away from the steam from the damp shirt. Then turn the same area to the outside and press until it is dry.
2. Then each sleeve: first iron the inside then the outside of the cuff, flatten and smooth the sleeve, press, turn over, and press.
3. Next the back of the shirt: stretch it little by little across the board, and iron till dry.
4. Then the shirt fronts: first iron the inside of the button strip, turn to outside, iron around the buttons and rest of shirt front; repeat ironing the inside of the buttonhole area, the outside, and rest of the shirt front.
5. Last, the collar: first iron the back side, reverse it, press carefully so there are no wrinkles on the front of the collar, and fold collar and press on the inside and outside.

After those detailed instructions, Mother didn't assign me the chore of ironing shirts, although Dad wore a white shirt and tie with a suit every day at the taxi stand. (He cared about dressing right as a businessman; for many years he resisted wearing the new short-sleeved white dress shirts.) I don't recall doing much ironing for the family, except my own clothes in high school.

The message I took away from learning this task: Do it the right way, no skimping, no rushing just to get done. I never forgot this skill. Even if it is antiquated in the age of "wrinkle-free" or "permanent press" fabrics, I still use it occasionally ironing my husband's all cotton shirts—not something feminists would approve of. And I taught it to my children, a daughter and two sons (for the boys a necessity since they do more ironing than their wives).

Other so-called feminine experiences with my mother were fun, and I enjoyed spending time with her. She taught me to embroider, and briefly I was interested enough to carefully thread the colorful skeins into leaf and flower patterns stamped on pillow cases or dishtowels. I also learned the simple chain stitch for crocheting but no more; these crafts quickly went by the wayside, not capturing my fancy. I did like the idea of sewing clothes. Mother had made my First Holy Communion dress, and later simple "broomstick" skirts. In high school she and I made a couple of sheath style skirts for me. I have continued to sew a few items from time to time, but mostly window swags and curtains—a practical activity to avoid costs of professional decorators.

One memorable event taught me the hazards of homemaking. I had the tendency to "not hear" or dawdle when Mother asked for help. On a couple of occasions, she pulled my hair to get my attention, get me moving. Then something happened, really pulling my hair, but not by her. I was standing by the Maytag wringer washer in the middle of the kitchen. At ten or eleven, I already knew how to put clothes into the rollers. This job I liked. Suddenly, "Help!" I screamed. The wringer had caught my stringy hair as I bent too close. "Help!" My head had been yanked right up against the rubber rollers. There in an instant, Mother pulled the cord. Scared but safe, I felt the small bald area at the top of my head. I don't recall much fuss or tears from me. Maybe she showed me or I figured out how to pull back my front hair to cover it, secured with a barrette. It soon grew back.

My learning about babies took place by osmosis. Brother Bobby had arrived when I was six. I watched in fascination as my mother sterilized glass baby bottles, mixed the Dextri-Maltose formula, and filled the bottles to refrigerate. I wasn't even aware of breast feeding. Bottle feeding was the new way with babies, and Mother must have welcomed it, with her oldest son being thirteen. Then more of the "nitty-gritty" aspects of babies surfaced. I learned along with her that formula had its down side. Poor Bobby was always terribly constipated, often crying in pain for hours, and on more than one occasion I watched as Mother applied the enema remedy, which seemed to help. If present, my dad had such a graphic way of joking about this, saying the baby "was shooting out marbles" when the enema finally delivered the goods. That problem got solved when cereals and solid food were added to the baby's diet.

I witnessed Mother's caring for others, not just family, because she involved me in this. When I was around nine or ten, we often went with her neighbor and close friend, Mildred, to the hospital to visit Mildred's mother— "Mom Darkey" suffered ongoing serious complications from diabetes. The three of us would walk the four blocks for the evening visiting hour. With little contact with grandparents, this was my first experience with an older, sick person. I liked to go and don't recall being bored or restless while the three women chatted.

Mother was also kind and caring toward Mae, a young woman with limited intellectual ability who rented one of the small units in our apartment building. She had two "illegitimate" children and may have received some type of government child support, but my mother ran her own welfare agency, giving her food and clothing at times. Mae was involved with a more-or-less homeless man, similarly impaired, plus alcoholic; "Boomer Bill" worked for Dad's moving business and was allowed to sleep in the truck during good weather. When Mae had yet another baby, Mother tried to educate her, warning her about sexual relations with this man. On another occasion, when my dad's youngest sister, Aunt Katie, had her second baby, I was sent to help her for a day at their coal company home in Longacre, about two miles away. No doubt, Mother's example of kindness and generosity to family, friends, and acquaintances added a caretaking element to my identity.

As I got older things changed, bringing more balance between my tomboyish, carefree, physical pastimes and my feminine side. It took a shameful experience, around age ten, for me to pay more attention to my appearance and become more responsible for myself.

A warm summer Saturday afternoon, I was at the school playground. Meanwhile, back at our apartment a car pulled up in front—inside two women, sisters, and their niece Joann. They sent her up the steps to get me.

"We're here to pick up Janie," she said. Mother, befuddled for a moment, busy with two little ones, quickly called for Eddie back in the boys' bedroom.

"Eddie, where's your sister?" she said while trying to hide embarrassment from Joann, who was waiting politely in the living room.

"I think she's at the playground."

"Run down there and get her. Make her come quick."

When he came shouting for me, I suddenly remembered catechism lesson. I was to be picked up by two women from the Church and driven, along with their niece, for class. I ran fast ahead of him, saw them in the car, ran up the steps, and found Joann waiting.

"I'm coming, be ready in a minute." She stared at me. I didn't want her there. "Go tell your aunts I'm on my way." My feet were dirty from playing in sandals on the school yard. In the bathroom, I wiped off my face with a damp washcloth and pushed my hair back, a bobby pin to hold it. In my room, I put socks on my dirty feet and quickly changed clothes, pulling a play dress over my head. But I couldn't find my good shoes—till I looked under the living room couch. I somehow managed to get ready and go with them.

That day humiliation slammed my spirits down, but no tears. I had long noticed this family at Sunday Mass, especially their niece, maybe a year older than me, always so well dressed. I had felt envious, but thought that her nice clothes looked more suitable for an older girl. Now for a moment I allow my sense of hurt and neglect to surface, that Mother had not kept track of me, made sure I would be ready on time. At the same time, my guilt takes over: she had five other children at the time and did her best. I should have been more responsible.

From this point on, I grew up fast and assumed care of myself, such as bathing, grooming, selecting clothes and dressing. Maybe Mother helped with these routine activities and I have simply forgotten. I fondly recall the times when my young Aunt Alline briefly lived with us while Uncle Charlie, Dad's brother, was in the Army: she would brush my hair and I would brush hers. Why don't I remember that kind of intimate attention from my mother? If I felt neglected, I was good at keeping any sadness deeply buried. I do remember Mother once treating my head for lice with the protocol of the day: gasoline meticulously applied to the scalp, then a thorough shampoo in hopes of removing the odor. No recollection of personal shame or whether there was a school infestation.

I don't recall that my family paid much attention to my appearance. Being the only girl meant I never had "hand me downs," but there was no abundance of clothes. Mother did say on several occasions that the color red suited me. As early as second grade I noticed with a certain envy a classmate's blond hair done in long curls and thought of another girl as being pretty. As a teenager, I studied *Seventeen Magazine*—for clothes, bras, makeup.

Mostly I liked myself and my appearance, though always wishing to be a little taller than my five feet two. From showering with other girls after high school gym, I thought my breasts were too big. But my skin was good, very few pimples, and I sensed others' approval of my looks. During high school, with my expanding awareness of and desire for social status and Emily Post's guidebook on etiquette, I began paying attention to wedding announcements in the newspaper and forming ideas of a proper wedding. But not much fantasizing about a husband, a dress, or my own wedding—that would come in my distant future. By then I had shifted away from my childhood thought that I would never change my name for marriage.

Unconsciously, I may have begun facing the reality of being a girl. Two unpleasant grade school memories linger. I became frightened when I saw two girls fighting on the playground, shocked at this behavior from girls. Then one day in my sixth-grade classroom I was walking to the pencil sharpener. I was wearing a teal blue, faille type fabric dress with the typical tie back belt, maybe a "church" dress. A boy in the class (from one of the hollows), going in the opposite direction, approached me and put his fingers on my budding breasts, saying, "Titties." Stunned with disbelief, I saw that no one else had seen or heard this and I told no one. I didn't have enough sense to try to sort out what had happened.

Not that I was aware at the time, but being a tomboy as well as a girlie-girl turned out a good mix for me. Back then I was just myself, unaware of such labels. Experiences both within and outside the family were tweaking my developing identity. From my mother I absorbed certain qualities: sensitivity to others' needs, management of tasks, tolerance, acceptance of change, and a tendency toward submissiveness. With my older brothers, I played hard and competed, admired their school achievements, and harbored my own aspirations to excel. With my younger brothers, as I got older, I naturally fell into a mothering role. My dad conveyed my specialness as a girl, but his perspective also meant I was vulnerable and in need of protection, which unconsciously left me cautious, wary, but not openly fearful of others or the world. And just like my brothers, I received our parents' strong message: work hard, achieve, fit into American society, and honor yourself and your family. Now as I ponder the identity of the woman I became, I take a closer look at my mother and other women in my young life.

My mother was not simply a model of "femininity," she was also a competent woman. She was never fussy or preoccupied with my appearance—or her own—although she took pains to look nice when going out in public. While she more than fulfilled the role of submissive wife, other characteristics added to her strong identity. In everything she undertook, she showed a "can do" attitude, strength, and ambition. With courage and resourcefulness, she managed her large family, she had survived the deaths of two children, and she kept our lives stable during and after our father's terrible accident.

Early on Mother told me the story of how she had been smart in school and wanted to become a teacher (although I doubt she ever told my father about this). And throughout my childhood, I saw her own ambitions, not just goals for her children. She subscribed to a book club and ordered and read popular religious novels. Even with childcare and household responsibilities, she also contributed to the family income. For several years Dad owned a small diner next to the taxi stand. Mother kept some of the institutional-size pots and pans at home, cooked spaghetti sauce, meatballs, and chili and sent these items in a cab to the diner, ready to serve to customers. Then for many years she sold her large loaves of homemade bread. This small money-making enterprise started when she gave a loaf as a gift to neighbors; afterwards, to her surprise, many of them put in regular orders insisting on paying one dollar a loaf. Later, around the time I was in college, when Dad owned a tiny neighborhood grocery store after the taxi business was declining, Mother worked at the store when Dad couldn't, and I also filled in occasionally if needed.

Even as a young child in the 1940s and later, I also saw women around me (wives and mothers) who held jobs: younger aunts working as waitresses and several teachers that I admired in junior and senior high school. When we were around eight, my girlfriend Gigi and I played at being secretaries. She had a bunch of order pads from her mother's waitress job, and we would set up an "office" outside on the steps, writing stuff on these, pretending to answer a phone for our jobs.

Other female family members had jobs. A cousin, after finishing high school, joined the Air Force. One of my aunts, wife to Dad's youngest brother, had been in the Waves. And later, I was aware that my Aunt Alline worked as an X-Ray technician at the hospital; she told stories about a female physician there from Germany and her "modern" views about sex and women.

So even our isolated, provincial town was beginning to reflect subtle, embryonic changes in the definition of what it meant to be a woman. Maybe I was unconsciously impressed by these competent women and my mother's ambitions. I just know that from about age eight a powerful dream was hatched in my imagination, a private plan to leave this town.

Other experiences likely nurtured the dream as well. School life continued to add more substance to the plan, since the one constant was my high grades and excelling on standardized tests. I proudly took home report cards and scores. With one straight-A report card, my mother said, "You can always do better." She was proud but still gave a message of humility so that we kids didn't get too full of ourselves. Gradually, I imagined myself becoming a gym teacher (all that tomboy, physical activity still a powerful part of my identity). I was confronted about this idea at a high school basketball game in my junior year. Sitting with my cousin Mary Ann on the gym bleachers, she asked what I wanted to be. When I said a physical education teacher, she said, "Janie, you're too smart to be that." Truthfully, this was an eye-opener for me, so I then set my sights on becoming an English teacher.

Now I can be thankful for the childhood afforded by my large Italian-American family and for the mix that I absorbed of today's so-called masculine and feminine qualities. My older brothers lent me a kind of physical and mental toughness along with ambition expected mostly of boys of my generation. With my younger brothers I gained a sense of comfort and competence with caretaking. From my dad, despite his excessive strictness during my teen years, it was clear that he loved and valued me and that I should settle for nothing less from an intimate partner. Perhaps most of all I am my mother's daughter, and I mean this in a good way. I never set out to fulfill her thwarted ambitions, but I did accomplish a career before marriage. But certain aspects of her submissive and passive nature continue to flow through my body. And not always for good.

In writing each chapter here, the darker reaches of my psyche struggle to come to light. Although I still like myself just as I did growing up and throughout my life, I now glimpse certain long-denied qualities in my character. I see my flaws: submissiveness, denying feelings, excessive sense of privacy, and a need to keep the peace. Although I do better at feeling my difficult emotions, I still suffer in deciding if and how to share them with others who should know and care; too often I expect catastrophe if I speak them. Privacy about personal matters was the norm for my mother's generation, but my sense of privacy and reticence about my feelings and views far exceed my own culture's standards. At other times, the "me" who is cool-headed, unemotional, and unsentimental dominates. Somewhere along the line I over-learned from Mother, or perhaps the whole family, to ignore feelings, keep silent, trust only yourself, and get on with life in the here and now.

The bottom line: I admit that I am not the modern woman I thought I was. But now tiny cracks in my old persona are allowing new messages to creep into my brain: "Try something different, don't suffer in silence, speak up, trust that you will not be destroyed." Will I be able to listen to and heed this voice? Maybe if I keep exploring how I got this way, change will come.

CHAPTER 6

Family and Food

In 1966, WHEN MY HUSBAND and I were living in London, England for a year, I could not find anywhere in the city the pepperoni and black olives I wanted for making a pizza. Appealing to my mother back home, I explained my predicament. A couple of weeks later a greasy package arrived in the mail. We dug in right away, but plenty was left for pizzas.

A vivid memory—I was nine years old, standing in front of my parents' bedroom window at the apartment peering into the shadows of dusk settling on the mountain beyond our street. In my hands a small stained brown paper bag filled with ripe black olives that I must have gotten from the refrigerator. So tasty. I really liked these olives, so different, maybe the first time I had tried them. Nearly in a trance, I kept eating and eating while watching the darkness descend. Suddenly, I felt sick at the stomach. I'd had too many, done something wrong, so I quickly put the bag back in the refrigerator. No one noticed or mentioned later that half of the olives were gone. Maybe I'd learned a lesson! What could it be?

Besides my own first and second families, we were surrounded by a huge extended family, all living nearby. My father's parents in Smithers, his seven siblings, and their spouses and children were important in our lives. Now I've made some discoveries never imagined. We had loving visits and lots of contact with uncles, aunts, and cousins. But there's no nostalgia here about "over the river and through the woods to Grandmother's house." Big Poppy's angry rants kept us children distant from the DiVita grandparents, although every Sunday our family made the obligatory visits to their home.

Writing this memoir led to an unexpected discovery: my brothers and I were deprived of close relationships with grandparents—no pampering or making us feel special, no stories from the old country. The same was true with my mother's parents but for different reasons. We didn't fit the common mold of Italian families who enjoyed warm relationships between the generations. This difference made a difference and was partly responsible for our family's unconscious distancing from its Italian heritage.

Until my Grandmother Maruca died when I was three, my mother's parents continued to live in Adrian, nearly a three-hour drive from our town. So I never knew her, but a picture taken after her funeral shows Mother in a black maternity dress holding me. After my grandmother's death, Grandpa Maruca moved to the New York City area to live with his adult children there. I remember only one visit by him to our house—I was seven and making my first Holy Communion. He was very quiet, spoke only Italian, and did not pretend to an affectionate relationship with us kids; he also had "palsy," which kept me respectful but somewhat aloof around him. I once saw my mother shaving his beard in the living room; that makes sense now: his hands shook so much he couldn't have managed a razor.

With my dad's parents, Big Poppy and Big Mommie, it was impossible to feel close and affectionate. Every Sunday we piled into one of Dad's cabs, and he drove the family for the required visit. We knew what to expect: Big Poppy was scary as he railed against his sons. He demanded that they bring him whiskey and wine—he did the pouring—as he and the men sat at the kitchen table where he sometimes lodged his pistol. For us kids the visit meant giving a kiss and then escaping the kitchen where Big Poppy held court: my brothers would scramble outdoors with cousins and I would huddle with my mother and grandmother in the living room.

My memories find me in that darkened room, sitting on the arm of the navy mohair upholstered chair, fingering the fabric. Although I couldn't understand the Italian my mother and grandmother spoke as they sat close together on the couch, I knew they were talking about Big Poppy. I worried that he could hear them, and even tried to warn them, putting my finger to my mouth, "Shhh!" Yet their talking continued along with my fear. Amidst this atmosphere and hubbub, the women moved in and out of the kitchen, trying to ignore the yelling, cooking the dinner, and waiting for a good time to serve everyone.

I don't recall feeling close to my grandmother or her "making over" me, although I was her namesake (the third granddaughter named Phyllis after Filippa). Maybe Big Mommie did spoil me a bit. She would occasionally fix my pasta with olive oil and broccoli or spinach. I must have dared to say I didn't like tomato sauce; I think she made mine like that because that was how she liked hers. She took her coffee with sugar and heated milk (my preference too as an adult). One of her favorites was a purchased frozen ice-cream treat, a kind of jelly-roll type of chocolate cake filled with vanilla ice cream, rolled, and cut in thick slices. I doubt their refrigerator had a freezer compartment back in 1944-1945, so I guess the package was used all at once and shared with the children. The family may have brought her this dessert when her health was failing.

She died at age sixty-eight, when I was eleven. I remember standing beside my mother at her casket which had displaced the furniture in the darkened living room. In a nice dress, hair fixed as usual, she looked like herself at rest. As directed, I kissed her, dumbfounded as my lips met her frozen stone forehead, but no questions, no tears. I was not taken to the funeral. After her death, we no longer made the Sunday visits.

All the grandchildren were fearful and confused by Big Poppy's behavior, but the adults simply accepted it, and my parents gladly let us kids keep our distance. Now attempting to understand him, I consider some facts just discovered. He had had zero schooling in Sicily and probably started working in the sulfur mines as a child and possibly experienced the rampant child abuse linked with that workplace. Illiterate and ignorant, he must have found both the old and new worlds confusing and frightening. His view of life would have consisted of his country's most rigid cultural traditions and myths. Surviving the hard work and oppressive conditions in the West Virginia coal mines must have seemed an improvement over the horrific work conditions left behind. In America he succeeded in supporting his large family and owning property.

But why all the ranting? Clearly his weekend alcohol binges could have triggered grievances that occupied his psyche. He may have expected a level of financial support from his adult sons that never met his standards. His paranoia and disappointment no doubt infuriated him even further as they asserted independence and left the family home place he had set up in Smithers. Instead of the old country structure of family togetherness, one by one they moved out, with the youngest four sons marrying "American" women. Perhaps he saw his offspring as denying their Italian heritage as they established their own families. These speculations would be my most charitable interpretation. Or he may simply have been consumed by rage for unknown reasons.

Overall, the lack of loving care and attention from the DiVita grandparents, along with our own conscious avoidance, diluted the influence of the old country culture, with good and not so good results. When Mother and Dad left Smithers behind, they likely had several motives—more room for their growing family, closeness to Dad's work, escape from the place where two children had died, and distancing from the fury and control of the family patriarch.

Our parents took a chance that the new location would bring happiness and independence, while still allowing them to respect the older generation with Sunday visits; however, those contacts ended with Big Mommie's death. More and more Montgomery became our world and our relationship with our parents intensified. They and our tightly-knit family became the major influence on our characters and personalities. We siblings too would experience, as we got older, the spark of desire for independence from family while also unconsciously pledging love and loyalty.

As a widower, Big Poppy remained distant and angry, although his sons continued to visit him at times without their families. On rare occasions, word got out: "Big Poppy is coming. He's on his way, walking to Montgomery." A chain of phone calls alerted everyone in the family, eliciting fear of a terrible fate about to befall if he visited. I am unsure whether he ever actually came to our house; perhaps he went to see my dad at the taxi-stand. After I left home, he apparently came once for a Thanksgiving dinner. When he began a rant at the dining room table, my mother, who had become more outspoken by that time, said (in Italian, no doubt), "I will not have you ruining my family's dinner." Dad got up, called a cab, escorted Big Poppy to the door, and sent him on his way. But he apparently still had plenty of gumption. In his early seventies, he had a nineteen-year old woman living in his house. When he later married her, the family was totally scandalized. The story is that my dad and Uncle Tony arranged to pay off the woman to divorce him and leave town.

In our household the evening meal was considered sacred, and we knew to be home before Dad arrived. When I was little, around six to eight, I didn't like certain foods (spaghetti, meatballs, peas) but that soon changed. Mother made all dinners from scratch, and we were blessed with tasty Italian dishes, traditional American holiday meals, and occasionally one of her food experiments, some of which failed. Once she made beef liver in tomato sauce, the smell was terrible and the meat like leather; at least she didn't make me eat it. She also tried new recipes that she saw in magazines. One item was a ham and buttered white rice casserole, which led several family members to ask, "Where's the sauce?" (I know she was disappointed, as I have been on occasion by my husband's cool reaction to new recipes.) Every birthday was celebrated with a homemade cake, the birthday song, blowing out candles, and a kiss from everyone. I don't recall gifts being part of the tradition, but that may have changed after I left. Mother was in charge of food preparation but we kids sometimes helped.

Spaghetti and meatballs were served family style, the pasta and tomato sauce mixed together, put on a large platter, and passed around. She made the sauce, using a skillet to fry the tomato paste in a little oil, watching and stirring as it browned, careful to not burn. This would go into a large sauce pan, along with water and other items like onions, and canned to-mato sauce. Meat balls were made with ground beef, bread crumbs, egg, and sautéed chopped onions, mixed with her hands and formed into balls to fry in a heavy skillet, then added to the sauce to simmer an hour or two. A salad too might be part of this meal: iceberg lettuce with vinegar and oil mixed together by my mother's hands, no concern about keeping the greens crisp in those days.

We always had Mother's homemade bread but didn't appreciate it for the treat it was until we got older. Every other day she made it, filling the large pan (the size and shape of a dishpan) with a well of flour, then adding the yeast, oil, salt, and water, and kneading the mixture with her hands. With a little oil, she would finish with a big, smooth round mound, make the sign of the cross on top, and cover it with a damp cloth. After the first rising, she would roll sections of dough for large bread pans, and cover them to rise again. Coming home after school, we were intoxicated by the delicious aroma of baking bread and could hardly wait for a slice slathered with margarine. If it was still in the oven, my younger brothers' friends made a habit of hanging around long enough to have a slice too. Her bread was standard fare with meals and evening snacks of olives and parmesan or provolone chunks.

When we were younger all of us were present for supper. Dad might miss a meal if he couldn't get away from the taxi stand. Once we all had jobs and school activities, supper time became more flexible. We quickly learned to eat early or late or make our own meals as needed.

There was nothing in town that could be called a restaurant, but as we got older, I'm sure we all had enough change in our pockets at times to go to Eddie Kelley's (was it a drug store, a confectioners' shop?) to sit in a booth for a hamburger. Or we went to the College Drug Store soda counter for a sandwich. I remember Gene as a youngster saying he occasionally got a marshmallow sundae from the dime store, this flavor since, if he spilled any on his white shirt, Mother would not notice. On rare times when my dad took one or more of the boys to Charleston (such as to buy them a suit), they would report eating a "plate special" at a small restaurant. But there was no such thing as the family or parents going out for a meal. Home was where the serious cooking and eating took place.

GET TOGETHERS AND STOPPING BY

As for visits and shared meals with Dad's family, we probably had the most contact with Uncle Tony and Uncle Joe, the brothers closest to his age. They and their families often "stopped by" after suppertime for snacks at our house, and we would visit them occasionally for a planned Sunday supper. Tony and Catherine and some of their kids might come briefly on a Saturday evening and sometimes Tony alone on a weekday evening. Other uncles, aunts, and cousins also stopped for informal visits.

With everyone around the kitchen table, Dad made drinks for the men, typically Four Roses whiskey and coke or 7-Up, the women and kids would have soft drinks, and my mother would set out whatever snacks she could put together. Talk was free-flowing about everything—goings on in town, family, people, etc. The youngest kids often sat on my dad's lap, and Tony, who was a city policeman, and later chief, would blow his whistle delighting the little ones. The alcohol for the men was just part of the hospitality. At these kitchen-table gatherings over the years, I remember standing behind the chair of an aunt or uncle, just listening, not thinking, feeling happy belonging to all these relatives.

Besides talk about work, jobs, neighbors and children, the conversations often included politics, the coal mines, local events. Dad's two sisters were married to coal miners. Among his brothers, Tony was a policeman in town, Joe worked for a mortuary, Frank had several different jobs, eventually leaving West Virginia and owning a jewelry store, and Charlie and Jimmy, after returning from the war, each owned a gasoline service station. My parents were life-long Democrats and supporters of unions. The talk sometimes sparked disagreement, especially in the face of mine strikes and workers' suffering. During one of these periods, Dad's youngest sister, Katie, and her coal miner husband had an occasional meal with us, and Mother sometimes passed on canned goods in a paper sack as they left.

I remember a scene with talk about an upcoming city election, probably for mayor and city council. Uncle Tony laughingly reported that he had been out "electioneering, getting a little Black on me." I guess he had to worry about keeping his job as policeman, which was determined by who ran the city government. I was too young or too ignorant to be alarmed by his remarks. Comments about

Blacks were not common in our household, although the adults sometimes shifted to Italian when they didn't want kids to understand. On more than one occasion, they used an Italian word for Blacks, which I learned later was derogatory.

A memorable tradition was our Sunday morning breakfasts after church. These began once we moved to our house on Third Avenue, just two blocks across the tracks from the Catholic Church. One or two aunts and uncles and their kids would come by after church, and Mother would cook breakfast for all, including our family.

As family members came in the front door talking, she quickly changed from church clothes. Then she hit the kitchen, started first mixing a large batch of biscuits, put the bacon on to fry, and kept up with the conversation. She made what she called "drop" or "lazy" biscuits, just spooning the soft dough onto the cookie sheets. With her magical timing, she knew when to start the eggs, frying them in a large skillet, spooning bacon grease to finish them off, and placing them on a large platter. She managed to get everything ready at the same time. Others and I helped, placing the food on the kitchen and dining room tables and pouring coffee. Everyone dug into eating, while conversations went in several directions. And, yes, to an outsider it would have sounded loud, but not to us.

This informal family ritual took on a life of its own. My mother didn't have to "wait" on everyone but she was in charge. I am not sure whether she ever felt "put upon" by this tradition. But I wonder how we always had enough food for such a large group, often around six to eight relatives plus our family. I believe now that she planned for it and made sure to buy enough during Saturday's grocery shopping.

The family most often at the Sunday breakfasts were Tony and Catherine and their children from Smithers Hill. Mother and Dad and we younger children occasionally had a Sunday meal at their house. Since several of their kids attended our grade school in Montgomery, their boys sometimes came home with my brothers for school lunch. "Stopping by" was a typical pattern since we lived in town; the relatives living a mile or two away had to come there anyway for shopping, doctors, other appointments, and church. In fact, unannounced visits were common during that era, the way people engaged with family and friends—no preplanning, no appointment, no imposition.

Going to visit Tony's family on a Sunday was an adventure, mainly be-cause of the precarious road leading to their house on the hill. It was a steep trek on a dirt road, no switch-back engineering. We kids would sit in the back of the cab rooting for Dad to make it up the hill, gunning the motor all the way till we reached the dirt crossroad to turn on, about halfway up the hill.

Coming back from the visit, we would all sometimes go to the movies in Montgomery. My dad would take our family, along with some of Tony's kids in the cab, to the theatre, and their dad would pick them up after the show. We all got in free as my brothers and two of Tony's sons worked there. One memory stands out (I was probably eleven). Dad dropped us off at the Kayton Theatre. As we trekked in I heard the doorman say, "There must have been thirteen people get out of that car." My face burning, stung by this comment, I may have wondered if his remark was meant as an ethnic slur. Regardless, it tagged my family as lower class—not good enough. Later, when I was a cashier and worked with this doorman, I remembered his words and never liked him.

The visits and meals at Uncle Tony's and Uncle Joe's homes offered experiences different from our household. Uncle Tony and Aunt Catherine lived in a house he probably built, but now the layout reminds me of Italian village homes. The main floor had a kitchen and adjoining dining area and a bathroom; upstairs were three bedrooms and a living room. Displayed there, an impressive formal photo of Catherine's brother, Frank Yaquinta, who was a chief petty officer in the Navy, along with unusual souvenirs he had sent, one a gray heavy stone statue of a leopard. Catherine's other brother Dominic lived across a path in a house nearby with his wife Connie; this couple surprised everyone by marrying late in life and starting a family.

Aunt Catherine cooked a tasty dish we never had at home: chicken pieces in tomato sauce with pasta. When I stayed overnight with my cousins, Phyllis and Mary Ann, who was my age, I got to know Nonna, Catherine's mother, who lived with them. We three and Nonna slept in a double bed, with my cousins warning me to not bump against Nonna, as her legs were painful from having been burned years before in a house fire; she always wore heavy tan cotton stockings, even in bed. Although my cousins had a close loving relationship with their grandmother, I was a bit wary: she had once yelled, scolding me in Italian when I climbed on one of the peach trees in their yard. I was scared and didn't know what I did wrong, only learning later as an adult about the fragility of fruit trees.

Visiting Uncle Joe's home was always enjoyable, especially because of Aunt Maxine; she was friendly, talkative, affectionate, and had the most wonderful Virginia (Southern) accent. We also got to sample her food specialties—light dinner rolls, cornbread, pot roast, and other dishes we didn't get at home. On more than one occasion she stopped by our house in the middle of the day, headed for the kitchen, and started a batch of cornbread. Mother welcomed her, pulling out and greasing a large cast iron skillet for the batter. An unexpected treat!

The contacts with Dad's family were pleasant and friendly, with everyone seeming to get along. How did this happen, given their father's lifelong pattern of angry outbursts? I think they intentionally rejected his hostility to family, though this is not to say there were never minor jabs and criticisms among in-laws. My mother noted in her Memoirs that Father Doyle, our priest, had once told her that it was a wonder that Dad and his brothers turned out as good as they did, saying, "From the example of their father they could have all been gangsters (p. 62)."

Only after I left home did I hear about a feud between two of Dad's brothers, then adults. It apparently happened when one of them decided to pay a couple of nephews for helping him on a home project, while the other one denounced this action, arguing that pay was not expected or appropriate for family help. This spat eventually got resolved but "hard feelings" went on way too long.

It was interesting how the wives of my father's four younger brothers fit in with the DiVita family. Of course, they were all "American." The Sunday visits that featured Big Poppy's meanness had mostly ended by the time these women married their husbands, but they knew the history and the family's estrangement from him. From time to time these aunts all visited and were close to my family.

When Uncle Charlie was in the Army, his young wife Alline had lived with us and felt like a big sister to me. She was funny and fresh and talkative, and made every one of us kids feel special--we loved her dearly. Aunt Maxine was a lot like her, and we missed her and our times together when their family moved to Charleston. We didn't see Jimmy and his wife June as often but we had pleasant times together. Once when I spent a day with her at their house soon after their marriage, she showed me how to make a mayonnaise chocolate cake.

Uncle Frank's wife Muriel was a little different, more outspoken. I remember her telling a story about being in a meeting with our parish priest, maybe for catechism lessons before they married; she said she saw the priest put his hand on the thigh of a woman sitting next to him. On occasion I heard family members criticize Muriel's candid remarks. I think now that she was just being herself and didn't accept some of the DiVita family notions about women and didn't care whether she fit in. Still her visits with us were friendly. Their son Franklin played with my brothers, Bob and Phil, and was sometimes seen as the instigator of the boys' trouble-making. One story I heard—when the boys complained about having no baseball, Franklin left and returned twenty minutes later with a brand new one, no questions asked. (Of course, he matured into an upstanding citizen!)

I have never forgotten something Aunt Muriel said (which got back to me). During my adolescence, she remarked privately to another aunt about my developing breasts, "Look at that, they will be down to her waist by the time she's sixteen." On hearing about this, my feelings were hurt but I told no one, though the aunt telling me was outraged. Muriel was simply being herself, which was her right, just as she always made sure everyone pronounced her name correctly (not Merle). Unlike the DiVitas, she spoke her mind. Uncle Frank and his family moved out of state during my teenage years, so we lost face-to-face contact.

HOLIDAYS AND SPECIAL TREATS

For holiday dinners—Easter, Thanksgiving, Christmas—the relatives celebrated at their own homes with their children. The exception was an occasional picnic for the Fourth of July that might involve several families. For those events we typically met at a state park such at Hawk's Nest or a county park such as Beckwith, easily a twenty-mile drive. A certain amount of begging from us kids was necessary to convince Dad to go. Probably with good reason as I now realize. This was not the era of portable folding lawn chairs to lounge in, so the long day meant the adults had to sit around a hard picnic table or on a blanket on the ground while the kids madly gave the swings and monkey bars a workout or pestered for permission to go to the pool (if there was one). The main event was the food which each family prepared and all shared—plenty of home fried chicken, potato salad, green beans, and pies and cakes—no Italian fare unless it was snacks such as olives and homemade bread.

My father's involvement with food meant fun or surprise. Although Mother and at times my older brothers did the main grocery shopping at the local A & P Store, Dad sometimes independently bought special foods. This became a family tradition that we looked forward to. Probably because of being in business, he was able, especially around holidays, to get certain foods at wholesale prices. I remember routinely seeing twenty-five-pound bags of flour and one-pound packages of caked yeast. He may also have placed special orders through the Cavalier's Italian grocery store in Smithers. One day he came home with a large package of veal steaks, something we had never had. He supervised dinner that night: the steaks along with sliced onions broiling in the oven gave an aroma that left our mouths watering. That meal was a treat.

Cavalier's Grocery must have had a direct source from New York for Italian specialties. From time to time, Dad brought home artichokes and ripe olives, also green olives and lupino beans for curing in brine. But the dried black Greek style olives with pits were the best! Mother would spread the wrinkled olives on a cookie sheet, add a little crushed red pepper and garlic powder, and heat them in a warm oven for about twenty minutes for plumping and then devouring as snacks with homemade bread. Another treat was ricotta cheese, which came packaged in large round cardboard cartons, maybe three or four pounds. This we would eat, just spooning it from the container or on a saucer, not in lasagna or desserts. Never since then have I tasted ricotta cheese as good as that. While these kinds of Italian items are common today in most large supermarkets, that was not the case back then. Only as adults have my brothers and I come to appreciate how lucky we were to sample these delicacies.

Dad oversaw the production of his major food specialty, Italian sausage homemade from scratch. His recipe: buy a large fresh pork picnic ham, cut it up, and put it in the hand grinder clamped to the kitchen table; to the ground meat, mix fennel seed, crushed red pepper, salt, black pepper, and garlic powder. Using an attachment for making links, he finished the sausage process. His gift: to have the sausage oven-broiled and ready for our feast when we returned from Christmas midnight mass. Afterwards we would open presents. We probably had his sausage at other times as well, but Dad was our hero for the Christmas Eve celebrations.

His sense of humor often came through at meal times when he added his special grace: "In the name of the Father, Son, and Holy Ghost, whoever eats the fastest eats the most." Following his recipe, I occasionally make Italian sausage, though using the food processor and skipping the links. My two West Virginia brothers, Phil and Richard, now keep the family traditions going, often joining together to make large batches of Italian sausage links and, at Christmastime, Mother's Italian fruitcakes.

Maybe there were lean years, but we always had good food. I don't remember emphasis on presents or even asking for a present except once during college. The year I was twelve was memorable: Dad bought the Christmas presents himself at the last minute and sent them home in a cab, not wrapped. When they arrived around nine p.m. on Christmas Eve, we were thrilled. I got pink double-knit pajamas. I think Beatrice, the young woman who answered the phone at the taxi stand, ordered the gifts from the Sears catalog, but maybe Dad helped with selections. We kids were probably thinking there would be no gifts as nothing had been wrapped and put under the tree. Mother never offered her thoughts on these presents. Later as a teen, a kind of second mom, I took charge and ordered Christmas toys for my younger brothers.

On occasion Dad cooked other dishes he thought would be special. One thing he attempted more than once (which Mother dreaded to see) was chicken meatballs. I remember him in the kitchen one Sunday afternoon. After having a few drinks, he was deboning cooked chicken, pulling it off with his fingers, a cigarette dangling from his mouth. He seemed intent, so she just left him alone. He used egg and bread crumbs as filler to form the meatballs, then started frying them, hoping they'd stick together. Maybe a taste for me, but I was never interested in that dish.

We differed from some Italian-American families when it came to holiday meals. Our traditional American meals featured turkey, ham, roasts, potatoes, vegetables, and pies—things everyone liked. For Christmas or Thanksgiving, my mother was up at up at five a.m. to start the all-day baking required for a twenty-five-pound turkey. But we didn't have spaghetti or lasagna to go along with the meal (which was common with urban Italian-Americans). Occasionally she made Christmas "baccali" (dried codfish soup, not a favorite of mine) and more often Italian fruit cakes, biscotti, along with traditional American/Southern fruit cake. Later, as adults with our own families, when any of us came back home to visit, our family went into holiday mode. The meals once again became the centerpiece for celebration.

Looking back, I see my brothers and me mostly taking for granted our large extended family—they loved us and we loved them back. But until now I hadn't realized that we were deprived of the close relationship with grandparents so typical in Italian-American families. Big Poppy's rages led his adult sons and daughters to distance from him and set up their own independent homes. Without intention, this also brought a certain detachment from their Italian heritage. They had less incentive to speak in Italian and gave no thought to teaching their children the language. While they wanted to fit in with the local community, all of Dad's siblings stayed close among themselves and preserved the sense of *famiglia*. For me, that meant more layers of love and belonging.

It seemed normal to have all these DiVita relatives who, like us, had complicated personalities and problems. The adults shared their worries and complaints and received family support. Yet no one fell apart or gave up—they just dealt with whatever came their way. In this we were ordinary families, like millions of Americans: parents got up every morning, cared for children, did duty on the job and at home, and kept striving for a good life. Today's generation may not grasp the simplicity of life in the 1940s and 1950s, in that small town in West Virginia. As children and youth, my brothers and I were comfortable in and accepted that world as our given fate, even as we imagined our different futures in the larger society.

Like other second- and third-generation immigrants, at some point we realized the gifts from our Italian heritage and began to reclaim and rejoice in then. My brother Gene made two trips to Italy and obtained some family documents. More recently, my youngest brother Richard and Cousin Charlie, along with their wives, have spent time in Sicily and sought out family information. Seeing their videos and hearing of their adventures and discoveries, we all feel a new closeness with the old country and its traditions. But mostly we marvel at the courage of our ancestors. Charlie's extensive research has produced new information about our Great Grandmother DiVita and relatives in Rochester, New York. Although we have had a couple of large reunions with many extended family members attending, these have unfortunately become rare as people have aged and scattered across many states.

My brothers and I have reached a stage where we want more contact and make it happen: we set up mini-reunions for ourselves and invite cousins, nieces, and nephews to attend if they are able. For me, these gatherings offer an opportunity to express and demonstrate my love. It seems a chance to make up for a certain isolation and emotional distance during my years devoted to career and my own family. Although my husband and I liked to travel and made numerous trips back to my parents' home, today, more than ever, I feel a new sense of closeness, am more comfortable with my feelings, and want to share them. In our recent reunions we seem to step out of our shells of individuality and honestly engage with each other's lives; embrace our Italian heritage; honor our mother, father, and two oldest brothers who are gone; discover new family stories and re-tell old ones; enjoy good times, good food, good wine; and finally, create new contemporary memories for our family.

CHAPTER 7

Our Town: Location, Location, Location

ONE NIGHT AFTER WORKING ON this chapter I dream that I am in my home town. Walking down a side street I see on both sides that the buildings have been entirely remodeled: everything is white and bright with huge windows, looking somewhat sterile but also much like store fronts in a new mall. The buildings all seem to be empty and I do not enter any store.

Another warm summer afternoon with nothing much going on. I was sweeping the kitchen linoleum floor, like Mother told me. She picked up the ringing phone, talking less than a minute.

"Janie, come here. I need you to do something."

"What is it?" She seemed excited and I couldn't imagine what she wanted.

"They have nylon stockings at Murphy's. I think they're letting you buy two pairs. I need you to go quick before they're all sold out."

"Will they sell them to me? How do I find them?"

"Just look around the women's counters and you'll see them. Look for a line. Get in it and stay in it. Get the shade called 'Gunmetal' if they have it, or just get two pairs of any kind. Here's the money. Just go straight to the store and straight back home."

I headed out the door of our apartment. I was ten, knew the way, and had been there by myself before. Still a little scared though. I understood—the war had meant no nylon stockings, and my mother had talked about this.

Now I have learned more of that situation: "The shortage persisted into 1946 but by March, Du Pont was finally able to ramp up production and began churning out 30 million pairs of stockings a month. Widespread availability of the stockings ended the period of 'Nylon Riots'."[4] At that time there were other shortages too. When I was younger, it was fascinating that every kid in our family had a "ration" book with our names that allowed for buying the restricted grocery items.

I ran down our street, Fourth Avenue, to the section where it ends and slides into Third Avenue, a traffic light there. No cars, so I crossed, rushing on two more blocks, past my dad's taxi stand, not slowing down to see if he was there, and on to the "dime store." I easily got the stockings and was proud of my accomplishment—I could get around in our town by myself.

Before Montgomery, West Virginia, became our hometown in 1940, we lived a mile away and across the Kanawha River in Smithers, an even smaller village with dirt streets. When my parents made the move, they were excited and hoped for a happier life compared to the daily stress endured at the DiVita family home place. Our new town shaped much of the evolution of our family—my parents, six brothers, and me in the middle. Even with its paved streets, there was no escaping dirt with trains running through the middle of town pulling coal cars. Here I spent a long time growing up—until I left at age twenty.

A current online description of the town in those days (1940s and 1950s) called Montgomery "the commercial center for the surrounding coal mining and ferro-alloy industries; a boom town with a hospital, department stores, and the college."[5] The hospital also offered, in conjunction with the college, training to become a registered nurse. But there was more: a high school and elementary/junior high, a segregated Black elementary and high school, two dentists, and several physicians. The three or four drug stores sold food at lunch counters and booth areas. Then the usual—two movie theatres, two banks, two furniture stores, two hardware outlets, a large G. C. Murphy store, an A & P supermarket plus a couple of small neighborhood grocers, women's and men's clothing stores, a small department store, a piece goods shop, a run-down three-story hotel where some local old men lived, several Protestant churches, and the Immaculate Conception Catholic Church, which my family attended. Montgomery could meet most of the basic needs and wants of area families. One other important point, since West Virginia was a dry state, there were no bars, and so-called 3.2 (non-intoxicating) beer was available at only two places in town, these, of course, off-limits to my brothers. A State-run liquor store, however, sold alcoholic beverages.

The town sits squeezed into a valley, between the Kanawha River and a mountain range to the north and another mountain range to the south. Across the river, U. S. Route 60 takes you twenty-five miles west to Charleston, the State capital. The railroad runs through the center of town, east and west, parallel to and directly across from Third Avenue, the main street. The seven east-west streets, less than a mile long, sit in the narrow valley. You could count them starting from the base of the south mountain: Fayette Pike, First, Second, Third Avenue "uptown," with five blocks of businesses, then Fourth, Fifth, and finally Sixth Avenue running along the river. The eight north-south cross streets are shorter; the entire town area consists of about one and one-half square miles. Typical residences when I was growing up were modest frame houses, some shabby and deteriorating, along with a few nice two-story brick homes with larger yards. People always said that Montgomery was land-locked and couldn't grow.

Photo (source unknown) posted March 4, 2016 by David Ramsey on Facebook site: "I Grew up in Montgomery, WV": https://www.facebook.com/photo.php?fbid=1311161718900265&set=g.223454277701101&type=1&theater&ifg=1

The apartment we moved to first now reminds me of a miniature city tenement because it was surrounded by concrete. At 124 ½ Fourth Avenue, it sat close to the sidewalk, the sidewalk next to the road, and just beyond the road, the railroad tracks. Twelve concrete steps led to our entrance; a concrete pad fronted the finished basement space below, which housed a mining equipment sales business. Adding to the tenement feel—at the back-right side of the building was the entrance to two other adjoining small apartment units upstairs. Although I didn't know it at the time, my parents owned this building.

Now I see the town as a mini-version of America's "melting pot." It included a few families representing diverse backgrounds: Italian, Lebanese, Syrian, Arab, Hungarian, Irish, Jewish, Scots-Irish, Blacks, and English, who were the majority and the town's founding fathers. The town was segregated. I encountered few Black people and was unaware of the location of their "section" of town or the segregated schools. One Black family lived about five houses from us, but we didn't know them. Walking by there, I occasionally saw an old man, probably a grandfather, sitting on the porch of the ramshackle house, with a couple of very young children. Of course, when I worked as a cashier at the theatres (also segregated), I sold tickets to Black customers. Around 1955, a young man from South Carolina became the first Black student to enter the local state college. Two years later during my student teaching, I had one or two Black students in my class. So integration was underway by then.

Unlike Smithers, our previous home, Montgomery had a variety of immigrants but not a high concentration of Italian-Americans. In my eighth-grade class section, my cousin Mary Ann and I were the only students of Italian descent; now I realize the class also had one student each from Jewish, Syrian/Arab, Lebanese, Hungarian, and Slavic ethnic groups. The high school had more ethnic diversity as it served students from Smithers and surrounding small towns.

The fact that Montgomery was not a "Little Italy" created a difference that made a difference and one of several conditions that diluted our family's connection to the "old country" culture. Without the high concentration of Italian immigrants, we were likely protected from the worst stereotypes. Away from the Smithers neighborhood, my parents did not consciously distance from their heritage; they just wished to escape the daily criticism and meddling from the DiVita family and other Italian compatriots. In town, they felt free to run their own lives and pursue their own ambitions. There, without conscious awareness, we all ended up making friends from several different cultures.

Unlike the experience of some Italian immigrants in large cities, our town seemed relatively free of the most hurtful of stereotypes. We had no parochial schools, and our local Catholic church did not celebrate saints' festivals with public parades—the kind of thing that led to suspicion and criticism of Catholics in urban areas. Also missing was the rampant stereotype of Mafia mobsters and newspaper charges of Italian immigrants' support of Mussolini during the war. With all local children in public school, we felt just like everyone else. I sensed acceptance by the community—from school, church, neighbors, friends, and people who worked in the local businesses. Only occasionally did we feel prejudice, although some people may have kept negative attitudes private.

What does it say about me that I didn't define myself then as Italian-American? I was just myself, no different from other kids; my younger brothers have reported the same response. I recall only one troubling situation. When I was around six and playing a block behind our apartment with two kids from a doctor's family, they called me a "Tally." Knowing this was a bad thing but not why, I ran home and told my mother. I was shocked that my quiet, unassuming mother immediately went to their house and told their mother that her children's behavior was unacceptable.

Although my parents wanted to fit in with the community, they did not reject their Italian heritage; nonetheless, loosened ties resulted. They still spoke Italian to our DiVita grandparents, but the Sunday visits ended with our grandmother's death. Even before, Big Poppy's alcohol-fueled angry ranting allowed us kids to avoid adults' Italian conversations, and our parents made no attempt to teach us the language. They occasionally drifted into Italian with relatives if the topic was not for our ears, or in fun they might call one of us a name such as *testa dura,* hard-headed/stubborn.

Fitting in was important for my dad's business; he had to interact everyday with customers and enjoyed this. And he dealt with other business people, especially bank owners and employees—his need for loans was unending. He made friends and was included in some social activities, such as poker and gambling groups. My mother also enjoyed contacts with a variety of friends and neighbors without regard for their ethnic background.

Our parents seemed happy living in the town. When we kids occasionally asked if they would like to visit Italy, the answer was always a definite no. They also said they knew nothing about the Mafia, except that it started to protect immigrants from harassment and violence. They did not deny their Italian-American identities, but as they embraced life in their hometown, we did the same and simply felt like full-fledged Americans, which we were. My mother was born in America and Dad was a naturalized citizen.

Compared to the urban environments where many Italian immigrants settled, our location was extremely isolated and provincial. Unlike cities, our town didn't have parks, public libraries, museums, organized sports for children, or professional sports teams to follow, so we remained unaware of these limitations. But we appreciated the small-town events and pleasures. The town was patriotic and celebrated certain holidays with a parade. I remember a Memorial Day parade that ended on the Montgomery Bridge, with a wreath being tossed in the river. I also recall at least one city "festival" on a Saturday night; it offered a few carnival-like games, food, and jeep rides for entertainment. Another happening that sent our household running to the front porch to watch—the high school band practicing and marching, majorettes leading the way.

What can I say—not a lot of excitement! On the other hand, we didn't have daily exposure to crime and danger. Our family was shocked to hear that my mother's sister's son in Brooklyn, New York, was in a juvenile detention facility. Mother's big city relatives occasionally stopped by for an unexpected visit. What a surprise! Gesturing wildly, they talked rapidly and incessantly, outspoken, not holding back thoughts and feelings—so different from our family. From such experiences, we felt a sense of innocence and ignorance, a kind of inferiority that we tried to overcome through higher education and later by embracing the wider world. Our town's simple, unsophisticated atmosphere seeped into our identities and personalities, tempering ambition with a sense of hesitancy about spreading our wings.

We knew that life in surrounding areas, the "hollers" near the coal mining operations, was much harsher than ours. Yet school was something of an equalizer in that regard. While I was aware that some kids came on the bus from these locations, I don't recall disparaging talk among my friends, though the "townies" could have been cliquish. One experience made an impression on me. I was a freshman and, as a Homecoming attendant, went to the after-game school dance. A boy I knew from out of town, friendly, nice, smart, also in the Homecoming court, asked me to dance. Once we began I was startled to feel his hand against mine. It was so rough and calloused that I instantly realized the hard labor he must do in his family: probably hauling water into the house, chopping wood for heating, working in a garden. Yet this boy had been elected by classmates.

Our name was spelled Divita (no upper-case *v*), and for most of my life pronounced "Da vit' ee," (accent on second syllable and last syllable as if ending in a *y*). We grew up with this pronunciation and never questioned it—until my older brothers' college professors pronounced the final *a* as *a*, not *y*. But through our college days, without concern, my siblings and I answered to both pronunciations. Who if anyone told my dad or his father on arriving in America how to pronounce their last name? We knew that Ellis Island agents had told Dad that his Italian given name, Liborio, would become Benny, and so it did. That familiar name likely ended up a good choice for a man who wanted to fit in the society and eventually run a service business. The West Virginia townsfolk probably said our last name to the best of their ability, and our elders accepted it. Only gradually did we learn that the correct Italian pronunciation should be "DaVeeta" and the *V* should be upper case.

Our parents had always told us the name meant "of life," which I liked. As older adults and after Brother Gene had visited the Italian homeland, some of us chose to reclaim the original Italian spelling, DiVita, despite worrying that others might see this as "putting on airs." Another Italian family in our area reinstated their original name Bria for the anglicized Bree.

Growing up, my brothers and I happily regarded this town, this state, as home. It was all we knew until we gradually began to see bits and pieces of the world. Only later in life did we learn about the history of the coal and chemical industries, the limited opportunities for jobs, the corporate exploitation of the land and residents, the extreme dangers, accidents, and deaths associated with the mining industry, and seemingly ongoing governmental corruption. It was not until I was required to take a college course on West Virginia history that I learned about the Hawks Nest Tunnel disaster, one of the country's worst occupational catastrophes resulting in hundreds of workers' deaths from silicosis.[6]

Before all the public outcry against strip mining and revelations about the State's industry in general, as we kids were growing up, we simply sensed the importance of coal and chemical operations. Even driving by the Union Carbide plant in Belle, with the rotten egg odor miles away, we just joked about it. We felt a sense of patriotism and pride that these industries were the life line for our town, thus mirroring the view of most adults there.

As kids, we were immersed in growing up, having fun, and being part of our small town. Brother Eddie, just fifteen months older than me, and I spent a lot of time on the apartment steps watching the trains go by, especially hoping for the war-time troop trains so we could wave to the soldiers hanging out the windows. We jumped rope on the concrete pad, and the sidewalk transformed to a rink for roller skating, good enough except for the cracked and buckling areas—for these we just slowed down and hopped over. We stayed outdoors as long as possible, scurrying home for supper before Dad arrived. Simple pleasures—that was our life.

Back to the dirt—as young kids we didn't notice it. A couple of vacant lots behind the apartment, just dirt and scattered weeds, served as our playground. The house next door had a yard with no grass, but the bare ground was perfect for playing marbles. At six years old, I, along with Eddie and girlfriend Gigi, devised a project to clean an old abandoned shed behind a neighbor's house to make into a playhouse. We spent two days sweeping out years of grime, spider webs, and bugs, and carrying buckets of water to scrub the rotting floor planks. After all that work, I don't recall playing much in it.

The playground at our two-story tan brick elementary/junior high school, just four houses down the street from our apartment, functioned in lieu of a city park. It was also open for several weeks in summer with supervision by a few high school kids. This was the closest that we neighborhood kids came to a summer camp experience. The front playground was paved with ancient blacktop and the sides and back were dirt. I loved going there in the summers, staying the whole time, it was open—for dodge ball, the climbing bars, the swings and slide, and organized games. I played hard, got dirty, and didn't care. At least until one time—when I was supposed to be at home, cleaned up and ready for a church family to drive me to catechism lessons. That shameful experience probably started my war on dirt and concern with social status.

On Fifth Avenue, where I went to play or visit friends, a few houses had nice yards with grass, flowers, and fences. As I got older I noticed differences between the streets and the quality of houses in our town. At a slumber party I was impressed with a girlfriend's two-story brick home; it had carpet, dark woodwork, and expensive looking furnishings. After her parents' divorce, my friend and I would get together occasionally when she visited with her dad at his small apartment near our house.

When we moved to our remodeled two-story frame home, five blocks west but still on the street facing the railroad tracks, I liked our house. But at twelve, I was becoming critical—the red brick siding looked fake compared to real brick homes on the street across from us, beyond the railroad tracks. Our house had a small front yard adjoining the sidewalk (finally with grass and two small Rose of Sharon bushes), but the back yard remained dirt, despite many attempts to grow grass. After all, my three younger brothers hung out there and kept up the family tradition of playing hard and getting dirty.

The many trains passing through town contributed mightily to the dirt problem. Until I was eleven, the black iron monster engines, steam powered with coal, pulled hundreds of open cars teeming with coal. Soot deposits and daily powdering with coal dust were just part of life. Many times I would sweep off the front porch, only to see it sullied again by the next passing train. So yes, the town was dirty, but it was only later as a teenager that I complained about the dirt, about the same time that I imagined gaining higher social status. Dirt, however, had not been a factor when, at age eight, my vague private dream appeared: I would leave this town when I grew up.

Why this notion of leaving so early in life? I wonder if it was an unconscious reaction to family stories of how our family came to live here, how our parents' fathers had been told to go to West Virginia for work in the mines, how my parents had no choice about where to live. It was as if they had been deposited by parachute, a note attached saying, "This is where you will live, and this will be your name."

When my parents married in 1928, the coal, chemical, and railroad industries were growing, the workforce of immigrants essential. My dad was thankful to have jobs: starting at age fourteen, the coal mines for many years, a bottling company, tending his father's tiny grocery store in one of the hollows, road construction. He may have "willingly" become entrenched in this locale, whereas my inner voice whispered that I could have a choice—I could leave this place.

Why did I envision my future elsewhere? Here's an early fantasy. I am five or six, and winter drags on with lots of snow. I am looking out the large front window of our apartment, toward the mountain that rises past the railroad tracks; it is covered with snow. So tired of the snow, I imagine taking a water hose to spray the mountain and melt it all away. Was this an early sign of wanting to control my environment? My fantasized egocentric omnipotence? Stage one for control freak? Or simply having no happy memories of playing in the snow and having fun?

As I got older, part of wanting to leave and feeling little connection to the physical environment of Montgomery may have come from a sense of its smallness and constricted environs—just one and one-half square miles locked in between the river and the mountains. You could easily fast walk from one end of town to the other in fifteen minutes. Maybe I thought this small place would not fit my later yearning for an independent life. From junior high on, part of my motivation was to start fresh with my own identity, unfettered by my family's history and status, but by no means to renounce them.

This dream of leaving did not mean that I was angry or hated the town or that my family's place in the community was terrible. Since Dad owned a business, we were probably lower middle class like most other families there. I had friends, liked the people, and felt a sense of belonging. This was true for my parents and brothers as well. In some ways the whole "village" participated in our upbringing. Once when I was about twelve, walking in town along with two girlfriends, all of us feeling adolescent "high jinx," I said "Shit." By the time I got home, my dad had heard about my language from the owner of the men's clothing store who had been standing in front as we girls walked by. Dad was fond of telling us kids, "I will know everything you do." The community had a role in helping us conform to the expectations of our family and the town.

While difficult to admit, I now realize I had little feeling for the natural environment. There I was, surrounded by Nature with a capital "N," with a river running through it and dark, thick-forested mountains to the north and south. But for me, little feeling for nature! I can explain or find excuses. My parents had little time for leisure in the outdoors, or leisure of other kinds for that matter. Although Uncle Tony occasionally took his boys "camping" or "fishing," not so my dad, not interested. More important, he had the taxi business that required working long hours, including weekends. Mother too had unending responsibilities.

They devoted themselves to the demands of providing and caring for their large family. Mother bounced from the kitchen cooking, to the washing machine, to hanging the laundry on clothes lines, back to the kitchen ironing, all while taking care of kids. Dad drove or walked to and from the taxi stand; there he took calls and arranged cabs for passengers, taking a brief break only to chat with the owners of Cater's produce market across the street. Following our parents' seriousness about duties of daily life, we kids adopted the same attitude as we got older: helping with family chores, getting jobs, and focusing on school. We also had fun and pastimes, but until teen years these took place mostly at home, not outdoors, not with nature, not so much in the larger world.

So there were few outdoor recreational experiences and no talk of the beauty or wonders of nature. Some of my friends told about their travels. One boy offered exciting descriptions of the Mammoth Caves in Kentucky as well as his annual summer camp experiences. Others mentioned hikes to a mountain top visible from the town's bridge called Devil's Tea Table. I listened but was silent, having no adventures of my own to tell.

The lack of time and money, but also our parents' over-protectiveness, prevented meaningful encounters with nature. We had the rare picnic only after much begging. We would meet some of Dad's family for a brief venture at a state park or a creek-side location where we carefully waded, trying not to fall on the slippery, slimy rocks. On one occasion my older brothers were allowed to swim/play at the pool in a county park. The city pool in our town was off limits—our dad worried about drowning, always saying he could not swim. We never had a family vacation.

I remember only two weekend visits to my mother's remaining West Virginia brother, Uncle Al, who lived in the rural area of Adrian, over one hundred miles from our town. On the drive, we kids noticed the winding road, trees, and mountains, and blabbered, hoping to see deer, foxes, or rabbits but spotted none. Once there, no walks to explore the rolling hills and meadows, but it was fun getting to know new cousins, enjoying "country" type food, and joking about the outhouse and rules about not peeing in the bathtub.

Outdoor excursions were rare. When I was nine, Dad permitted me to go with the Girl Scout troop and leader for a Saturday morning hike to Devil's Tea Table. There we cooked and ate breakfast and then returned—no time to explore or commune with nature. On our frequent visits to relatives living nearby, driving in the car with Dad, I may have noticed the mountains, especially how roads had been carved through them, leaving rock formations visible and subject to slides. I was more likely to notice coal barges on the river and ask about mining operations along the highway, such as coal tipples, slag heaps, coke ovens. Perhaps my first experience of being in awe of nature came on a drive to a picnic. Dad stopped at the Hawk's Nest Park Overlook for the scenic view. Peering into the New River Gorge below, I momentarily ceased thinking, maybe for the first time in my life letting my senses soak up the beauty and power of nature here in my home state.

What else? A brief academic exposure to nature came in my sophomore biology class when Mr. Clonch took us on a hike up a nearby mountain to collect leaves and learn the names of trees. By then, I knew about the mountains harboring copperheads and my mother's fear of snakes, these critters often getting into her childhood rural home and into the bedsprings. But I didn't fear nature or avoid outdoor experiences; I just had so few opportunities. On our senior picnic trip to a large park in Charleston, I met my first horse, mounted with some help, rode briefly, and survived. Surprised myself! No more horse experiences until I was married.

From childhood, nature's flora and fauna rarely captured my fancy, not counting hunting for four-leaf clovers, except when I noticed the beauty of flowers and trees when walking by the yards of the nicer homes. Later, being immersed in the study of literature through three academic degrees, I often felt inferior on reading great writers' lush accounts of nature, their emotional responses, even transcendence with it. I could only vicariously experience their encounters. I still sense my first adolescent enchantment with the sensuousness of "The Apple Tree," a short story by John Galsworthy. Otherwise, I have few childhood memories of being enthralled with the natural environment.

As a teenager, I was somewhat tuned into weather and occasionally noticed stars and the evening sky. I liked the feel of the sun when I would get out on the roof outside my bedroom window to gain a tan. And if I was home during a thunderstorm, I liked sitting alone on the front porch, enjoying the heavy downpour, the thunder claps, and the earthy scent of moist dirt and grass. Not being outdoors much at night, I mostly remember occasionally viewing the evening sky, the moon, and stars through a window and briefly feeling a sense of loneliness.

Nature and me—maybe my limitation stemmed from my personality, my lack of attention to the physical world. I realize I was more tuned in to my own musings and to people rather than the natural environs. When walking throughout the town—both business and residential streets—I often felt a certain wariness and walked fast, intent on getting where I was going, completing my task. At age eleven I would zip by on the opposite side of the street to avoid the gaze of men sitting in front of the run-down Faymont Hotel. On the way to junior high school, I eventually took a longer route to escape the exhibitionist standing naked in front of his glass storm door facing the alley behind our house. When my mother and I were out together, she occasionally asked why I walked so fast. I never said. Now I think my personality probably kept me too grounded in the here and now business and risks of life, barring me from tuning in to nature.

As I moved into teen and young adult years, a conscious desire for social status infused my dream to leave. I entered the adolescent stage of analyzing and finding everything short of my standards. Just because I didn't share any of this doesn't mean I didn't think and feel it. I was ashamed of the current social status of my family. I hated that our home was so close to the sidewalk and a busy street and right across from the railroad tracks. (So were all the solid brick homes on Second and Third Avenues.) Our house was probably better and larger than those of my best girlfriends, but I hated its fake red brick siding and the back yard where the grass never grew. I didn't like sitting on the big front porch, so close to the sidewalk, probably wanting to avoid others' seeing where I lived. I sometimes felt embarrassed with my big family that left the house looking messy, "over lived in." The sense of shame hit hard one summer day. A bunch of us were in the kitchen having a snack/dessert of watermelon. Brother Gene's friend, David, from one of the town's high-status families, was there, and at some point he said out loud or on leaving, "This place is swarming with flies."

My brother Phil recently reminded me of the contortions he and Brother Bob went through adjusting the television antenna on the roof. First off, our next-door neighbor had given us their old black and white set when I was a sophomore in high school—we could not afford to buy our own. When the picture was fuzzy or clouded with snow, Dad would send one of the younger brothers up to the roof and then yell directions through an open window. I may even have witnessed these dramas but repressed them as assaults on my dignity. How utterly lower class! No wonder I avoided sitting on the front porch.

So when my shame occasionally escaped, banging at my mind's door, my private dream was at the ready, promising my future independent life. I held on to the dream like a talisman—a precious stone with many facets secreted away in my pocket. Feeling it soothed the pain of humiliation. I would oversee my life. I would live somewhere else, a more beautiful place with a nice home. I would have a career based on my talents and abilities. I would have interesting, enriching experiences. I would fall in love, get married, and have my own family. I might as well say it: I would live happily ever after. At the time, I thought the dream was quite practical and within my reach. But I was unaware of how naïve and provincial I was about life and the world. How could I have been otherwise, given the family and town that nurtured me?

Reliving the experience of growing up in our town in the 1940s and 1950s forces me to rethink my relationship with Montgomery. As a young child, I sensed the town's good qualities Then the physical smallness was a good thing: I could easily walk anywhere, knew all the shops. It was like feeling comfortable and secure in my own skin. Unaware of the advantages of city life, I didn't know what I was missing. My life was provincial but I didn't know that word. Gradually during college, learning about the world from books, more than ever I knew that I wanted a life that my hometown could not offer.

Other young people in that environment likely saw much more of the wider world than I ever did, so even with a college degree, I ended up a naïve, unsophisticated young woman. My family didn't have the means or time to take us on trips. And my dad's restrictions on me were greater than those for both my older and younger brothers. As teenagers, Frank, and maybe Gene, were allowed to go to New York, probably on a bus, to visit my mother's relatives there. Ed went on the senior trip to Washington, DC. The younger brothers enjoyed several trips away from home during high school and college.

Travel away from home anywhere was not in the cards for me. I was eleven when my Uncle Joe and Aunt Maxine wanted to take me with them to Virginia to visit her family—Dad said no. I was nineteen before he taught me to drive. While I may have been smart in school and always had my nose in a book, as some of my relatives said, I came up short on experience outside my hometown.

I understand now my dad's perspective, not warming up to the idea of picnics or taking us to visit Mother's relatives. Over two decades of my youthful life, I remember only two trips to visit Uncle Al and Aunt Gen in Adrian. I saw my mother's sadness that she was so cut off from her family. For Dad, any kind of family trip meant taking one of the cabs out of service and keeping him from the business, from assuring that fares were recorded and turned in. Sunday was the only day we could visit our local DiVita relatives since that was a slow day for the taxi business. Yet I know my dad did take a cab out of service to travel several times to an event he liked: the Indianapolis 500 Race. I wonder if this was a sore point between my parents.

I see how my youthful personality and family dynamics colored my perception of my hometown. Our intense family life centered on work and responsibilities, and I naturally came to be grounded in the here and now of daily life. In other words, I was not given to sentiment, dreaminess, or fantasy. For our parents, life was serious business—work, duty, taking care of family—and my brothers and I followed suit. My preoccupation with the routine tasks of living constrained my capacity for imagination and feelings. My own limitations left me without deep emotional attachment to my hometown and state.

I differ from others who look back on the place where they grew up and bask in a sense of nostalgia for the locale's beauty, quaintness, history. My warm feelings are now tempered by awareness of the many adverse, damaging, harmful outcomes, past and continuing, that have plagued my home town and West Virginia. The town has lost its commercial status: businesses and jobs have disappeared since big box stores have opened a few miles down the river west on U. S. Route 60. The population has declined by half since 1950. Most recently, our beloved state college has been closed and relocated to another town, Beckley, forty miles away. There's more. In 2017, the State Board of Education approved closing the Valley High School built in Smithers in 1977, which replaced our former Montgomery High School. With that decision, students will be bussed thirty miles to a high school in Oak Hill, or fourteen miles to another county if that school will accept them. Except for fond memories, my two alma maters essentially obliterated.

Publicity about the State seems to be mostly negative, such as the *New Yorker* articles about the Elk River contamination (April 7, 2014) and the

Martinsburg battle against opioid addiction (June 5 & 12, 2017), although this latter problem exists in most states. A recent brochure from Creighton University in Omaha offered a course for seniors to do community outreach service and advocacy in West Virginia—the dire needs of our state akin to a third-world country. Although small towns and rural areas have likely borne the brunt of declining socioeconomic conditions, there are bright spots: larger cities, especially those with institutions of higher learning—Charleston, Huntington, Morgantown, Lewisburg—are doing well.

Thinking now about having left my home town and state, I don't feel that as abandonment or lack of caring. My education, especially the Master's Degree from West Virginia University, left me looking for a college teaching position. I took the first one offered, which happened to be out of state. After that, I willingly accepted that my husband's career would determine our subsequent moves and employment. While I never felt any emotional pull to return to West Virginia to live, I never stopped caring about its people and future. Hearing of the State's socioeconomic troubles saddens my heart, that my childhood home and many residents must endure problems that often go unsolved. Still, I have much to be thankful for: my upbringing in that locale, happy reminiscences of friends from the past, and love for family members who remain there.

My meaningful experiences with nature began in adulthood, and not in my home state. Not for me the "wild, wonderful West Virginia," touted by the new tourist industry, although intellectually I can appreciate the State's beauty and breathtaking rugged wilderness. Today, I try to nourish my imagination, expand it. I consciously look intently at nature and open myself to experience it, and am again and again awed by its beauty—the shimmering Florida Gulf and warmth of its beaches, the majesty of the Rocky Mountains, the solace of Michigan woods and lakes, the vista of the Midlands prairie, the splendors of Europe.

Most adults dream of the kind of place where they want to live—perhaps influenced by their childhood environs, but also by individual identity and personality. My dream centered mostly on achievement and respectability, bourgeois values no doubt. As for where to live, my vision was general. A place opposite of my home town: a city, a nice house with landscaped yard and grass, a safe neighborhood to raise a family, and access to career opportunities and interesting entertainment and cultural activities. As I came of age, this bill was met by locations with a mix of urban and suburban characteristics— no more constricted small towns for me. Eventually, together with my husband, we have lived in such places: Buffalo; London, England; Washington, DC; Pittsburgh; Grand Rapids, Michigan; Omaha; Fort Myers, Florida. The one exception was a two-year stint in small town Athens, Ohio.

Although our homes have been in the suburbs of cities, today we live my husband's dream, that is, on thirty-four acres overlooking and backing on a man-made lake just outside Omaha. This place suits both of us, and although suburbs are encroaching, we don't demand perfection. We love the wildlife of the prairie: rabbits, deer, foxes, hawks, owls, but also skunks, moles, voles, groundhogs, and coyotes. We have plenty of grass, but I have made peace with the devouring deer and am satisfied with very few landscape plants and flowers. The vista of hay fields and the lake brings a sense of peace, respite from demands of daily life. Still, like my parents, I remain consumed by duty and devotion to work projects of my own design.

Memories of our town have revealed its complicated influence on my identity and character. I have also unearthed another piece of my self-discovery puzzle: admission that shame at my family's low social status partly motivated my plan to depart and make my own way in the world. Unconscious seeds of embarrassment sprouted early on and later grew into a thriving resolve to become someone unquestionably worthy of respect. The next question: was it just my family, or was I myself not quite good enough?

CHAPTER 8

In the Name of the Father

STARTING FROM THE TIME THAT we lived in the apartment, church and religion enveloped my life. When I was seven years old, my mother allowed me to go with a neighborhood girlfriend, Barbara, to the local Baptist Church. What a surprise! We made lanterns with colored construction paper and proudly carried them home. Not what I was used to. In our somber Catholic church, I sat quietly, listening to Father Doyle's sermon, imagining that he paused long enough between thoughts for me to repeat them in my mind.

Two early church scenes remain seared in my memory. At age eight, Mother and I were seated, along with toddler brother Bobby, who kept pushing my hat off my head and laughing, while I cringed with embarrassment. On another occasion, about a year later I was seated beside my mother as usual, but she didn't notice that I was sniffling, miserable, with an awful runny nose, probably wiping with my hand. But I didn't tell her or ask for help. Finally, the woman next to me, youngest of four adult Irish sisters, stalwarts of the church, flipped a tissue in my direction, with what I perceived as an attitude of contempt.

Perhaps the most memorable "religious-like" experience occurred earlier, when I was six, on a visit to the L. family in Smithers, godparents of my brother Eddie. Mother called ahead letting Mrs. L. know we were coming. From our apartment in Montgomery, Dad's cab driver took the old bridge across the Kanawha River for the one-mile trip and deposited us on the unpaved main street. The L. family lived upstairs in a stucco building, the first floor housing their business, a small local "dime" store. We walked to the back entrance, Mrs. L. coming out the upstairs door before we even knocked.

"Comare," she said, in a high lilting voice, hugging my mother first, then me. "Come in, come in." Always smiling, probably in her fifties, less than five feet tall, a round, squat figure in a print house dress, Mrs. L. had twelve children.

"Comare," my mother answered, offered another hug. "We won't stay long. We haven't seen you for several months." But we always stayed an hour or more.

The entrance opened to a large kitchen area with a huge white metal table in the center of a light-colored linoleum floor. Sunshine streamed through the tall upstairs windows creating an almost heavenly brightness. Once we settled at the kitchen table, Mrs. L. hustled about, bringing "orangeade" for me and fancy store-bought Italian cookies. Then she and my mother began drinking coffee and continued the rest of their conversation—in Italian. At some point Mr. L. came upstairs from the store, more hugs and smiles, and handed us a box of cookies to take home.

As the women resumed their private conversation, I sat at the table, had my snack, and watched. Although I couldn't understand, their voices flowed like a gurgling creek at a picnic spot. Sometimes their faces and bodies glowed and sparkled with energy but from time to time turned dark, heavy with frowns. What were they saying? I imagine now that it was about their children, husbands, in-laws, life—both good and bad.

Two things happened to break my trance—first, seeing their adult daughter M., who was disabled and, second, going to the altar. Before we left home my mother must have explained that M. was not and never would be mentally "normal," for her age, so I knew to be respectful. Jabbering announced her arrival in the kitchen. She was about five feet tall, a somewhat heavy figure, shapeless in a loose, blue-patterned cotton smock dress, a type of clothing I had never seen before. With short black curly hair streaked with gray, she smiled a lot, talked to herself, and occasionally flapped her arms or yelled words out loud. My mother and I quickly said hello and returned her smile politely. Then Mrs. L. led her shuffling out of the room.

Later the women's Italian conversation paused and we went to visit the altar. Leaving the kitchen, we passed through a short hallway into a small darkened room. All was quiet so I knew to behave as if in church. The only thing in the room, the altar was set up on a table against a wall. Covered with a plain white cloth, it held a small crucifix in the center, surrounded by several miniature woodblock colorful pictures of saints. Two lighted votive candles sat on each end. It was beautiful but strange to see this display in a house. Soft voices again in Italian, maybe prayers. I just stared at the altar, not praying, but aware this had to do with God. Since we didn't know any other family that had a home altar and my mother never explained this, I believed that the L. family was somehow closer to God than we were. When I was older, I thought the altar meant that the L. parents accepted from God the burden of their disabled daughter.

Thanks to Mother, the Catholic Church was central in our lives and Dad tacitly approved. Our experience of God came through attending services and catechism. My brothers and I were baptized, made First Communion, and were confirmed. All the brothers served each in their turn as altar boys. Mother was the force for devoutness, and she also lived her faith in daily actions and caring for people. Even with the responsibilities of her own large family, she showed kindness and generosity to friends, neighbors, and the DiVita relatives.

As kids we knew she hoped Gene would become a priest but also sensed that Dad did not share this dream, and it never came to pass. Occasionally, we begged Dad to go to church—he mostly just dismissed our entreaties with a smile. Every year's Christmas Midnight mass was especially inspiring, but we were happy that Dad stayed home and prepared the meal for our return: broiled Italian sausage that he had made himself. While not a church-goer, he embodied a large cache of Christian virtue, was generous to a fault, and believed in his own essential goodness. I remember two stories about him from Mother. She said he was proud that he had never been in jail. And his mother, Big Mommie, had told that as a youth in Sicily, Dad was selected for the role of the boy Jesus in a church festival.

Catechism was serious business. With our copy of *The Baltimore Catechism*, we kids approached this task as we did all learning: reading assignments, listening to our priest, and answering his questions. Most sessions were held at the church on Saturdays, but I recall some lessons in one of our public elementary school classrooms. When I was in fourth or fifth grade, one class left my face stinging with shame at my wrong answer. Father Doyle had asked the question, "What is a Mormon?" My hand flew up, I heard this word as "moron," so I proudly threw out my answer as someone with very low intelligence, only to have our priest smile and correct me. I'm not sure of his reason for asking about Mormons, but it must have related to catechism much more than my word did. Lesson learned: pay closer attention!

The move to Third Avenue at the west end of town put us two short blocks from church, easy walking distance. Our newly-remodeled house featured only three religious decorations. At the foot of the stairs hung a small picture of the Sacred Heart of Jesus. A wall in my parents' bedroom held a small carved wooden crucifix that opened to reveal materials for the Catholic last rites, the sacrament of Extreme Unction. And a kitchen wall featured a picture of the Last Supper superimposed on a small slab of wood.

My mother and I always attended church together, a routine as normal as going to bed at night and waking up the next day. Sunday mornings meant rising early enough to arrive for the eight-thirty a.m. mass at our church across the tracks, never to the eleven-a.m. service at St. Anthony's in Boomer, a mile away; both churches comprised one parish with the same priest. Of course, taking communion meant you could not eat or drink anything beforehand. Perhaps there was some yelling to get the brothers up in time to leave early for altar duty. As each of them started college, this church role naturally fell to the younger brothers.

For the three-minute walk, unless we had to wait for a passing train, Mother and I carefully maneuvered over the railroad crossing beyond our street and moved quickly for the last block of the trip. We were almost never late, but I often felt self-conscious walking up the aisle to find a seat. In those days church was a dress-up affair, and women and girls wore dresses, heels, hats, and gloves, even in summer. Later in the sixties, the lace mantilla, popularized by Jackie Kennedy, became a substitute for a hat. I don't remember ever having this head dress, and I had left home by then.

Growing up, I felt myself to be a devout Catholic and close to God, as much as possible for a child. Once on hearing "Ave Maria" on Brother Frank's record player, I felt a deep sense of awe for its beauty without understanding the words. For catechism, I didn't mind the rote memorization, but this mostly afforded an intellectual understanding rather than spiritual feelings.

As an adolescent, however, I found the Lenten season especially moving; the Wednesday evening Stations of the Cross left me entranced—the darkness, the incense, and the priest moving up and down the aisle, stopping at the stations pictured on the stained-glass windows. I was horrified by the suffering of Christ, all this for our sins, but at that time never quite realized the full meaning of the Resurrection.

We kids and Mother always "gave up" something for Lent. Probably candy for me. One year Mother gave up sugar in coffee, and after Lent she never used sugar again, just milk, or later the Cremora brand of powdered creamer. Every Holy Saturday, the day before Easter, she recounted the Italian tradition for that day: chasing all the evil spirits from the house with a broom. She never enacted this ritual, but we kids might have teasingly pretended to do it.

Attending Sunday Mass every week could sometimes feel routine and mechanical: except for kneeling, standing, and sitting, parishioners had little overt participation, such as singing hymns or giving prayer responses. (All that came later with the English Mass.) I grew up with the Latin Mass and enjoyed a private religious experience from following the English translation in the Sunday Missal provided.

I welcomed any kind of variation from the usual church routine. Once or twice a priest, a seminarian from our own parish, said Mass. His visage always seemed stern, although my perception may have arisen from the gossip that he was extremely devout and tough on people in confession. Another diversion came when three or four nuns from Charleston occasionally attended our Sunday service. Except for movies, this was my only experience with women who dedicated their lives to God. With their black flowing robes, veil, and the tight white wimple seeming to choke at their necks, they struck me as saintly, mysterious figures obviously holier than the rest of us Catholics. I never had any inclination toward this vocation, and no one in my family ever mentioned it as a career option.

An occurrence that shook my usual notions about church occurred one summer when I was in my early teens—our church sponsored a "Mission." This meant that several out-of-town priests, maybe Franciscans, came to conduct a week of daily evening services. My recollection is that my mother and I attended, or maybe she insisted that I go on my own. The goal seemed to be encouraging a personal relationship with Jesus. The tone and message felt emotional, kind of like a tent meeting, and it left me somewhat embarrassed by its departure from the kind of "cool" Catholic religion that I was used to.

Much of my perspective of Catholicism likely stemmed from the nature of our small, poorly equipped church and the limited social experience offered. I recall very few church-sponsored events that could be called social. With only the sanctuary and no meeting room, there was no after-church fellowship time with coffee and rolls, although my mother and I on leaving Mass would say hello and speak briefly with others.

Through the years, she and I attended a few special events offered: one "lawn fete" on the grounds of our church and another several years later at St. Anthony's in Boomer. Makeshift booths offered food and baked goods and simple carnival-like games for children. St. Anthony's, the newer church, had a large basement meeting room and kitchen; next door on the grounds stood the priest's rectory. Mother and I attended two other Saturday evening events at the Boomer facility, getting a ride from one of Dad's cabs: once for a Thanksgiving-type turkey dinner and on another occasion for a spaghetti dinner. Much later, after I had left home, our Immaculate Conception church in Montgomery had a special fundraiser and subsequently built an adjoining education room.

Every Sunday we usually got a copy of *Our Sunday Visitor*, a Catholic newspaper/newsletter, which I read cover to cover. One story in1950, when I was thirteen, made a lasting impression on me. The article reported Pope Pius XII's canonization of Maria Goretti, a twelve-year old girl in Italy who, in 1902, fought off a young man who attempted to rape her. She first became a martyr, dying of her stab wounds but preserving her chastity, and then was granted sainthood. Reading this account charged my emotions in different directions. Because I too was Italian and close to her age, I identified with Maria's fear and suffering. But I was shocked that such lurid details would be in a church article. Not to mention that I greedily soaked up the information about rape while feeling horrified. Although I had a strong reaction at the time, I did not, in my mind, automatically link sex with assault.

Entering adolescence, I became less devout, shying away from the abstraction of God, moving toward more mundane self-centered interests. I was not above praying for good things for my life, such as school honors or awards, but didn't think to ask for help for my family, though God knows we were fast approaching the point where we could have used divine intervention.

Around this time the prospect of confession brought the scary specter of admitting "bad thoughts and acts"; thankfully, the priest knew this was code for sex and didn't ask for details—just three Our Fathers and three Hail Marys for penance. Once standing in line for Saturday confession, I was shocked to see a teenage girl from a prominent Irish church family openly crying. I couldn't believe this unseemly emotional display that allowed everyone to imagine her horrible sins.

My adolescent analytic tendencies had begun to elicit questions about faith. On one occasion when our new priest, Father McDonald, gave me a ride home from catechism, I naively attempted to ask him about the lack of morality that I heard about among certain teenagers at our high school. He offered platitudes, nothing near the intellectual discussion I hoped for. That experience may have started my serious doubts about Catholicism. Yet, surprisingly, remarks made at home suggested it was okay to question religion, especially Catholicism.

Through the years I had heard family conversations (some not meant for my ears) about the Church. One of my uncles had called Mother a "religious fanatic." Then too my dad, who rarely went to church but willingly cared for the younger children, was also critical at times. He labeled as "hypocrites" people who went to church but did not live their faith—he said he saw some of them engaging in "crooked" practices in their businesses, even sin in their private lives. Nor did priests escape his purview as word got out about their less than stellar behavior.

One day, accidentally overhearing a private conversation between my parents, I was embarrassed to hear Dad's angry disdain of priests and Catholic doctrine. It was a Saturday after supper and I was in the dining room and about to enter the kitchen when their words led me to shrink back.

"Jo, what's the matter with you? Are you crying?" my dad asked.

"I don't know. I just can't get it out of my mind" she said.

"What are you talking about," he asked again.

"From confession, this afternoon, what the priest told me. Said it was a sin to use birth control," she softly replied.

"Why did you say anything to him? It's none of their damn business. This just burns me up."

After that I retreated upstairs to my bedroom for a while. But at another point my mother actually mentioned something to me, coming almost out of nowhere: "If we didn't use something, we would have even more children." Now I can imagine her sense of frustration that led to this personal revelation to a teenage daughter—it left me speechless.

I have learned recently that my mother's religiosity increased after I left home and was manifested in more dogmatic ways. I don't recall her nagging us kids about church, but maybe that was because we were all so compliant. I do remember a situation where she likely intended to strengthen my faith. I was probably seventeen and for some reason wanted a pair of white kid gloves and mentioned this as a possible Christmas present. When I opened the box, the same size it would have been for gloves, she had given me the *St. Joseph Daily Missal*; I'm sure I stifled my disappointment. Of course, now I treasure it, along with several pairs of her own white cloth gloves that I have. But I am shocked at my own self-centered neediness back then. The family's income was way down, and my giving a suggestion for any gift was insensitive.

Later, after I had left home, Mother put much energy into making sure certain family members adhered to the tenets of Catholicism. I heard from one of Frank's children (they lived with my parents during their growing up years): "She pushed Catholicism; everything was about Catholicism." A younger brother of mine also said she was adamant for him during high school to serve as altar boy, not just for Sundays, but for daily masses. She also had a way of reminding you of God when you least expected it. When my brother Phil got news of his military deferment, he off-handedly said he guessed that he just got lucky; she jumped in to remind him of the power of prayers—hers.

Early on Mother took it upon herself to convert a young cousin, Charlie, who spent a lot of time at our house with my brothers his same age. Charlie's father resented the priest for denying him and his Protestant wife a Catholic wedding and was uninterested in sending his son to the Catholic Church. With Mother's influence Charlie attended catechism, became confirmed, and served as an altar boy. His parents went along with this, though they may have privately harbored some ill feeling toward my mother. She, I think, truly saw this boy as almost another son in the household. Today, Charlie remembers her with great love and appreciation, although he has not stayed a Catholic.

After I left home I remained faithful in my young adult years, still on automatic pilot, never allowing my doubts to keep me away from Mass. I assumed that my future marriage must be within the Catholic Church. I even thought that if unmarried partners had sex, they should not use birth control except as approved by the Church—never mind the sin of pre-marital sex. Of course, my evolving beliefs were inconsistent.

During this time my interest in contemporary philosophy led me to read the Existentialists: Kierkegaard, Sartre, de Beauvoir. The notion of making existential choices despite living in an absurd world made sense; however, this new perspective never really breached my automatic commitment to Catholicism (perhaps more accurately labeled commitment to my parents). I am not proud of insisting on a Catholic wedding service while having had doubts about my religion for years. For the sake of my parents, I needed the Church's blessing—I could not disappoint them (meaning have them think badly of me). My fiancé reluctantly agreed, but he often joked that from attending a series of catechism lessons he had converted several priests.

About a year after the wedding, my husband and I decided to try attending the Episcopal Church. Even this was no strong personal commitment on my part but simply my shifting allegiance to please my husband instead of my parents. On a visit home, I mustered the courage to tell them about this change. My mother's face, pale with shock, spoke her disbelief and disappointment, but she offered very few words. My dad, on the other hand, said, "It doesn't matter as long as they go to church. That's the important thing." His quiet acceptance immediately lifted the dark cloud threatening my soul, and the discussion was over. But Mother felt my leaving the Catholic Church as a betrayal; she mostly hid this thought, allowing it to surface gently and indirectly only in her Memoirs.

Although my six brothers and I were brought up in the Church, we escaped potential further indoctrination since there was no Catholic school for us to attend in town or anywhere nearby. Our adult approaches to religion were likely influenced by our parents' peaceful management of their differing religious viewpoints. Three of us left the Church, although one left and returned. The other four have remained involved, with the faithful siblings apparently seeing themselves as "modern" Catholics: following conscience rather than strict Church doctrine. As adults, we accept our different religious lives but have rarely spoken in depth about this. The lack of sharing may be active avoidance of potential conflict or simply acceptance of each other as individuals. Our childhood family life would have trained us well for either motivation.

My experience with religion has left me with a deep sense that there is a right way to live and that the teachings of Christ can be a guide, not necessarily the teachings of the Catholic Church. I came later to believe that ritual and church affiliation were not necessary for my belief in God. When our children were young, my husband and I attended the church denomination of his youth. Then his aversion to organized religion ended that effort. As young adults, our children have had various views on religion, from one being agnostic to the other two being early participants in fundamentalist churches, with neither now highly involved in a religious denomination. While we often celebrate Christian holidays when we can be together, we don't have serious or sustained conversations about religious beliefs. Not surprising, this topic the elephant in the room.

My spiritual life remains, as much of my life, a very private domain for which only I am answerable and have no need to share. I cannot compartmentalize the doctrines of the Catholic Church; I don't attend any church but I accept Christianity with my own interpretation. My childhood religious experiences influenced my current position—still a believer but open to meanings of God and life beyond my understanding. I am happy to allow that people connect with God or find meaning in different ways, and some through formal religious institutions.

I continue to cherish my dad's honest questioning about the Catholic Church as well as my mother's undying faith, which she openly embraced and lived throughout her life. On religion and other issues, they had differences, but acceptance and tolerance dominated, not argument or rigid judgments. As a child in the Maruca family, my mother attended Protestant services since there was no Catholic church in their area. I doubt that the DiVita family of Dad's youth and young adulthood, without a car and a mile from the nearest Catholic church, ever showed up for Sunday mass. In the Italian culture, an anti-clerical sentiment was common; baptisms, weddings, and funerals were important, not regular church attendance.

My parents' holding somewhat different views on religion was another difference that made a difference in their marriage, parenting, and ultimately in my identity and personality. The Catholic Church became another aspect of my upbringing that I left behind. But in its place, I experience a strong sense of spirituality and meaning in life that remains with me.

CHAPTER 9

School: My Sanctuary

JUNIOR HIGH, SAME OLD SCHOOL, but now we claimed big-kid status. We trudged in and out the back doors, the Fourth Avenue entrance, where the inside stairs led to the basement gym and to the second floor. Classrooms on this upper level housed the seventh and eighth grades, signifying our brief elevation before mutating downward again as lowly freshmen in high school.

It was out of these doors on many a sunny afternoon that Barbara, Saralee, and I left the building to start our walk back home, they to their same Fifth Avenue houses across the street from each other, me to our new home a block further west. Lugging our books to our budding bosoms, we hear jabbering. Who was trailing after us? Two or three boys we had known probably from first grade. Now intent on what? Pestering us?

It wasn't so much their goofy taunts or smiling faces but what they did. Some days they sneaked up close behind us, struck matches, and threw them at us. (Freud would have loved this.) Other days, they ran up behind us and as they passed, spit a "lugie" at our hair. (Freud would have loved this even more.) We girls either yelled at them in pretend outrage or just ignored them. We enjoyed the attention. We were all changing—even if ever so slightly.

For that era and a small town (population then around 3,000) tucked away in a southeastern West Virginia valley, our two public schools had decent physical facilities. (I doubt that was true for the two Black segregated schools that I never saw.) Montgomery Grade and Junior High, constructed of tan brick, had two levels and the gym and cafeteria kitchen in the basement. The asphalt playground in the front offered the minimal swings, slide, and a set of metal bars for climbing and walking across with your hands; the west grounds had no equipment just the solid dirt where we played dodgeball. Every grade school classroom featured combination bolted desk-seats with a top that lifted for storing books and supplies, a cloak room, a picture of President George Washington, blackboards, and a large square metal heating vent high on the wall with a thin strip of crepe paper attached, this to signal that the furnace was working.

In our household school was the domain of the kids, and we were accountable for what went on there: maneuvering in that world and meeting its requirements. Our parents sent us off each morning after breakfast and for the rest of the day expected us to take care of school business. At home in evenings more of the same: no one told us to do homework. When we brought report cards every six weeks, early on Mother passed them on to Dad to sign, but later she took over, signing "Mrs. Benny DiVita." Our parents did not meddle, there being few opportunities, since schools back then did not encourage communications and no such thing as parent-teacher conferences. We took seriously the unspoken family mandate to do well in school. Mother was proud, though never effusive in praise, when I brought home good report cards and high scores on standardized tests. She helped if asked: calling out my spelling words for an upcoming test and even in high school doing the same for my French vocabulary words.

It's no wonder that school became a sanctuary, a kind of second home. It gave me a world outside my family, and for whatever reasons I liked learning about that world and always felt I had a lot to learn. That's just the person I was. Even now, seven decades later and without my report cards, I can name all my grade and junior high teachers. Although they differed in age and personalities, I liked all of them; however, Miss Holder's stern visage and attitude left me wary and cautious in her fourth-grade classroom. Sometime around fifth or sixth grade, when I had been in Girl Scouts a couple of years, I decided to quit this group, thinking that school work was keeping me busy enough.

Without preaching, our parents pushed the importance of school, trusting that we were in good hands there. So back and forth we walked. From the first to sixth grades, when we lived at the apartment, just four houses away from the school, Eddie and I and sometimes a cousin or two quickly ran home to a fast lunch that Mother had ready for us. Back thirty minutes later, we re-entered classrooms greeted by whiffs of banana peel deposited in waste cans—a lot of bussed kids brought a packed lunch from home.

Starting in sixth grade and during junior high school, I became more aware of changing rules and roles for girls, and some of my own new feelings. First, I knew my body was maturing and intuitively took this in stride. There was no school-based education about puberty. But as I encountered changes, I mostly muddled through on my own, not really understanding some of my own reactions.

I now regret how I treated a sixth-grade neighbor boy I had known since first grade. He and I were at his house in the yard playing with his football. When I got off a good kick to him, with my right leg flying up in the air, pushing my dress up, I said something to him about looking up my dress. Why this remark when I was having such fun? The painful expression on his face said I was dead wrong, so our play session ended.

My own sexual feelings were likely emerging, along with unconscious awareness of my parents' unspoken fears of my growing up. When new fluorescent lighting was being installed in our junior high school, the work went on during classes. Over several days, I noticed one dark-haired young male worker sitting aloft his tall ladder and thought him handsome. I felt his eyes meeting mine. Was he gazing at me or was I gazing at him? Or both? These kinds of pleasant yet scary feelings I mentioned to no one.

Unconscious memories about things sexual must have dictated silence and privacy. Somewhere in my psyche was a Big Mommie story told to my mother—no doubt a warning for her new daughter-in-law—and passed on to me. A group of friends were together visiting at a home (in Sicily no doubt). One of the women yawned, then a man across the room yawned. When the woman's husband noticed this, he construed their behavior as a secret signal between the two of them that proved his wife's unfaithfulness. Obviously, some horrible fate awaited her. The moral: sexuality for women is a dangerous business.

After we moved to our Third Avenue home, now a six-block walk to my junior high school, lunch options changed. Only two blocks from school, at the Henderson Drug Store, my friends and I could get a hot dog with chili and coleslaw for fifteen cents. Service was quick as the store had prepared them in advance, but we didn't mind if they were a little soggy. During this time I also ate the twenty-five-cent lunch at from the school cafeteria, supervised by Mrs. Williams, the "home ec" teacher. I really liked certain foods I had never had at home, told my mother about them, and asked her to make the tasty white bean soup and grilled cheese sandwiches like the cafeteria served. She did.

One day, in line for the cafeteria, we seventh-graders must have been un-supervised because a boy from my class standing behind me was stooped over hiding something in his hands, then furtively showing it to kids in front and behind him. What can I say? It was my first peek at pornography, and a mild one at that. His little soft-cover booklet with white pages, about five inches square, displayed black ink cartoon-like drawings of a "naked" man and woman on each page. That's about all I remember, although he may have fanned the pages to create a sense of movement. There was giggling all around, but no discovery by a teacher. The year before, when I had attended a girlfriend's birthday party and played "spin the bottle," I kissed this boy, a longtime school friend and liked by everyone. Just a quick kiss and back in the room we came. I didn't have enough sense or know to allow myself to feel something from a kiss.

My grade-school love for recess shifted to unabated enthusiasm for ju-nior high gym class, with a passion for physical activity co-existing with my commitment to excel academically. This half-conscious goal seemed normal for me, not requiring any special effort. I liked school, plain and simple, and didn't see myself as that different from others. I knew my older brothers had been good students, and my best girlfriends also made good grades, although I don't remember ever comparing tests or talking about our report cards.

After our move to Third Avenue, during my junior high years, I made a new best friend, Joanie. She lived in a house behind the paved alley running by our backyard. I knew her from grade school, and she was a top student, so we could have felt some friendly competition between us for grades. After school we two would play with her volleyball in the al-ley, just serving it back and forth across an imaginary line and keeping it aloft till one of us missed the return. I remember wearing my first pair of jeans or dungarees for this activity, probably borrowed from my Brother Ed. Joanie's father had a reputation in our household—joking that he occasionally hit and knocked over garbage cans sitting in our backyard when he tried to park his car in the garage in the alley. The cause—he was often intoxicated. That time frame was probably before I became aware of my dad's own problem with alcohol.

Joannie and I didn't walk to school together as her mother drove her and two younger sisters to the school. After eighth grade when my friend moved with her family to Charleston, she attended Charleston Catholic High School. We regularly exchanged letters, and I was fascinated to hear about Catholic school groups like Sodality, her activities and classes, her teachers. For the first time in my life I began to share personal details about my life, at least my school life. I think our correspondence lasted all through high school. I vaguely remember initiating contact with her after college, maybe even visiting her in Charleston—she was engaged I think.

I had favorite grade and junior high subjects but never ignored any class and don't remember having a boring day in school. I liked getting books from the school library but back then we had no contests or summer reading programs to inspire us. In grade school my preferences ranged from fairy tales to James Fenimore Cooper's adventures, such as *The Last of the Mohicans* (where I paid close attention to descriptions such as "he lay with her"). I also liked *Little Women* and Nancy Drew mysteries. In high school I read the books required for English classes, such as *Silas Marner and Great Expectations*. On my own I was fascinated with the romance in *Jane Eyre* and *Wuthering Heights* and also read religious novels that my mother had at home, such as *The Robe* and *The Silver Chalice*. Rather than imagining myself in the roles or adventures of characters, I think reading was a way to learn about the world. Math was never a favorite subject, and although I got good grades, anxiety plagued me in junior high when we took daily speed tests on basic arithmetic and then exchanged papers to grade.

For high school, a much shorter walk, just two blocks from our house. I made the trip there alone, since my former walking partners' homes were not on my way. The three-story beige brick building was large enough to accommodate an average student population of about 500; the two sets of inside stairwells at each end of the building may have been designated one for "up" and the other for "down" traffic. The gym and a band room were attached to the rear east side. We had lockers and three minutes to change classes, which might meet in classrooms on any level. There was probably a brief freshman orientation on the first day of class where we received a schedule based on the curriculum previously selected, college prep for me—no guidance counselors back then.

The high school served students from a large area, including very small towns: Smithers, Boomer, Alloy, and much smaller crossroad locations on highways near coal operations: Eagle, Mt. Carbon, Deepwater, Longacre. I made new acquaintances and got along with everyone in my classes and don't recall any students being harassed (but I could have missed that).

MONTGOMERY HIGH SCHOOL
1955-56
MONTGOMERY, WEST VIRGINIA

I have one troubling high school memory—of my own making. As a brand-new freshman, I was pursued by a junior or senior boy from out of town; for a few days I met him before or after school at the stairwell, where he briefly held my hand, telling me he liked me, until I realized I should not be doing this. Looking back on his questionable appearance and my silly crush, I can say now that my dad's strictness with me at that time was much needed. I was no judge of boys or men!

It was high school that finished off most of my emerging identity, which might fit several labels that are common today. Nerd, Brainiac, School Junkie: these tags would have fit, but I didn't see myself as that different from my girlfriends and a few boys I knew who cared about grades. And it wasn't totally about getting good grades. I just felt that I had a lot to learn. But I was certainly aware of my brothers' high school accomplishments: Gene had been class valedictorian, Frank had been in plays and band, and Ed, two years ahead of me, also a good student, was on the high school Student Council. I was determined to follow their footsteps, make my family proud.

My teachers, on seeing my consistently good grades, came to expect a high level of performance from me, thus adding further incentive to my own obsession, but school also included moments of fun and some occasional rough spots for me and for teachers. Mr. Clonch, my sophomore biology teacher, routinely administered true-false tests in which he read aloud the questions, while we put our twenty answers on a sheet of paper. He sometimes kidded, calling me "poker-face DiVita," telling the class that my expression never revealed whether I knew the answer or not. Then I was shocked with my difficulty with Typing class—I got a C for the first six-week grading period. After that, using the strategy of slowing down and aiming for accuracy not speed, I brought the semester grade up to a respectable B. But clearly no secretarial talents.

And back to math, never a favorite. Although my curriculum required two years of algebra and I did fine in Algebra I, I was never confident in Algebra II. One of my worst, and most shameful moments, came during a test, when I glanced, undetected, at another student's paper to confirm my answer for a problem. My guilty conscience assured I would never commit such a violation again. Geometry class restored my confidence in math. I loved this class, probably had a girl crush on my beautiful teacher, and earned A+ both semesters. Still I was glad to be finished with high school math and beyond: my intended English major had no further college math requirements.

Most teachers offered interesting classes with a good mix of levity and seriousness—but not Miss L. Her first-year French class was mostly enjoyable but in the second year I felt sorry for her. She had no control of the class, and some of the boys were outright disrespectful. Pacing desperately in front of the room, often stifling tears, she allowed their antics instead of sending them to the principal's office. Her incompetence with discipline problems created a powerful example that fueled my later anxiety about becoming a teacher.

While getting good grades was a priority, I also participated in a few extracurricular activities. Early on I had recognized that I had absolutely no talent for drama or singing, and band was out of the question due to Dad's restrictions, but I joined the French Club and the High-Y and earned membership in the National Honor Society.

My fondness for sports continued and once forced me to deal with a gym incident at home. In a class or maybe a noon intramural game, a hard-thrown basketball hit me squarely in my right eye. While not requiring attention from the teacher or anyone else, by the end of the day, when I went home, I had a very black eye, a true shiner. I was probably fourteen and living with my dad's strictness that had intensified in my teenage years. I recalled his anger, although short-lived, that always erupted whenever any of us got hurt. I worried about what he would say about my injury and mentally predicted some horrible fate because of it. My mother may have also commented about his expected reaction, thus amplifying my own anxiety. A ready solution dawned on me and worked: I simply avoided being in Dad's presence for five days, until the purple, green, and gold striations on my eye and cheek had faded away. Nothing to be proud of for either of us. He didn't notice my absence or ask about me. Maybe this was the period when his increased drinking at the taxi stand often left him missing for family suppers.

That successful escape no doubt further reinforced my deep-seated tendency toward avoidance. Had I been more rational, I could have asked myself:

what could Dad do besides show some brief anger? He wouldn't interfere with school, wouldn't take me out of gym, wouldn't go and talk to my teacher. He might have even smiled, saying, "You look like hell." But my automatic coping pattern was hardly rational when it came to my dad. Yet I knew he loved me.

About this same time, I had an experience that increased my mostly unconscious worry about Dad. The memory has remained intense, I know it happened, but I cannot recall specific details. About a week in advance of an away football game, I had asked if he could give a ride to me and my two best girlfriends to Ansted, about twenty miles away. Barbara's uncle, the team coach, would bring us back home but could not take us since he had to arrive a couple of hours early. I am puzzled why I would have asked this favor. I had never been to an away game before. Maybe I thought it would be easy for Dad to take us since he had three or four cabs. Maybe I wanted to impress my friends, save the day and get us a ride, feel like a normal teenager. Driving one of his old 1946 gray Packard cabs, he put me in the back seat, and we picked up my friends. Almost immediately I smelled the liquor on his breath. The trip, the game, the ride back—I have total amnesia. Except we all lived and I never told a soul.

One-trial learning was enough to keep me compliant regarding Dad's view on dating. He had put the kibosh on that option when I was a freshman and asked if I could go on a date with a boy from school. Because of his scathing lecture about the boy and his family and all the bad things going on in our town, I never asked again. I'm sure I had a reputation in high school: "Janie is really smart, but she doesn't date." No worry about fending off offers. I never talked about my peculiar status with anyone, and my job schedule gradually allowed me to drift away from close relationships with my girlfriends. I wasn't the type to brood about missing the dating part of teenage culture. It may be hard for others to believe, but I was happy with the good stuff in my high school life.

A surprising honor came unexpectedly in my freshman year: I was chosen to represent my class in the school's homecoming "court." At that time selection didn't involve nominations or campaigning. The school just voted one day in homeroom for any girl they wished to name; the one with the most votes became "Miss Greyhound" (typically a senior); the names with highest number of votes for the other three class levels would be in the homecoming court. I draw a blank as to how boys were selected as our escorts. The whole event was exciting. Mother and I shopped for a wool suit for me to wear in the parade and the festivities on the football field. I loved the huge golden mum corsage and went on to the dance after the game, not a date of course. The school later expanded the tradition of homecoming, by also electing a "Mr. Greyhound." (In 1963, my brother Phil, captain of the football team, was selected.)

As I moved through high school, even with Dad's strictness, I had a social life of sorts. I had friends and talked with them before and after classes and in club meetings. I went to football and basketball games with girlfriends and occasionally to an informal dance afterward if there was one. And I did attend two proms even if they didn't qualify as exciting dates. For my sophomore year I don't remember who my escort was, but I liked my outfit: a full-skirted lilac strapless, ankle length dress with crinoline. Since we bought it in Charleston, Dad would have driven my mother and me, so he must have agreed I could attend.

My prom memories for my senior year are more vivid. It was common for senior girls to invite an outside escort, so I asked a college boy, a friend of my brother Ed's. I knew him slightly as a nice enough guy, but harbored no romantic feelings for him. On my own, I selected and purchased my prom dress from the local department store. I liked it because it was different, not strapless—white chiffon floor-length overskirt with a scoop neckline ending in the tiniest of sleeves. As was the custom, we had pictures taken before the event by a local photographer. One of my girlfriends, whose father was the Methodist minister, had an after- or before-prom party (all very proper and sedate).

I orchestrated this last prom experience for myself, made sure not to end up an outcast. I don't recall if my escort asked me later for a date, but if so, it didn't happen. Some years passed before I noticed among family photos that Mother had cut him out of the prom picture showing us both together. Was this how she wanted to remember the event? Was it a mirroring my own reaction?

My graduation from high school must have been exciting, but I remember only snippets of a few events. My senior yearbook picture still haunts me, yet I selected it. What the other photo proof choices looked like, I don't recall. Having attended several class reunions in the past, I was shocked to see that picture on my nametag. Who was that person? My face, my somber countenance, no trace of a smile, eyes dull, serious. Although I keep asserting in this memoir my typical positive, upbeat mood, that picture may capture something else—a girl burdened with unspoken sadness and an overwhelming sense of responsibility to family, Yes, I had my dream, I would pursue it, I would achieve it, but that photo showed tension on my young face: the me that I kept buried. Would I ever figure out what I owed my family, what they owed me, whether I could leave for my own life and still be a good daughter?

Commencement happened, and again only memory fragments. I don't recall being in a cap and gown, having pictures taken by family, or whether my parents attended commencement, although surely my mother would have. Here's what I do remember. I was named salutatorian of my class of about one hundred. I had to give a brief speech (wherein I mentioned something about the early conflict in Viet Nam, of which I knew nothing). And I probably had a moment of disappointment in not being valedictorian as I recognize my sense of competitiveness back then and even now.

The next evening I walked to the school for the senior class dinner. I was wearing white sandals with a little heel and a full-skirted, knee-length dress made of a light crinkly fabric with delicate white and aqua stripes. I was happy and met up with several friends at the dinner table to enjoy this last graduation event. My public and optimistic persona, not the sad little girl in my senior yearbook picture, was back in business.

I left high school in much the same way as I began, with anticipation and excitement that I was getting on with my life. School and family had been my ever-present dual safe havens. I had no sense that each might be in competition for my soul. And I didn't expect that to change: after all when fall came,

I would still be living at home for college, just a five-minute walk across the street and railroad tracks and up the hill. But I sensed a new shakiness in my family, signals hinting its foundation was weakening, though not exactly crumbling. Events happening were beyond my control: sister-in-law Betty's profound depression, Dad's drinking, his declining income.

I had fulfilled my expected role: the compliant, perfect daughter. But I could not fix the complicated family problems. The future would find me maneuvering in these two worlds, college and family, in and out the revolving door, mostly not getting jammed up on either side. Unlike home, which seemed plummeting in a downward spiral, the college experience that awaited me offered a bright beacon that would guide me toward my dream of leaving.

CHAPTER 10

Two Women

IT WAS THE SUMMER AFTER my sophomore year in high school. Coming down the stairs around ten in the morning, I answered the ringing phone, the caller asking for me; after hanging up I looked for my mother. In the kitchen I figured, where soft sounds of music from the radio on the counter reached my ears; she kept it on pretty much all day. When I spotted her at the kitchen doorway, I held up both arms silently but wildly waving her to come into the living room. Then I blurted it out.

"I got the job--cashier. That was Mr. McKay. I can work at both movie theatres. Start right away."

"You need to talk to your dad, ask him. I don't think he even knows you applied," she said. Dread rose like flood waters in my fifteen-year old body, washing away my excitement. How could I ask him when I already knew the answer?

She pointed to the kitchen, "He's still here, reading the paper. Just go in and let him know. He'll be leaving soon." And so I moved to find him. How I forced the words from my mouth, I'll never know,

"Dad, I got the job as a cashier at the movie theatres."

Looking up from his paper, "What the hell? What are you talking about?"

"I applied and I just got a call that I got the job."

"You're not gonna do that." His words came crashing down and hurt, even though I had known exactly what he would say.

Scared and hopeless, I managed one word, "Why?"

"Just because I said so." What was he thinking? That his daughter doesn't have to work, that he can support his family? Then, to my surprise, my mother quietly spoke up.

"Benny, I don't see why not. Her cousin Mary Ann works there. Your brother doesn't think there's anything wrong with it. He lets his daughter work there. They're both the same age. Jane just wants to make a little money of her own."

"I just don't like it. I know what goes on in this town." Silent, my heart pounding, I waited for him to start naming all the bad people and bad stuff.

But Mother kept up softly, "You know, her brothers worked there and Eddie still does. "I'm sure it will be all right. Can't we just let her try it?" He didn't argue back, didn't say no again, and went back to his paper. So I had the job. I couldn't believe it.

My mother, she had come through for me! I was still reeling. She stood up to him and won a battle. For me. And a critical one—a job. That was the summer of 1952; in fall I would start my junior year in high school. Little did I know then how important that job would become for me. At the time I never wondered if my mother would continue to take my side. Nor did I ever consider that, since she and I were the only two females in our household of seven males, we should stick together.

Just four years before, the house remodeling was nearly finished. We were excited—we were getting ready to move. It had been fun to go after school, walking the six blocks alone, and watch a couple of workers, at times plastering, then later varnishing the doors and woodwork a dark walnut shade. Fascinating how they placed the mesh metal lath into the walls and then slapped the plaster blobs onto it and finished it in a rough swirl pattern. I made sure to stay out of their way and they mostly ignored me.

School was out and moving day just a week away. One warm, bright afternoon, I was outside sitting on the concrete steps leading to our apartment—basically doing nothing. Suddenly my mother was there sitting beside me.

"Jane, I want to tell you something." Her face looked drawn, tight, not a frown, but worried.

"What is it?" I was curious as she seemed so different.

"Your girlfriend, __, you know you were playing at her house maybe last week, I think."

"What about it, what about her?" I couldn't imagine why she was talking like this. I had permission to play at her house, less than a block from the new house where we would be moving. She was eleven, same as me.

"Something happened to her. Her uncle, he forced himself on her. He put a towel over her face."

That was it. Stunned, I knew what she meant but didn't know how I knew. I had never heard words like rape or sexual assault. Mother stood up and started up the steps. The conversation was over—no questions from me and nothing else from her. Was I feeling shock, fear? How can you know when you can't tell anyone? My mind was churning, trying to sort it out.

I remembered playing at my friend's house several times in the past. Once I noticed her father and her mother in a bra and skirt lying together, embracing on the couch in the living room. Definitely a shock—that didn't seem right! Recalling that scene got me wondering if things were all messed up in their household and that was why this happened to __. Were they trashy people? At the time, my mother's follow-up silence seemed normal. I didn't show any emotion or upset, and it had probably taken all her courage even to tell me this much. After that, I heard nothing more, just that my friend and her family moved away. About four years later they returned to our town and __ graduated from our high school. I didn't have any classes with her, but we spoke if we happened to see each other. Neither of us attempted to renew our friendship—I don't know why.

Menstruation as a topic had not come up with my girlfriends, although one had asked me when I was eleven, "Have you got 'M' yet?" I somehow knew enough to say no. But I am not sure how I knew. Back then, there was no film on puberty shown separately to fifth-grade girls and boys. It was around this time that my cousin Mary Ann (my age) asked me if I knew where babies came from, and I had to say no. She smiled and blurted out, "From your pussy." Shocked again. Then silence—no questions from me.

How does it go? You become a woman—when you get your "period." I had never heard this word, not before, during, or until long after it happened to me in our new home, in late summer of 1948, as I neared my twelfth birthday. My mother had never mentioned the subject. Some months before at the apartment she had pointed out deodorant ads in a magazine (not sanitary protection ads) and then admonished me, "Never take anything from a man, not even a stick of gum. They'll expect something in return." I gulped, but as usual said nothing. This was her attempt at "sex education" for me. I had no idea at the time if other girls in that era got such a message from their mothers.

Here's what happened. One hot August day a routine trip to the toilet surprised me, yet I somehow knew what it was, calmly found my mother, and told her. She immediately got me the needed supplies, showed me the upstairs bedroom closet where Kotex pads were kept (presumably hidden away from the eyes of my dad and six brothers). Although I wasn't aware, Mother at thirty-six years old was still having periods. Did she tell me that? I don't remember that she gave me much more information, but maybe she did—that it would come once a month. I do remember I said, "Don't tell Dad." It seemed normal for our brief conversations to often end in silence without questions or explanation. The unspoken message being "Enough Said"—I should simply understand. From then on, I combed the newspaper and magazines looking for words about sex.

Gradually and inadvertently, more information came my way. From one-trial learning I got a strong message about female modesty. I overheard Dad tell my mother about an adolescent girl in our town that I knew: one his cab drivers had seen her undressing one evening in front of her bedroom window, shade wide open. Then another conversation not meant for my ears—my parents' talking about using birth control and Mother's confessing to the priest. And once Mother had even openly said to me, "If we hadn't used something, we would have even more kids." Then there was the time I was brushing my hair in front of the vanity mirror in my parents' bedroom and happened to look in a drawer. I know now what I saw was a diaphragm, but then only guessed it had something to do with sex and birth control.

At some point more graphic information came my way. It's amazing that I skim read a couple of stories from Boccaccio's *Tales from the Decameron*. This book sat alongside other classics in the dining room bookcase. Mother had ordered the set through a book club and obviously never had time to look at them. The final *pièce de résistance* of my accumulating sex education—I was cleaning the bedroom of my oldest brothers, when I saw Ovid's *The Art of Love* on the night stand and glanced at a few pages before quickly putting it back. Since this happened shortly before my brother Frank's wedding, I figured he was getting himself educated. Still, interesting stuff.

In our new home, for many reasons, I began feeling and acting more grownup. I asked Mother to have my first and only birthday party when I turned twelve—assuring permission by volunteering the party would have girls only. She sensed this was important to me, so she and I planned the party, the food, the games. Six or seven girlfriends arrived and all went smoothly, but I have no memory of details, except it was just us—no brothers hanging around.

I did not find it odd that Mother and I were the only two women in the household, outnumbered by males: Dad, three brothers becoming young men, and three younger active little boys. You might think that we two women would have become allies and in some ways we did. But not exactly—our relationship was complicated.

I continued to help with household tasks as needed and when asked but never felt burdened with more than my share. It seemed normal to help hang clothes to dry on the lines in the back yard and rush to bring them in, wet or dry, when a thunderstorm threatened. We didn't get an automatic dryer until a few years later, and even then, sheets and other heavy items got sun-dried to save on the gas bill. Mother counted on my help, especially with the younger boys when their antics were wearing down her patience. They got into trouble with her—made messes, jumped on furniture, wildly played cowboys, chasing each other with cap guns. When she went after them and they would crawl under beds, she called me to get the broom to push them out of their hiding places. Mother never nagged, even about my messy room, with clothes piled on every surface. She saw me as able to manage my life, and with her endless responsibilities and constant worries, she silently appreciated me as a good daughter.

Although Mother and I spent time together, it didn't quite add up to intimacy. We always went to church services together. Sometimes we worked as a team in the kitchen with meals and cleanup. As a young adolescent, before I got my job, she and I often walked together "up town" as a Saturday evening "event." No serious goal, maybe window shop or pick up needed items at the "dime store" or talk with my cousin Phyllis, who worked there. These outings gave her a break from childcare and housework, and I also looked forward to them. We also felt a sense of closeness when we worked on sewing a clothing item for me. In junior high, I described a "weskit" vest-type garment that I wanted, so we bought a pattern and the wool tweed material and she taught me as she used the sewing machine. The same thing in high school: we made a couple of wool sheath skirts for me, only I was the one using the machine for these. Thanks to her and my interest, I learned to sew without ever taking a "home ec" class.

My Saturday evening walks to town with Mother ended once I started working. I typically did a Saturday evening shift (but never a midnight movie, nor did I ever attend one of these). With my small earnings, starting at twenty-five cents an hour, I saved money for buying my clothes and pretty much made these decisions alone. The rare joint shopping trip with my mother was for big items—a winter coat and on another occasion, a dressy suit to wear as an attendant in the Homecoming court in my freshman year of high school.

As for wearing lipstick or shaving my legs, I guess I asked my mother, but it must have been okay as I don't recall any argument. I also draw a total blank as to how I got my first bra. For way too many years afterward, I would gaze at the *Seventeen Magazine* models, looking for one with a figure like mine. I always thought my bosom too big, my figure too curvy. Showering with other girls after gym class, I admired their small breasts compared to mine. On my own I finally discovered underwired bras that fit well. I became more confident about my appearance as I sensed approving glances from others.

It seemed my mother had so much to do in caring for the younger boys and the household that she naturally let me manage myself, seeing me as a dutiful, obedient daughter. And I didn't have to struggle to meet her expectations: I mostly felt grownup, not needing her constant attention, especially when I compared myself to one of my girlfriends. On the walk to junior high school I would pick up two girlfriends who lived nearby. We usually met at S's house where I waited while she got ready. As I watched her mother comb her thirteen-year old daughter's hair, this seemed odd to me—I had been doing my own hair for as long as I could remember. Maybe I had to grow up too fast in my large family. S's mother had only two daughters and no husband—very different from my mother's large family.

Mostly, I didn't feel ignored or uncared for, but I'm sure I blocked my troubling feelings and needs. One occasion reminds me that I did act on my feelings—surreptitiously. I was about twelve and we were living in the new house when I went with Mother and Dad to a concert in Charleston to see Phil Spitalni's All Girl Orchestra. This was a big splurge that I am sure my dad had arranged. He may have remembered this orchestra from the radio, perhaps because of the Italian conductor. It was exciting to see all the talented women in lovely evening gowns and hear such beautiful music.

On the drive home I was in the back seat of the car with Mother. This part is not clear, but maybe another couple was with them, the men in the front seat and women in the back. I intentionally moved—lying toward my mother, putting my head on her lap and keeping it there as if I were sleeping. I pretended sleep, stayed put, wanting this closeness with her, and getting up only when we arrived home. Why this reaction? I had been out with my parents, spent time with them at this event. But apparently my need for affection and closeness arose and I had to get it this way. I don't remember displays of affection toward us kids from either of my parents. She probably treated me just like she did the brothers—not showing any special attention because I was a girl.

Another situation with Mother has always troubled me since it reinforced my already strong tendencies to ignore and withhold difficult feelings. I was thirteen. It was evening, dark outside. My mother, three younger brothers, and I were the only ones at home, just sitting around the table talking in our brightly lighted kitchen—not meal time. At the end of the kitchen was a door to the back porch; to the left of that door near the top was a small clear glass window, about two feet by three feet—no curtain. At some point, I saw the face of a man in the window, peering at us. Someone we all knew well, someone in the family—my cousin's new husband (she was around twenty and he, eighteen).

Our eyes met for a moment. I blurted out for all to hear, "I see __ in the window." When they looked up, he was gone.

My mother said, "No, you don't. That can't be." I knew exactly what I had seen but didn't argue, and she didn't go to the porch to look. I don't think she ever told my dad about this. It was part of her nature to think the best of everyone, and in this case, she was close with my cousin and would allow no threat to her niece's happiness in her new marriage. That time I knew what I was feeling: scared, then hurt and shocked that my mother just dismissed what I had seen. But I did not complain, could not tell her.

That wasn't the end of the man's strange behavior. What happened later was frightening and again left me suffering in silence. During the first year of their marriage, he was accused of and maybe charged with rape. Somehow the charge was dropped, perhaps because my cousin's father "pulled some strings." Then he also started turning up in our neighborhood.

There he was again, sitting in his old black Packard parked on our street, three houses from our home. Just sitting there behind the wheel, staring straight ahead. This became a pattern: he showed up at least two or three times a week, but I never knew when or why he might be there. I was scared and dreaded leaving our house anytime I had to walk toward town because it meant going in the direction where he parked. Once out my door and on the sidewalk, I walked fast, never looking in his direction. He never acknowledged me, and since the criminal charge, he had no longer showed up at family gatherings. Why was he there and why couldn't I tell anyone in my family? Didn't my brothers ever see him and wonder about his sneaky behavior? For good reasons, I believed he was there to watch me (the word *stalking* wasn't used back then). Even during their courtship and after the wedding, I had felt his silent, intense staring at me, so I had rarely even talked to him, except for routine family-type hellos. But there's more.

Before the marriage, I had overheard my parents' discussing my cousin's fiancé. Dad said that he knew things about this man and he was "no good." Through his taxi business and meeting many people in the area, my dad said he heard about and saw a lot of bad stuff that people did. This criticism did not sit well with Mother. For many years she had been my cousin's confidante, listening with compassion to her complaints about her father and her feelings and secrets, such as crushes on unavailable men. So my mother knew of how her fiancé was now the love of her life and how thrilled she was with the upcoming wedding. My mother argued (rare for her) with my dad that the "rumors" could not be true and that he must not ruin his niece's chance of happiness by bringing his information to her or her family. She won the argument and Dad kept silent.

I'm sure there were difficult discussions—recriminations and blame—between my parents afterwards, when this man was arrested a second time. That occurred probably in their second year of marriage, after she had their first child and was pregnant with the second. This time the charge of rape resulted in a trial, conviction, and a long sentence to a state prison, where much later he died. I never told my parents about his pattern of sitting in his car on our street. I feared that if my dad knew, he would go after him, maybe even kill him. Once he was gone and I felt a tremendous sense of relief, I still did not tell anyone. These experiences left me even further entrenched as a private person.

While my mother had convinced Dad to let me take the job as theatre cashier, she was not curious about or attuned to what I might be experiencing during my teen years. I hesitate to say this since I felt close to her and we shared activities, especially earlier, when we lived at the apartment. Back then she occasionally took me for the two-block walk to the Valley Bell Dairy Store, where we got strawberry milkshakes.

Now when I say that Mother didn't see me as needing her understanding as I was growing up, I bear some responsibility for that: she never asked me about personal stuff, but I also never volunteered anything about my feelings. Maybe that was just the nature of life in that era. I can only believe that she agreed with Dad's strictness and over-protectiveness with me. Why wouldn't she? I never complained about it to her. The situation, when she dismissed my fear and experience of seeing the man peeping in our window, left me bewildered, even more wary of sharing feelings with her.

More than ever, I continued my pattern of denying my feelings, worrying about others, avoiding conflict. Should I have felt neglected, uncared for? Perhaps, but if I did, those feelings didn't last long. Whether through denial or determination or both, I didn't harbor resentment toward my mother. My character simply didn't allow it. I just carried on with my life, concentrated on the here and now. I must have found solace in my private dream of an independent life, but I did not see this as escape from family.

As I now admit some disappointment in my mother, I also see how I failed her. She was more likely than me to show her feelings in times of stress or worry. From time to time, beside herself, she would run to the bathroom to get a cold, wet washcloth to put on her face, saying, "These hot flashes, I can't stand it, this change of life." Then she would calm down and go back to what she was doing. I don't think she expressed this frustration in front of my brothers, just to me. I kind of knew what she was talking about but not really. Since she rarely showed strong feelings, her response left me somewhat embarrassed. Although I might have been sixteen, seventeen at the time, I don't remember ever saying a comforting word.

Then there was my reaction when she had bursitis in her shoulder. She asked me to rub a pain-relieving ointment on the area. In her bedroom, she removed her blouse, lay on the bed on her stomach, pulled away her bra strap, and I applied the ointment. It seemed strange to be touching her, touching her skin in this way. But I got past the weird feelings, finished, and heard her thanks. Good thing I wasn't planning to be a nurse! Why this squeamishness at touching her? Maybe because I don't recall having much physical contact with our parents—no hugs or goofy playfulness—just a quick kiss from everyone after blowing out birthday candles. Then I tell myself, *Of course, I had this, cuddling, holding, soothing, when I was little, Dad bouncing me on his lap as I had seen him do with all the babies and toddlers that came to visit.*

Another incident comes to mind when Mother was pregnant. I was thirteen and okay with this. I imagine her condition could have been embarrassing for my oldest brother who was in college in our hometown and had a girlfriend. In a weak moment she confided to me that she was upset, at age thirty-seven, to be having another child. This intimate revelation left me speechless. Once again I could offer no words. She likely did not expect anything and probably felt guilty after uttering the thought, maybe even confessed it to the priest.

Several months later, the day before the Fourth of July, we were going to have a picnic—drive to a park or spot where there was a creek and celebrate the holiday with several of our uncles, aunts, and cousins. We kids were excited because picnics were rare in our family. The next morning Mother had all the food prepared (I had probably helped): fried chicken, potato salad, deviled eggs, desserts, and assorted other foods. There would be cartons of ice cream kept frozen with dry ice—fascinating to watch the icy vapors rising from the box.

Then Mother began saying she might not go. I was crushed by this: "You have to go with us." She said that she wasn't feeling well but no explanation. I was disappointed and felt no sympathy for her. We went without her. Three days later, in the middle of the night, July 8, 1949, she gave birth, at home, to my youngest brother, Richard. I had no idea the birth was imminent: she hadn't been able to say the baby was coming any day. Her friend Sarah, a talkative, jolly young woman who had been there for the birth, told me that Mother screamed once or twice, but none of us kids sleeping upstairs heard or woke up, unless the older brothers were aware. Again, no further questions from me.

Even in high school and college, I was still unable to express understanding and compassion for what my mother was going through. Her worry and frustration grew as family problems piled up. The taxi business was failing, money was very tight, Dad had developed diabetes, his abuse of alcohol was getting worse, and my brother Frank's wife was struggling with severe depression.

I saw Mother continue to cope with and manage whatever came her way. She educated herself about Dad's diabetes as well as trying to learn everything she could about alcoholism. Her frustration spilled over when he would not follow his diet, although she prepared healthy foods. It was maddening for her to see him drinking despite the diabetes; after a while she gave up nagging him. From time to time she would tell us kids that alcoholism is a disease.

During this period, when she talked about her worries, maybe I listened, maybe agreed with her, but probably not much more than that. I didn't feel burdened by her worries or compelled to try to fix problems. I tell myself that I showed concern and caring by helping her in any way I could, such as with chores and the younger boys. But it's painful to admit that, amidst all the family troubles, I remained so cool-headed. Or was it cold-hearted? At that time I was good at burying uncomfortable feelings and compartmentalizing my life.

More and more I managed to live in two mostly separate worlds—engaged with family when I was home but also enjoying my individual identity through school, job, friends, and my private dreams. I participated in the family world with enthusiasm not resentment, not thinking myself better than any of them, not ashamed of them but just of our situation. It was natural to be involved with family stuff. I gave my mother home permanents, set her hair in rollers after a shampoo, cut my Aunt Mary's hair, listened to the family gossip. But my own dreams I kept private, not needing to share them with anyone.

Looking back, I know now that Mother was the woman in the family, bearing all the adult responsibilities of that role. I was perhaps a woman-in-process, in-training. We interacted daily and shared some activities together. We got along well—no harsh words or criticisms from her—and I was certainly never argumentative or rebellious. Only once, when I was around twelve, she bordered on accusing me of meeting a boy at the movies; the fact was that I had run into a boy I knew and he sat beside me, but no planning was involved.

Simply from my mother's presence and conduct, I absorbed much of her identity, personality, and character, learning what it means to be a woman. Surprisingly, for her era, her feminine identity was broad and deep. As I moved into adulthood and a professional career, we might look like two very different women, but this would be a superficial perspective. As I was growing up we shared similar personality qualities. We were both even-tempered and more rational than emotional, characteristics that allowed us to have a smooth, steady relationship but also kept us at a certain distance, preventing true intimacy.

In that sense, to some extent, we failed each other. In psychological terms, from an early age, I kept my difficult or painful feelings to myself if, in fact, I even allowed myself to experience them. Mother was better than I at expressing feelings, but neither of us was good at empathy and validating each other. From the culture in that era, the life message was: "Suck it up, carry on, move on, do what you need to do, take care of business." We were both too good at this, much better than even the culture demanded. Ultimately, we received a great deal from each other, and it came about silently, unconsciously, just from our presence together in the daily routines of life.

I now recognize that I gained a certain sense of power and autonomy from my mother. It was not her nature to want to control others, although she could make her preferences known in subtle ways. With me, I think she was so busy with family life that her benign neglect ended up supporting my independence. She never criticized my clothes, appearance, or make-up. She accepted my initiative and ideas on home decoration and activities for the younger brothers. I hated the linoleum flooring in our living room—she let me order a sisal rug I had found in the catalog for a reasonable price. Then when I wanted a headboard for my bed like I saw in magazines, she and Dad took me to Charleston. I remember selecting it, a plain limed oak headboard, cheap, on sale at fifteen dollars. And she too liked nice things, so when china pieces were available for a small price at the A & P store, that's how we got a full set of china. As I was becoming obsessed with social status, I ordered through her book club, Emily Post's bible on etiquette. Knowing everything in this guide seemed crucial to my future life dream.

I also absorbed other qualities from my mother that have lasted a lifetime and brought mixed results: an internal pressure toward submissiveness and passivity and difficulty asserting my needs. Like her, I became adept at assuming too much responsibility without complaint, working harder than others, and being too patient and too willing to find the good in people.

I may have had some influence on Mother too. She was proud, though never boastful, of my achievements in school, having a career, and managing my life. (Late in her life, she began saying openly, "My daughter is exceptional.") Perhaps I was fulfilling some of her private dreams. From time to time she had shared with me personal goals that were thwarted by constraints in her life. I marvel now at the many layers of meaning of one of her stories.

One evening when I was in fourth or fifth grade, she was calling out my spelling words for a test the next day. We were alone at the kitchen table.

"You know, Janie, I loved school too, and I was a good student just like you. But I quit."

"Why did you do that?" It seemed like an ordinary conversation at this point.

"I was finishing the sixth grade and always got good grades. I had a man for a teacher."

"What happened?" She had a serious, sad expression on her face that I didn't understand.

"When he told our class that he would be our teacher again the next year, I told Mommie that I wasn't going back."

"But why?" Somehow this didn't make sense to me.

"He had started looking at me a lot. Really staring at me. I knew it wasn't a good thing. It scared me. So I decided I couldn't go back the next year.

Mommie never asked why. But I'm sorry I quit. I got good grades. I loved to learn. I wanted to be a teacher."

What could I say? I couldn't think of anything, so I'm sure I said nothing. By this time I had forgotten my own first-grade experience of not telling my mother what Mrs. Allen did to me. I had been sick and missed a couple of days of school. We were supposed to be cutting and pasting in a workbook, but I didn't understand, so I walked up to the teacher's desk to ask. She quickly rose and walked me back to my seat, swatting me on the bottom the whole time. I didn't know what I did wrong and felt hurt, treated unfairly, but I didn't tell anyone. I knew that Mrs. Allen, before coming to Montgomery, when she had been Miss Wiseman, had taught my mother back in Adrian. For whatever reason, I did not let anyone in my family know what happened to me.

It looks like the pattern of silence and keeping feelings to yourself had come full circle with Mother and me. Though from different generations we had both overlearned submissiveness, passivity, and managing our feelings privately. Only in her Memoirs did my mother begin to break the pattern. After Dad's death, in several entries, she complained that he would never let her get a driver's license, although as an adolescent, she had driven her brother's car around the farm area. She had also wanted to work the voting polls, but he wouldn't hear of this. And she noted that she was hurt by his occasional words of "putting her in her place," diminishing her abilities. She also admitted in her Memoirs to having "an inferiority complex," being a "loner" from school age on due to her "Italian heritage" and fearing others' saying things to hurt her feelings.

During Mother's twenty-one years as a widow, she fulfilled some of her dreams and became more independent and autonomous. She devoted herself to reading and continued to learn, even keeping lists of the books (with authors) that she completed. She participated in an Italian language class. She kept diaries that spanned nearly thirty years, which became her Memoirs (totaling around one hundred and twenty typed single-spaced pages), an un-expected but treasured legacy to her family. She became a certified Catholic Catechism teacher and loved working with the children. She participated in several church women's organizations and enjoyed the friendships and social events. She managed her anxieties about traveling alone and the unpredict-able conditions of flying.

Many years later when I was a psychotherapist and professor, I was im-pressed by her continuing thoughtfulness and desire to learn. She had seen something on television about men who cross-dress and asked me to explain this behavior. Thankfully, by this point in my life, I was thrilled to have this intimate conversation with her.

Even now as I am approaching the age at which my mother died, I rec-ognize more than ever that I carry much of her soul and character in my be-ing. Yes, maybe I went a little crazy, over-achieving with four degrees and a professional life and wanting to have it all: marriage and a family too. But the story behind my experiences—how they began and turned out—are linked to the personality that I share with my mother. For good and not so good. My personal failures, self-imposed limits, and dissatisfactions often emerge as I struggle between independence and dependence and assertiveness and submissiveness. There's always a price to pay for my automatic worrying about others, assuming too much responsibility, keeping the peace, looking for the best in others, avoiding conflict, and being the rational adult in the room. These characteristics were most dominant in my marriage and with my chil-dren. In my professional life I voiced my opinions while respecting those of others; even so I admit taking on more responsibility and working harder than my colleagues on our joint projects.

My cool head dominated when I left home to make my independent life. I was excited with the new adventure of my dream and somehow couldn't feel my parents' sense of loss and sadness with my leaving. Not that I became dis-tant or lost contact. I just didn't realize the depth of their feelings. For several years on my own and until I was married, knowing finances were very tight, I sent money home, saw this as my duty. But I remained constricted with show-ing my feelings and understanding theirs.

When Dad and Mother in their later years traveled to visit with me and my family and helped with babysitting while I worked on graduate degrees, I hope I made up for some of my earlier neglect. We had many good times together, playing cards and Kismet and watching Dad build us a brick grill in our back yard.

During Mother's years as a widow, when she lived alone, I wish I had done things differently: visited her more often, called her more to express affection, caring, and empathy for her situation. Caught up in my life—marriage, family, and career—I counted too much on my three brothers living nearby to provide love and support. Now I also know how grateful she was to have Aunt Mary, also a widow, as her best friend: she had a car, could drive, and routinely took Mother grocery shopping and to other activities as well.

I did arrange later for my mother to come for three extended visits with me and my family, allowing her to know her grandchildren better. Still, I admit a lifelong difficulty with expressing my deepest feelings and showing affection. Even with those I love dearly, there often remains a distance in me that belies my tender emotions. I am now consciously taking the risk to speak my feelings and allow myself to be vulnerable.

CHAPTER 11

The Box Office

IN THE SUMMER OF 1952, when I started my job, at age fifteen, as cashier at the two theatres in town, movies were the primary entertainment for residents in the area—adults and children alike. The local owners were a major employer for teenagers in the vicinity. I was lucky that the job offer came and even luckier that my dad finally gave in and allowed me to accept it. Beyond my involvement in school, church, and shopping and window shopping with Mother, this job pushed me front and center into the larger community. Given my dad's extreme strictness and vaguely aware of my own naiveté, I worried how I would fare in this new adventure. I felt certain I could do the job well, be a good employee. But would I be accepted by co-workers? Could I keep up my good grades?

The Kayton Theatre sat across from the tan brick Post Office on Fourth Avenue and the Avalon on Third Avenue directly facing the college, West Virginia Tech, across the street and the railroad tracks. At the Avalon the box office adjoined the sidewalk, while at the Kayton the entrance and box office were recessed back about ten feet. Cashiers who occupied these work stations were clearly on display to passersby and customers. Inside the box office we sat on a comfortable elevated stool, and a half saloon-type door separated us from the lobby.

For a small town, Montgomery was fortunate to have two theatres. This meant up to three or four different feature choices in a week, unless a big Hollywood hit might run a week or more; cowboy movies featuring Roy Rogers and Gene Autry along with serials enticed kids for Saturday afternoons. In both theatres, racially segregated seating placed Black customers in the small left section of the auditorium, with whites having the large middle and right sections; there was also an upstairs balcony, and smoking was permitted. A benefit for employees was free attendance at movies for themselves and their family members. My starting wage was twenty-five cents an hour, and I don't recall ever hearing employees complain about pay or work conditions. The 1948 photo below, about four years before my job began, shows employees, including two of my brothers and two cousins, in front of the Kayton.

The work atmosphere was casual and friendly, and we could select shifts according to school schedules. The manager came only at check-out time at closing; this could be a little stressful as he and the cashier reconciled ticket sales with cash received. It was typical for ushers and the ticket taker to hang over the half door occasionally and chat with the cashier.

One afternoon, during the slow time while the feature ran, John, a college student, struck up a conversation with me, his head peering over the door to the box office.

"Do you know why poor families have so many children? he asked.

"No, why is that?" A little shocked at the question, I was interested but wary of him. I obviously came from a large family, and he was probably four or five years older than me.

He continued, "It has a lot to do with hunger. When hunger needs are not met, which happens with poor people, the sexual drive takes over for survival purposes, and people have more sexual activity. And more children."

"Really!" Being shy and not used to any kind of talk about sex, I didn't know what else to say. I figured this information was something he was learning in college, so I didn't encourage more talk.

Sometimes the conversations were just plain gossip, but not initiated by me. On another day an usher I knew from high school was hanging out in the lobby. Standing behind me in the box office, he asked, "Did you hear about Laura S.? She has mono. She'll probably miss a lot of school."

"No, haven't heard that." We both knew Laura as a town girl a year behind us in school.

"Yeah, mono," he said. "It comes from deep kissing. You know, she and Arnie have been going steady for a year."

"That's too bad." I knew Arnie as a young kid from my old neighborhood, now a freshman. I saw Laura and him come to the movies sometimes, sold them tickets.

"You won't believe this. But Arnie makes his sister Judy, she's sixteen, drive him and Laura around while they have sex in the back seat."

Wow! I also knew Judy and was not expecting to hear something like this. Shocked into silence, I couldn't imagine a boy of fourteen and a girl of fifteen behaving this way. So out of the realm of my reality. But later I heard about these two kids again. Funny, how a lot of the conversations at work were about sex. I was beginning to learn about the larger world. Of course, I wasn't even allowed to date. Was there ever such a naive and innocent fifteen-year old girl?

Yes, it was me, the most over-protected girl in my town, maybe in the whole state of West Virginia.

The job, however, brought a new level of independence from my family. At work, I became more of an individual and began to be comfortable chatting with other workers, customers, and people I knew who might be passing by. While this bit of socialization may seem a small thing, for a "quiet" girl like me it made a difference. From initial shock with John's conversation, I learned to enjoy small talk, playfulness, and joking with the other workers— most of whom were males.

By this time, I knew that my life differed from that of other teenage girls: my dad's extreme strictness was intended to keep me away from boys and boys away from me. After asking to go on a date during my freshman year in high school, Dad's harsh lecture and critique of the boy and his family convinced me he would not approve of my dating and would find fault with any boy. So I accepted his view, did not push the issue. I asked and got permission for two prom events and a college dance—with one-time dates not boyfriends. It may be hard to believe, but I did not obsess about my differentness and was not consumed by anger or resentment against my dad. Many other good things in my life made me happy, and I still had my private dream of leaving and being on my own someday.

Here's what I couldn't do:

- no participating in band, didn't even ask (Although my cousin in the same grade joined band and became a majorette, I told myself I had no talent for music anyway.),
- no dating (My high school and later college classmates knew, "Janie doesn't date."),
- no going on vacation with relatives (This was first forbidden when an uncle and aunt asked me go with them to visit her family in Virginia.),
- no walking home from work at 9:30 p.m. alone or with an usher friend (I had to call one of Dad's cabs for the two-minute ride.),
- no overnight senior trip (regardless of where it might be).

Here's what I could do:

* attend basketball and football games with girlfriends,
* participate in school clubs,
* visit occasionally with girlfriends and two girl cousins at their homes (When young I attended a couple of birthday and slumber parties, but no boy-girl parties as a teenager.),
* work at my job as cashier (but never work at or attend Saturday midnight shows).

Now I realize just how cut off I was from typical female teenage pastimes, interests, and leisure activities—all because I accepted Dad's restrictions and was complicit in not testing them. Not having close, regular contacts with girlfriends, I didn't share feelings about boys or clothes or makeup; didn't gush about teen movie, television, or music heartthrobs; didn't buy or trade records; didn't follow the latest dances, learn, or practice them.

In high school gym class, we had sessions to learn slow dances or polka, with teachers demonstrating (mainly to teach boys these social skills?). Initially a few girlfriends and I found this activity silly and talked about forming an "anti-dancing league," but being "good girls" we never protested.

I got some female socialization from my few visits with two teen cousins in Smithers. The older one had country music records (which I didn't care for). Once I went to a skating rink with them and to a Saturday afternoon movie in their town. There my cousin, twelve or thirteen like me, met a "boyfriend" and sat holding hands with him during the movie. I wondered that she could do this while I certainly wouldn't dare. It was at their house not mine that I occasionally saw and read movie and romance magazines. My older cousin tended to share more private stuff, once recounting how she had heard her parents having sex. But no personal talk came from my mouth.

Once I started my job, I had a ready-made excuse for skipping out on these cousins and my girlfriends. I spent my remaining time on school work and activities and home responsibilities. Serious-minded, quiet, dutiful, I remained mostly unaware of what I was missing. A dull, horrible life? Not for me, although again this may seem unbelievable. Honestly, although I thought at times about my differentness, I did not brood about it. For whatever reason, I was okay to live in the here and now and saw the glass half full, not half empty. Just more of my strange personality at work.

I wasn't totally unaware of pop culture of the 1950s. Mother pretty much kept the radio in the kitchen playing all the time and even commented on songs she liked, including some Hank Williams songs. Why not me? Just too private with my feelings? Maybe I was simply born this way.

When a next-door neighbor gave us a small black and white TV set (I was fifteen), I watched some programs along with family: "Tennessee Ernie Ford," "The Today Show," but once a week in the evenings I longed for peace and quiet to watch "Playhouse 90" by myself. Now I realize that being able to see any movie truly expanded my constricted world and kept me from being a total *naïf*. When our next-door Jewish neighbors moved, they gave Mother a bunch of novels. I read and loved them all—very adult content centered on Jewish life and characters.

Along with books, especially novels, the movies gave me a taste of life beyond the confines of my small town. Some captured pure fantasy but others offered slices of real life I could never imagine. From the time I started my job, I usually went to movies alone and liked it that way. Except for horror movies, still today, I could willingly see almost any film and find some enjoyment or value in it.

Despite the constraints on my life, my job in the box office diminished Dad's control of my life (which was probably why he did not want me to have the job in the first place). It afforded unique benefits that I didn't recognize at the time. There I sat—in the glassed-in box office basically on display—meeting and greeting at some point nearly everyone in town. Not a bad gig for a shy, quiet girl.

I grew accustomed to seeing college students pass by, mostly males, since Tech was primarily an engineering school. I waved to people I knew and briefly chatted with customers. I encountered all kinds of people. I recall one Black woman who always dressed in men's clothes, and while I didn't understand this, it didn't bother or offend me. When one of the older cashiers (a senior or college student) got pregnant, she continued working. There was probably gossip among employees, and I may have unconsciously seen her condition as a warning. But I was more shocked on hearing that a close girlfriend ended her engagement to a military cadet because he got his out-of-town partner pregnant and quickly married her. I probably saw a glimmer of truth in Dad's warning, "Men are no damn good."

Whatever I was learning vicariously about the risks of "romantic" relationships I did not talk about this with anyone. In my thinking I became prudish, maybe excessively modest. Although I dressed nicely and in current fashions, I was cautious about flaunting my figure and mindful that girls could get a bad reputation, but thanks to Dad, my reputation was never at risk. Still I felt the need to be extra careful in my behavior, as Shakespeare said, "Caesar's wife must be above suspicion."

My genuinely friendly feelings toward others co-existed with an unconscious wariness of boys and men. People probably saw me as a quiet girl, friendly enough, although some may have seen my reticence as "stuck up." As far as I could tell, my brothers too kept silent about personal worrisome events or feelings, so I didn't feel too different on that count.

Symbolically the box office perfectly captured my reality. The glass enclosure protected me—there to be seen, but off limits for personal engagement. It was no accident that we cashiers were all attractive girls. During the week we wore our usual school clothes, but Sunday was a dress up day, and I recall walking to work for my early afternoon shift in heels and the dress I'd worn to church. I realize now that I enjoyed the attention, the admiring looks, the gazes from men and boys, all while remaining safe and protected just as Dad required.

There he was again. Second day in a row driving by the Kayton. He was definitely slowing down the dusty pickup truck. Yes, slowing down. Just to stare at me? That's what it felt like. Again the next week, appearing about the same time every day when I was working—around four in the afternoon. I began to look forward to this, to him, to new feelings that left me tingling and alive, even while maintaining my demure, no-nonsense workplace demeanor. But I did look up and looked back when I could have averted my eyes and pretended to be busy.

I was twenty, in my last year of college, when the slow drive-by, the gazing, my excitement began and transformed my afternoon shifts. It was our secret. Although I sometimes read for school assignments during slow times, now my eyes studied the street starting around three-thirty.

When my secret admirer kept me enthralled week after week with his penetrating eyes, I must have felt emboldened by my looming entry into adulthood, independence, and the larger world. I cautiously welcomed the tingling warmth bubbling in my body that left me with new feelings, a glow that I hoped others couldn't detect.

Early fall, my last year of college and on schedule to graduate the next May. Still hot, sweltering days like summer. I had somehow become aware that my secret admirer and his parents were new immigrants. The talk was that they owned and operated a construction business. Just talk—no sign or name on his truck. Then I began to see him in church, along with his parents. When I dared to steal glances after mass, the three of them usually hurried away, not part of after-church chatting or back-slapping.

I started wishing I worked every weekday—just so I could see him. What was happening to me? Excited, eying the clock, spying for the muddy, black pick up, worrying that I'd be selling a ticket and miss him. His look, his gaze—electrifying. Didn't feel like a crush—teen stuff, a secret love for an unattainable person, a one-way street of silly emotion. I was twenty years old and had never had a boyfriend. I had enough sense to be shocked by my reaction: enveloped in longing for a man I didn't know. Definitely a man, not a college boy. Definitely older—thirty, maybe even thirty-five.

How could this be? Just driving by slowly, that steady stare lasting only a few seconds, yet I felt his hunger for me. I had seen these looks from men before, but never admitted feeling anything myself. With him I must have stared back. Did he see this? I figured (when I thought logically about this): he's new in town, doesn't know my reputation. I knew the talk about me: interested boys quickly learned—I was pretty but unapproachable, didn't date, was a top student, and had a strict Italian father.

The unspoken message behind Dad's over-protectiveness might have been that no one was good enough for me. What was he thinking: that I was a princess and he would decide what suitor would win my hand in marriage? I had long since decided I wasn't going to challenge him about dating—probably my own streak of pride. I would be in charge of my life someday.

Now I wonder why I didn't rebel against my dad's control. Lots of girls—even Italian girls—with strict fathers found a way: flirted, sneaked around, broke family rules, had boyfriends. But not me. Not even for someone who "turned me on." Or maybe with my strong feelings about this man, I could do things differently. Start by giving a smile when he bought movie tickets for himself and his parents. Find a way to get acquainted, an introduction at church, and then let my dad know. How long did those thoughts last?

Not possible. I had already been formed, stamped, imprinted with a personality incompatible with asserting myself or taking risks. My cool, rational, practical self clicked in. What am I thinking? Is this love? How can it be when I don't even know this man? Is this someone I could marry? I haven't even started my life yet. But suppose I had the nerve, told my dad—maybe I could do that, need to do that. I've never had these feelings before. Suppose we do start to date. Then it would all just fall in place, with me trapped even if I discover he's not right for me. It will be a done deal. Like diving into a swimming pool: once you've dived in you can't "undive." Something's not right. He knows nothing about my world and dreams. And I know nothing about him. If I'm so smart, I should know he'll be just one more person that I'll have to please.

This wasn't the first nor the last time that I would ignore my emotions in favor of a rational or practical choice. I remember that I did speak up once about something during high school, though in a joking manner. At the kitchen table with my parents, I said, "Our family is like a communist dictatorship." No one responded, they just didn't take it seriously, and I never said such a thing again. I was who I was and always would be.

During college, a classmate had told friends he really liked me, but since he never had the courage even to talk to me, I never had the chance to show that I liked him too. More than liked—a full blown crush that went on for several years. So it passed, I survived, and moved on with my life. Shortly before my college graduation, I agreed to have a young man from one of my classes stop at my house one evening to visit and chat. He knew I had no romantic feelings toward him, but his persistence won, and I finally said okay. I introduced him to my parents. No surprise—later my dad told me that he knew the boy's unmarried mother—he was a bastard child. Once again Dad's view of the world dominated and I didn't argue. But I sure got the message.

Despite my compliance, the job as cashier increased my self-confidence and sense of independence. I had a life outside of my family: people at school, co-workers, and townspeople got to know and like me as an individual, while also aware that I belonged to the DiVita family. My so-called two lives became even more separate and private during college in my hometown, but I never became estranged or distant from family: at home I was totally present.

Now I realize that the attention I got in the box office sustained me on an unconscious level. Even if I couldn't date or have a boyfriend, I knew I was desirable, attractive. I felt approval and admiration without the complications of real boyfriends. In a way, on reflection (and revising history?), not a bad tradeoff. In the long run it worked for me: without all the drama of teenage romantic entanglements, I had time and motivation to develop my talents, abilities, and personal dreams and goals.

As I would later learn in my professional life about Erik Erickson's stage of Identity vs. Identity Confusion, I experienced a kind of psychosocial moratorium, put on hold experiments with seeking a mate (a powerful female cultural imperative in the 1950s). My acceptance of Dad's strictness forced me to delay intimate involvements. And being socially immature, inexperienced, and naïve, I now see that I needed that time and space. Even in today's world with all the progress from the feminist movement, many teenage girls still make having a boyfriend their priority and let this goal define their value before discovering their own unique worth and identity.

There it is. Not a brash, adventurous, or angst-ridden teenage life. Just the beginnings of crushes and romantic, passionate feelings. And the willingness to wait and see for that part of life while I concentrated on the big dream: I would leave this place, be on my own someday, make my own decisions, have a career, fall in love, get married, have it all.

With each chapter, this memoir forces me to look at myself as never before, look for the darker puzzle pieces of my different life stages, the ones I kept in the box, never getting placed to make a complete picture. As a full image begins to emerge, can I accept the parts of me hidden away then and now?

CHAPTER 12

Dad and Alcohol

THE CHANGES MUST HAVE STARTED gradually and worsened quickly—a pattern that applied to my dad's drinking and to our town's economy. Looking back, I can now capture this insight, but I hardly registered these changes at the time, certainly did not see their connection, and did not see Dad's drinking as my problem to solve. I was busy living as a high school and college student. All I knew back then was that our family's income was down, Dad's taxi business was in trouble, and his drinking had increased. As far as the town was concerned, Montgomery in the 1950s seemed the same as always.

Of course, the town's and the State's economies had influenced my father's life since his arrival in America—specifically his ability to make a living, early on before marriage and later to support his growing family. Starting around 1914, at age fourteen, he had benefited when the coal industry was booming as part of industrialization; he got a job as a miner, continuing for at least ten years. His next main job, a laborer on road construction work in 1928, came about during a period of development and improvement of West Virginia's transportation system.

Shortly after his marriage in 1928, the Great Depression descended. The coal industry was hard hit and unemployment was rampant. The New Deal of President Roosevelt softened the blow somewhat with public works projects and eventually helped improve working conditions, rights to collective bargaining, and strengthening of unions and workers' benefits. Then the war years, from 1939 to 1945, added to the prosperity of the State's coal industry and the growth in electric power and chemical production.

Our existing family has no information about Dad's employment during the Depression, but he must have held jobs to support the family of six children born in this period. Our parents never told stories about the Depression or how they fared during these hard times. Regarding the taxi and moving business, an elderly neighbor has documented that it was underway in 1942, but it may have been in operation as early as 1940, when Dad moved the family to Montgomery. This time frame clearly would have offered a strong economic environment for establishing a taxi service in the town.

During my childhood and early adolescence, my father's income seemed sufficient to provide for us, although money was always tight. The older brothers had part-time jobs and contributed some of their earnings to Mother, who did the worrying about paying the bills. We had our home, clothes, food, basic furniture but somehow knew not to expect or ask for extras. During this period, I didn't worry about money. Typically, when we needed something like lunch money, we just asked for it; if Dad was not awake yet, Mother said to get it from the front pocket of his pants that hung on the bedpost in our parents' bedroom.

Memories—so strange and mysterious. I have quite a few images of my dad in our new house, the years when I was in junior high school through college. Changes began with his diagnosis of diabetes during my early high school years. But before that, when we lived at the apartment, my memories are few: he was rarely at home to spend time with us as a family. We knew he had to be at the taxi stand running the business, though he was home briefly for daily suppers and for most of Sundays. I remember him sitting on the hassock tuning the big Philco console radio, looking for Jack Benny or Amos and Andy. On another evening he was at the kitchen table having a drink and conversation with an ex-Navy man, one of his cab drivers, I think. A distinct memory at the apartment—I overheard Dad in a private conversation telling an adult male relative to do the right thing about his relationship with a woman he was involved with.

The changes mostly showed up at the new house. I wonder: do I have more memories of Dad there because I was older or because he was home more as the business declined or a combination of both? With the diagnosis of diabetes, he became resentful, a new attitude for him. He hated the restrictions on his diet but faithfully gave himself the insulin injections every morning. At times he and Mother had words about his diet and continued drinking. Still, he seemed to remain our typical Dad in temperament.

One memory now strikes me as a little funny, but at the time I was thinking about social status. The open archway entry to my parents' downstairs bedroom was next to the front door. Dad's habit on waking up was to go directly to the front door in his white jockey shorts and sleeveless undershirt, with hand over the front of his shorts, open the door partway, and bend down quickly picking up the newspaper. Then he got his pants on and proceeded to the kitchen table to read the paper. I was embarrassed by this behavior, perhaps unconsciously thinking: *So lower class—my future husband would never sit at the breakfast table in his undershirt.* At that point Dad was himself, still easy going.

Most of my early memories of Dad and alcohol were pleasant enough, taking place at the blue rectangular Formica and chrome kitchen table, usually at evening time when relatives stopped to visit. Wine or beer had never been part of supper meals at our house or the homes of relatives. Whiskey before and after meals was the beverage of choice. When relatives came by, Dad got the pint of Four Roses from the refrigerator and poured drinks for the uncles and himself, usually mixed with Coke or Seven-up. Drinks were just part of the hospitality, along with snacks like olives and parmesan cheese chunks. The women and children got soda pop, unless one of the younger American aunts asked for an alcoholic drink. These unplanned, informal social events lasted no more than an hour or two, and the drinking was not excessive. No youth or teen was ever allowed to have alcohol. It's possible that after others had left Dad continued to have another drink or two alone. If so, my mother would have worried about that behavior even if she didn't openly criticize it.

Another happy memory—when Dad was having a drink or two at home, he would occasionally break into an old Italian song; we kids didn't understand the words but enjoyed seeing him relaxed enough to try to sing, even if only a few words or one verse.

C'è la luna 'n 'menzu o' mari
mamma mia m'ha' maritari
figghia mia a 'ccu t'ha a dari
mamma mia ce pensa tu.
(And the moon in the middle above the sea
o mother I want to get married
o daughter who do I have to give you to
o mother please take care of this.)

All of Dad's brothers and sisters grew up with their father Francesco's weekend alcohol-fueled rages—the Sunday family visits dominated by his drinking, ranting, pounding the kitchen table, and berating his children. Yet their father's behavior did not seem to cause his adult children any worry about their own use of alcohol. I have no idea whether any of the uncles ever drank excessively in their own homes. But I gradually became aware of my dad's abuse of alcohol.

Mother agonized when he did not follow the recommended diet for diabetes and continued to drink. They sometimes argued, had words, not angry exchanges about this. She had good reason to worry as the many negative effects of excessive alcohol for the diabetic patient were well-known. I don't know if she ever resorted to pouring the whiskey down the sink or hiding it, but for a long time, she expressed her concerns to him and believed she could change him. She also began to mention to us kids what she was learning about alcoholism, namely, that it is a disease. When she said this off and on, I don't think she offered details and I never asked questions. Whether my "no questions" policy was due to my typical reluctance to approach personal family concerns, to being just a kid, or to my unconscious thinking that it was not my problem, I will never know. More changes in Dad's drinking, however, eventually drew me into the problem.

One early December evening around eight p.m., Mother, her face taut and drawn, found me at the dining room table doing homework and said, "I wonder why your dad hasn't come home yet for supper. He should be having a regular meal. I can't imagine why he's not home yet."

"Maybe he's on his way," I said, hearing soft music coming from the radio in the kitchen, but tuning it out, as I looked at my mother. She was over-wrought or else she wouldn't be telling me about this.

"Jane, why don't you call the taxi stand and talk to him, ask when he's coming."

"Okay, I will." And so I did. "He's not there. One of the drivers said he left to go home."

"Go watch out the front door window to see if he comes. I'll get his food on the table."

And so I did. Pulling the curtain aside a bit, and looking out, I could see a light snow falling and accumulating on the street in front of our house. This weather got me worried, but after about five minutes, when he should have arrived, I really got scared. I didn't want to alarm my mother, so I waited. Where could he be? It was a straight shot, five blocks from the taxi stand to our home.

After about ten minutes, I opened the door to get a better look at the street. Although I was freezing after closing the door behind me a little, I stayed a couple of minutes and then spotted the cab with him driving coming down the street. My initial sigh of relief quickly ended—the car was moving so slowly. Had he driven like that all the way home? Then he was edging, ever so slowly, to the right to park in front of our house. A strange thing—he parked the car in front of the house, turned off the motor and headlights, but made no attempt to get out. I quickly went inside and told Mother he was back, but hadn't come in yet. That started her on another round of worry. "What is he thinking? He's going to freeze out there." She was right about that. Dad always wore a suit and tie to work, but I doubt he even owned a topcoat. So we waited.

This became a scene that I witnessed on several occasions. He sometimes remained in the car sleeping for a while and coming in later. I remember see-ing him enter the front door and stagger into the kitchen. I have brief images of him at the kitchen table, food in front of him, falling asleep sitting up, chin on his chest. This picture was greatly different from the kitchen table family gatherings of the past, when uncles and aunts, laughing and talking, congre-gated for drinks and snacks.

With Dad's new pattern, he ate alone and at some point, on leaving the kitchen, would stop in the living room, sit in an upholstered chair, and fall asleep. Waking up later, he eventually made his way the next eight feet into the bedroom. Good thing, our parents' bedroom was not upstairs.

I must explain my brothers' and my reactions when we saw Dad "drunk" at home. I just avoided being around him, got out of the way, but not because I was afraid of him or of some unseemly behavior. When he was in that condition, he was not looking to interact with anyone, probably not even my mother. She put his food on the table and just busied herself in the kitchen as usual or even left the room. He was never angry or critical or wanting to pick a fight. And I don't think Mother confronted him about his drinking when he was clearly intoxicated. That's not to say she never confronted him about it—I'm sure she did. I do remember the words she used to describe his condition to us kids: "soused," "loaded," "stewed." As years passed and his drinking continued and her worry about his health and finances grew, she expressed her feelings more openly in front of us kids.

The thing about Dad was that when he was not drinking, such as the morning after, he reverted to his typical self and usual routine of getting ready for work, interacting with family as if nothing had been amiss the night before. But something was amiss that he could not imagine: he was losing the respect of his family, his authority as a father and husband.

The worst stage in my dad's alcohol abuse came after I left home, with my younger brothers witnessing our father's worst impaired functioning and its toll on the whole family. I heard of one scene that captured a low point. Dad had been gone for three days, without explanation or communication with Mother, although she assumed he was at the local seedy Faymont Hotel, drinking and gambling. When a taxi brought him home, droopy-eyed, black and gray stubble shadowing his face, he staggered into the living room, nearly falling as he approached the dining room, trying to get to the kitchen. My teenage brother, who had let him in the front door, remained standing there. He saw his mother enter the dining room from the kitchen where she had been sweeping the floor. As she approached, he couldn't believe his eyes and ears. She was screaming, "I can't take this anymore." Repeatedly she yelled just these same words, while swinging the broom wildly around in the air in front of her husband, not touching him. Within a minute or two she settled down. Dad, stunned, stopped in his tracks, turned around, stumbled away from her, and aimed himself toward the bedroom to go to sleep.

I never witnessed such a scene—my mother totally out of control—but while still in high school and college, I couldn't escape the facts: Dad was changing, now drinking at the taxi stand where he had freedom to do as he wished. He could keep a bottle in the desk in the back area, although this section was in open view. His drivers and customers likely saw him "under the influence" to varying degrees. He may have been careful to conceal taking a drink in front of them, while also deluding himself into thinking others could not detect his condition. Now I wonder if he also shared a drink with the two or three drivers that he regarded as friends.

The taxi stand at the east end of Third Avenue was the physical location of Dad's business. The cinderblock building, with white stucco on the outside, was small: around twelve by twelve feet inside with an added four-foot back area in full view; it held an old wooden teachers' desk and a tiny toilet room with a door. A dull gray linoleum covered the floor. Customers arrived with packages from shopping and sat on the built-in benches on two opposite sides of the room while awaiting a cab to take them home. Home might be any of the small towns or hollows within a few miles of Montgomery. During the 1940s and early 1950s, many people relied on taxis to get them back and forth to town where all the businesses were located.

As I entered my teens, I remember having strange feelings about the taxi stand. Why would I have gone there? Maybe to get some money from Dad? But not just to say hello as I did occasionally when I was younger. The whole place seemed seedy, dumpy. I felt uncomfortable, as if I didn't belong, but unsure why. Typically, besides my dad, a cab driver might be waiting to pick up the next fare, along with a couple of customers, and possibly one or two men just loitering about. I recall a few times standing in front of the jewelry store across the street from the taxi stand, hesitating to go there. I was self-conscious, maybe because it seemed to belong to the world of men, and I was an outsider.

For a time—not sure how long—a young woman named Beatrice worked at the desk answering the phone. With long, blondish, wavy hair and a slim figure, she was quite pretty. When I came by I must have said hello to her. I recall picking up vague vibes from my mother, some jealousy toward Bea. Maybe because Dad enjoyed joking, "lollygagging," and he carried on like that with his young woman employee.

After the end of the war, economic conditions in town began to shift in ways that impacted the taxi business and later contributed to the decline of the town itself. First, a boom period led to increased production of consumer goods. The auto industry especially took off after having stopped manufacturing cars around 1942, to focus on the war effort. Suddenly, civilian passenger cars became available and car ownership more affordable. People with jobs purchased automobiles on credit and provided their own transportation.[7]

With this development, the need for taxi service in our area naturally declined. For those who could not afford to own a car, many likely had friends or relatives who offered rides to do shopping in town. The only competition for the DiVita Taxi service was located a mile away, Marsico Taxi in Smithers. Both businesses began to see fewer and fewer customers needing taxis.

Then more changes. By mid-century, West Virginia once again experienced an economic decline that impacted towns dependent on the coal industry. Due to increasing mechanization in mining, many small coal operations closed, turning previously thriving communities into ghost towns.

Conditions resembling the very worst times of the Great Depression developed, as 80,000 unemployed miners, with 170,000 dependents, lived a marginal existence. State relief laws had no adequate provisions to help them. . .. During the 1950s, the state's unemployment rate was the highest in the country, at three times the national average. While most of the states' populations boomed, West Virginia suffered a loss of 7.2 percent as thousands fled in search of employment.[8]

The socio-economic changes impacting our hometown and the State certainly contributed to the decline of Dad's taxi business, but I don't know how his increased drinking figured with these changes. Did the loss of customers and decrease in income cause him to drown his worries in liquor? Or was his increased drinking already underway, rendering him less capable to deal with the changes taking place?

In 1950, Montgomery reached its highest population of 3,484 persons. Then came declines and continuing loss in population with each subsequent decade (down 13.9% in 1960, 15.85% in 1960, and losing more than 20% in each of the census reports for the next three decades). With these conditions many of the town's businesses closed. Most recently in 2017, the re-named State college, West Virginia University Institute of Technology, was fully relocated to the city of Beckley, forty-four miles away. The estimated population for Montgomery in 2015, was 1,596, a loss of more than half its residents from the 1950s when I was in high school and college.[9]

Photo (source unknown) posted March 7, 2014 by Bob Bragg
on Facebook site "I Grew up in Montgomery, WV":
https://www.facebook.com/photo.php?fbid=798152633532416
&set=g.223454277701101&type=1&theater&ifg=1

Now I must face my family's financial and living situation after I left home in 1957—what happened to my dad's business, his ability to make a living, and his health and drinking. By my last year in college, in 1957, the taxi business was still in operation but had declined so much that Dad had opened a tiny neighborhood grocery store in the east end of town. My mother or I occasionally helped tend the store if needed, and the younger brothers helped with stocking the groceries. This endeavor may have continued for another year or two.

When my brother Frank moved his family back in 1959, due to Betty's severe depression, he tried to help Dad get the taxi business back on track. He purchased at auction for cheap prices three or four old Packard cars for use as taxis. Then he, Betty, and their five children moved in with my parents the next year, at this point probably contributing significantly more than their share of household expenses. Still Dad was enterprising in trying to add income, though not always succeeding. He once brought in a load of watermelons in the moving truck to sell locally, and for several years in a row he did the same with Christmas trees, relying on his teenage sons to help with these projects.

The taxi and moving business closed around 1960-1961. At that point and for the next several years Dad spent more time at home while also trying to gain income from doing small concrete jobs around town. These included sidewalk repairs, and once even, contracting to build a homeowner a swimming pool. He sometimes took on jobs beyond his ability and resources, forcing my younger brothers to come to his rescue. Still he persevered.

During this period, although I had left home, my younger brothers have documented his continuing abuse of alcohol and their feeling that the family was very poor, with money lacking for necessities like clothes. With my teaching and later graduate school employment, I sent the family money and visited occasionally. Around 1965-1966, Dad was hired as a clerk at the town's State Liquor store, a political job obtained because of being a lifelong Democrat. For Mother, who carried the burden of bill paying, this new regular income seemed a Godsend, although Frank and his family continued to live at our parents' house and contribute financially. Betty had become very dependent on my mother's help, and even when Frank embarked on building a new home in town for his family, she remained reluctant to leave and live in their own home.

Sometime around 1972, a year before Dad's death, he started receiving a monthly check under the Black Lung benefits legislation. As Frank embarked on building his new home, Dad and my younger brothers helped with this project, working on some construction tasks. Brother Ed, who owned a small iron works company in California, also assisted, providing without charge the metal fencing and stair rails for the home. The family as always kept functioning as a team.

As I look back and try to make sense of my father's problem with alcohol, I have some hunches that are informed by my supposed professional understanding of addictions. However, during my years in clinical practice, I mostly avoided clients with alcohol or drug problems, referring them to specialists to address the addiction before I would treat their marital or relationship troubles. Eventually, I was forced to learn more because of addiction in one of my own adult children.

I could speculate to account for my dad's alcoholism, but without getting into any diagnosis or etiology, here I note briefly only his many risk factors. He may have been vulnerable from a genetic point of view, given his father's lifetime of abusing alcohol. Add to this his susceptibility from the childhood trauma experienced at the hand of his abusive, violent father. In addition, my father as the eldest child may have felt overly responsible for the well-being of his mother and siblings. Next, he had to endure the trauma of the deaths of his two children along with the burden to protect his living children. Dad's personality may have added risk as he enjoyed having a good time, maybe to the point of needing the excitement provided by alcohol: he also liked to gamble, didn't worry much about bills, and traveled to the Indianapolis 500 Race several times. Mostly, the good times he enjoyed were positive, with extended family and friends, but not always. His diabetes combined with drinking multiplied his risk and further damaged his physical and mental health. Finally, the environment took a toll as it interacted with the other risk factors. Owning his own business unfortunately offered a place where he was free to drink at will and a place of ongoing stress—keeping drivers, maintaining cabs, and dealing with the costs of doing business, such as auto accidents, and fluctuations in income.

Dad's problem drinking abated somewhat from time to time, yet it never ended. With the onset of high blood pressure, his health continued to deteriorate, although he easily managed to follow the doctor's order to quit smoking. Later, following exploratory surgery, he was diagnosed with pancreatic cancer that had progressed beyond any treatment options. He was approaching his seventy-third birthday when he died from congestive heart failure. No doubt a premature death for this good, decent man. A terrible loss for his family.

I have offered brief hunches about my father's risks for abuse of alcohol, not to explain it away, but to try to make sense of it for myself. It happened, and it affected our family, especially Mother. My brothers and I pretty much denied the painful feelings that his behavior caused for us. And that might have been rational to a degree or simply a rationalization. We may have sensed that his problem could have been much worse, so we just managed the hand we were dealt. Even with all the damage Dad was doing to himself and the agony that his drinking caused Mother, for the most part they handled this serious problem without falling apart, without horrible arguments, without extreme drama or violence. Although his alcoholism caused pain and tension between them, they related to each other in a decent manner. This consistency kept our household stable, likely protected us kids from being overwhelmed, and allowed us to stay on track with school and our own dreams. Most importantly, the nature of Dad's drinking and their steadiness kept us from taking on the self-blame characteristic of many children of alcoholics.

But there were unhealthy effects nonetheless. Besides our tendency to denial and blunted affect, I think both Brothers Frank and Gene themselves had periods of excessive use of alcohol. For myself, my strong tendency to deny the impact of dad's alcohol abuse on my life is just one category of my overall childhood and adult pattern to deny problems in general, withhold feelings, and maintain an excessive sense of privacy. Writing this memoir has unearthed these unhealthy character flaws of mine, along with many others.

CHAPTER 13

Across the Tracks:
College Miracle and Magic

It's 1950. Across the tracks, built against and on the mountain, the football field carved and flattened on the very top, sits West Virginia Institute of Technology, right here in my hometown. My oldest brother Frank attends the college.

One evening Mother and I, a sophomore in high school, took his suggestion to see a play by the Tech Drama Department that dealt with Jesus and his brothers. On leaving the theatre, I was thinking the production had been impressive, so different from high school plays. Then Mother said, "I can't imagine why Frank sent us to this play. It's awful."

Timidly, I attempted a response, but knew what she was thinking, "I thought it was interesting."

"What do you mean? It's blasphemy. That's not what the Church or Bible says about Joseph and Mary."

"Maybe it's just someone's interpretation. Besides it's only a play."

Mother was clearly upset, and she would likely confront Frank, ask what he was thinking. He was probably feeling like a sophisticated college student open to various explanations of the world—even the life of Jesus. Later I became like that.

Do I believe in miracles? Yes, but perhaps "ordinary miracles" might be defined as unknown confluences of the universe, seemingly random events and conditions, that come together and happen to bring a good result for some people. The presence of a state college in my home town: that was an ordinary miracle for my family! And yet another: that my Dad, an immigrant from Sicily at age thirteen, fifth grade education, appreciated the value of college. When he preached for us to get our education, he meant "go to Tech" not just "graduate high school." And that's exactly what we did—my six brothers and me in the middle, the only girl.

In the fall of 1954, it was my turn to register for Tech. Leaving our house, I crossed the street, stopped for the railroad crossing, mindful to walk carefully. Occasionally, there was a wait for a passing train. Scary to stand so close as it moved—at least the engines then were diesels. Until I was eleven, black iron monsters pulled hundreds of open cars teeming with coal. Soot deposits and daily powdering with coal dust drizzled on life in Montgomery. The railroad runs east and west through the middle of town, a mere one and a half square miles of valley hemmed in by a river and mountain of one side and another mountain on the other. Population around 3,000.

Imagine attending college in your hometown—a five-minute hike to campus, no dorm and roommate to adjust to, no fifteen-pound weight gain, no cutting classes. I walked east on Second Avenue to the college library. Excited but a little scared in anticipation (what I felt dozens of times trekking to my classes in the next three years). Since I planned to major in English, Dr. Allison, chair of the department, would be my advisor. I later learned that he had a PhD from Harvard, but the meaning of this took a while to sink in. Dressed in a light blue seersucker suit, white shirt, and gray tie, he had a pleasant appearance: mid-forties, somewhat heavy-set, pale skin, and prematurely gray, nearly white, curly hair. Together we set up my first semester schedule; he treated me with respect.

Proudly wearing my blue and gold freshman "beanie," I headed east, mounted the twelve concrete steps to the first tier on the mountain side, and entered the Student Center to buy books. From there another one hundred concrete steps and a couple of landings up the mountain took me to Old Main, the administration building, to pay fees and to scout the next-door Science Hall, the major classroom building. The rest of our tiny campus on street level: a dorm, a gym, and two blocks west, a print management building. The September 16, 1954, edition of *The Montgomery Herald* reported just over 600 students enrolled that fall, the second highest in Tech's history.

Thus began my life in two different worlds. Home, I was willingly tethered there by familiarity, love, and loyalty, while shrouding my long-standing dream to leave this place and make my own independent life. The other, college, I soon felt like I was hopping a magic carpet for exploring new realms beyond my imagination.

Back home my entrenched sense of privacy kept me from openly sharing my excitement about college. Maybe I talked with Brother Ed, who was a junior at Tech. At that time the family was focused on Brother Frank in the military, two children under three years old, his wife Betty with serious, recurring depression. They often drove back and forth to our home from his North Carolina Air Force base—until he later received a hardship discharge. Then Betty came to live with us as she was expecting their third child, while Frank took a band teaching position over three hundred miles away—the only job available on short notice. He drove back to Montgomery every weekend. Our family saw the crisis and jumped in to care for Betty and the two young children.

Change was no stranger to our household. Growing up with three younger brothers, I was comfortable with the unexpected appearance of babies, so it was normal, even fun, for me to diaper, feed, and play with my two adorable little nieces. Not a burden, just another aspect of home life. My three younger brothers who attended elementary and junior high school had to adjust too. Another change--my dad of the past, loving, good-natured, bouncing relatives' babies on his lap, had become different: resentful about his diabetes and still drinking. Mother, the glue holding the family together, attempted to meet everyone's needs and managed the household. Ed and I mostly studied at the Library where it was quiet, but still tuned into the little brothers' requests for help with homework. He and I also continued our jobs at the town's two movie theatres. At times, I wondered if I was on a collision course trying to negotiate my home life and my college experience.

In my other world at Tech I had finished my first year quite successfully and enrolled in summer school. I was also registered for two courses in the upcoming second summer session at Morris Harvey College in Charleston, having arranged a ride with several older women I had met in classes (no family car in our household). Summer school was essential for my plan to graduate in three years.

A summer public speaking course was my first class with Dr. Allison. (A close cousin my age was to be married on a Saturday class day, but I missed her wedding as school was my priority.) An upcoming assignment, a demonstration speech, left me lost for an idea. The day arrived, I finally had a topic and my props ready: to demonstrate how to apply makeup. Ahead of me one young woman showed how to create a fancy pear dessert. Next, a young man demonstrated constructing and using a telescope (this greatly impressed the professor). When my turn came, I already felt stupid, simple-minded, a frivolous female dealing with a superficial subject. Besides, I barely used any makeup myself. I sensed my professor's bewilderment and disappointment in me.

I don't remember exactly when the headaches began that summer, but the speech course triggered high anxiety. Aspirin brought no relief from the persistent pain. Maybe I saw our family doctor or my mother just decided on her own to give me paregoric. None of us realized that the main ingredient in this over-the-counter medication was opium! It worked, the headaches gone in a few days. After finishing the speech course, I never had such a headache again. But I remained doubtful that I could meet Dr. Allison's high academic standards.

Back home—as always, the good obedient daughter. Although my college experiences enlivened me, I couldn't detach from the worries of family life: Dad's failing taxi business, income down, Mother's constant fretting about bills and Dad's drinking. Betty was still with us, although with family help and support, she was managing her depression. My job as cashier at the movie theatres paid very little, but once I put aside enough money for the next semester's tuition and book expenses, I offered some of what was left to Mother.

The younger brothers had paper routes and grass cutting jobs, and they also contributed. But for whatever reason, I didn't feel overwhelmed by the home situation. I loved my family, was proud of them, didn't look down on them. When there, I was truly there, enjoying them, doing my part. Given my usual positive attitude, maybe I assumed that things would work out. Or perhaps life in my other world gave respite, strengthened me for family life. Maybe I was just cold-hearted.

My second year at Tech, I had two advanced courses with Dr. Allison. First, Comparative Literature. Realizing that high school English classes barely introduced us to great literature, I found this material amazing. We learned the concept of myth—creation, the hero, descent to the underworld. The array of authors expanded my meager perspective: Homer, Virgil, Cervantes, Tolstoy, Dostoevsky, Ibsen, Chekhov.

Dr. Allison lectured as if compelled to convey everything he knew about literature and its meaning for the real world. It was like a feast, me famished and ready to devour every morsel for nourishment, to grow in knowledge of literature and the ways of the world. He mentioned books, not assigned, but I kept a list. After the course ended, during the summer I started reading: *The Brothers Karamazov*, Ibsen's dramas, whatever I could get from the library. How can I explain the excitement, the joy? I read late into the night, woke up in the morning, stayed in bed, and picked up where I left off. Eventually, hunger pangs sent me flying down the stairs for breakfast.

The Survey of English Literature—the variety spoke to me, a first generation, unenlightened Italian-American girl sequestered in Appalachia. A selection from Cardinal Newman's "The Idea of a University" and Swift's "A Modest Proposal" expanded my thinking about argument. Then came readings from Coleridge, Wordsworth, Matthew Arnold. With a Hardy novel and Conrad's *Heart of Darkness,* Dr. Allison lectured about the philosophy, symbolism, and societal context of these works and pushed us, without preaching, to think deeply about the material. He constantly referred to the *intelligentsia,* people who know and think seriously about the world, life, art. The more he talked, the more I wanted to be in this group.

But so much to learn! My happiness in encountering this new life of the mind collided with fear that I wouldn't measure up despite the A's that I earned on essays and tests.

At home things remained the same, problems persisted, occasionally getting better for a while. The usual worries—the business, income, Dad's health and increased drinking, and Mother's distress with his behavior. Frank finished his year of teaching away from home, returned for the summer, then got a new teaching job, this time in Peterstown, West Virginia, just under one hundred miles away. In the fall he and his family moved there to try life on their own.

There was no change in Dad's overprotectiveness of me that had begun in high school, and I didn't contest this, just accepted his strictness and his view of the world. Even in college, I still had to call one of Dad's cabs to take me home after finishing an evening shift at work. Humiliating! But not surprising, my parents, with plenty of serious worries, showed no curiosity about my experiences at college. They trusted their ever-obedient only daughter would not add more burdens.

Back at Tech, besides academic learning, I began to have a bit of a social life and participate in extracurricular activities. I went with classmates to hang out at the College Drug Store in town. I remember being at some football and basketball games but don't recall if I went with friends. I joined a fine arts sorority (no sorority house) and participated in our fund raisers, serving dinners in the dorm cafeteria to the local Lions' Club and other groups. The sorority nominated me for Queen of the Year Book; formal draped head shot photos were taken of the five candidates and submitted to Esquire Magazine, which would make the decision. What a surprise when I got selected! As a sophomore I served on the Student Council, and the next year after taking a reporting course, I joined the yearbook staff. Although I liked certain boys and had an intense crush on a young man who had told others he liked me, he never mustered the courage to talk to me, much less ask me out. Too bad—for him I might even have challenged my dad's strictness. Or not.

My second and third years were enriching beyond belief. I had Dr. Allison for American Literature, Shakespeare's Tragedies, and a second semester of Comparative Literature. Again, he never viewed us as simple-minded undergraduates, aiming instead to capture our minds and souls for the cause of great literature as art and key to unlock eternal meanings of life. Although we students were poor or struggling financially, he warned us about materialism, the need to think beyond economic success, citing favorite quotes from Thoreau: "Things are in the saddle and ride mankind" or "A man is rich in proportion to the number of things which he can afford to let alone." Whether the material was *Huckleberry Finn* or *King Lear*, we soared with him into a realm of ideas that we barely understood. In Introduction to Philosophy he made sure to acquaint us with the masters of both Eastern and Western thought and encouraged our laboring through difficult treatises.

In my last year, a new unexpected aspect of college life. My friend, J, stopped me after class, suggesting we go for coffee at the Student Center. We had been acquainted since the previous semester but by now had become close—she a kindred spirit I sensed, like me fascinated by our literature classes. She was divorced, twenty-four, petite, with short dark brown hair and a bubbly, smiling personality. As we sipped coffee she started pouring out personal stuff.

"Did I ever tell you about my ex-husband? Not a pretty story. I shouldn't have married at nineteen. But I was lost after my mother died. I hated the idea of going back to that fancy women's college in North Carolina. When we met during Christmas break, we were together constantly, then set the wedding date for the end of my second semester. I hadn't cared about school. Now I know he was an escape. I could bypass my grief with Mom's death."

Uncomfortable at first, I sensed this the kind of talk girlfriends do, share deep feelings. Still, I struggled for a response, "It must have been agonizing to divorce with your little ones just two and three years old."

"He made it easy. Before long he was drunk every evening and tried knocking me around a bit. But Daddy told me to 'leave the bastard, move back home.' Now I can really focus on school and I love every minute."

What a surprise to hear such openness about everything—the men she dated, the ones she liked, the ones she laughed about. I was awestruck encountering this new phenomenon, a different kind of woman. Seeing her once in a dress with a low-cut neckline, exposing quite a bit of cleavage, I was shocked, realizing she was comfortable in her skin. Fine for her, just not my style.

On looking back, J. was important in my development. Not that I wanted to be like her, but here was a young woman who had experienced trauma and losses and survived. Unlike me, she knew her feelings, didn't hide them, and trusted me enough to express them. I didn't reciprocate at her level, but I began to open up. I invited her home with me one day for lunch (spaghetti and meatballs, which my mother prepared), and spent an evening overnight at her house, met her kids and dad, and saw another side of her—a loving mother and daughter (her dad too was a drinker). Our relationship loosened me up a bit about life. She was as close as I would come to having a "sister" who shared "girl talk" "life talk" and liked me for who I was.

My last semester brought more exciting learning but also a sense of acceptance from my small world of academia. For two more literature courses, Shakespeare's Comedies and Contemporary American Poetry, I had Dr. Kiley, a PhD from the University of Pittsburgh. He engaged us with humor and his mastery of the material, and he was friendly, often sitting and chatting with us in the Student Center. Dr. Olden, my professor for two years of German and Modern European History, an immigrant from Germany, also genuinely liked students and even invited our class to his and his wife's home for a traditional German dinner. Then I was hired as a summer assistant by the Director of Guidance to administer and grade tests when he was traveling out of town. Finally, my two major English professors had become informal, supportive mentors; they privately mentioned graduate school and encouraged me to seek an advanced degree. My career plan changed: teach for a while and save money for further education. The academic world seemed a welcoming place.

My graduation, May 26, 1957. In three years as I had planned, *magna cum laude*—a surprise to me, ranking number one in the class of eighty-seven. It turned out that on this same date Brother Gene would receive the M.D. degree. I don't remember the exact conversation, but I agreed with or maybe initiated the idea that my parents should travel to Richmond, Virginia, to attend his commencement. Frank and Betty would attend mine. I knew Mother and Dad were proud of me, but probably allowed myself only a moment of sadness that they would not be with me for the event. I don't remember much about the actual ceremony, no photos taken. I think Frank, Betty, and I drove together to campus and back.

What I do remember is afterward: being back home. They and the children must have left right away to go back to Peterstown. Once alone, I noticed that the kitchen linoleum was very dirty, so I decided to scrub and mop it. Wringing out the mop in the dirty water, I was nearly overcome feeling sorry for myself. This alien reaction descended as I remembered where I had been just hours before. My moment of triumph? The feeling didn't last long, I finished the cleaning job, and went on to the next thing—probably making dinner for my younger brothers.

About one week later I ventured again to the Tech campus. I had heard that Dr. Allison was leaving, taking a position at Cedar Crest College in Pennsylvania. Good for him, the type of school he deserved. I had always wondered how someone with his credentials ended up at Tech, figuring it was his only option when he finished his PhD and needed a position to support his wife and four children. I hoped he would be in his office so I could say good-bye and express thanks for all I had learned from him. I was a bit anxious, anticipating his always professional demeanor, not someone especially friendly with students. When working at the Avalon theatre box office on the street across from the college, I occasionally saw him hurriedly heading toward the town shops. He never made eye contact and never spoke. That was fine with me: I understood he was a professor not a friend. Yet, if he had looked my way, I would have smiled or waved.

Standing at his open office door, I asked if he had a minute. I mentioned his leaving and offered good wishes. He explained his new position would be at a women's college with a strong academic reputation. Still in awe of him, I managed a few words of appreciation for his teaching and explained that I hoped to go to graduate school in the future. He may have commented that I had been the best student he had ever taught, something like that. As I shook hands with him across his desk, I remember his exact words: "One piece of advice, Miss DiVita, try to find some joy in your life." And then I left—in a state of shock—that he had said something personal to me, that he had recognized my extreme seriousness about life, and that he cared enough to remind me that I deserved happiness.

Looking back, is it hyperbole to call my college experience a miracle and magic? I was never given to flights of fantasy or dreaminess, but now my heart speaks a deep gratitude: that unique exposure to academia made me who I am and was not simply a finishing touch for my identity. Change a few conditions, and I would be a totally different person.

My life unfolded in a small town in 1950s West Virginia, then and now one of the most exploited and poor areas in the country. Although I benefited from being in a stable but large family with a decent income most of the time, immigrants in that era certainly struggled for status. My brothers and I readily embraced our parents' ambitions for us and education as the rational path to a secure future—no fantasy shortcuts for us.

But on the way to gaining a college degree, a seismic shift in motivation shook my core. A joy in learning and gaining knowledge for its own sake coalesced with my dream of education as the means to leave my home town, have a career, and make a good life. Although always an outstanding student, I was unbelievably innocent, naïve, and socially immature, probably because of my father's extreme over-protectiveness. All of which left me time and motivation to soak up knowledge and ideas. It's unbelievable that I should have had a professor of Dr. Allison's stature at our tiny, pedestrian college, in our provincial town. Not just a teacher but a guide for what it meant to lead an examined life, he fed my nearly insatiable hunger to learn about everything. And the most valuable rewards came from within myself, not the external world. To this day, I get a twinge of excitement, happiness, at the prospect of learning—whether from approaching a novel, poem, article, or the challenges of my own writing.

Although I described my college and home life as two separate worlds, this is oversimplification: the worlds intersected at times, with both bad and good results that I understand now. When I encountered the character Falstaff in Shakespeare's *Henry IV, Part I,* I strongly disliked him, unable to appreciate his complex, amoral, even endearing comedic character. Instead my own unacceptable, unexpressed anger toward my dad's excessive drinking and moral failures elicited disgust. Then again, I abhorred, as Shakespeare intended, the tyrannical father in *The Winter's Tale* (but always aware my dad never approached the cruelty of Leontes, King of Sicilia). Still, like some movie audiences, I practically stood cheering at the play's magical ending, a necessary and fitting come-uppance for the King's unfounded, irrational vindictiveness.

Reflecting further, it was probably good for me to remain connected to my family during college. I was nowhere near ready to be on my own. I was emotionally immature: naïve, innocent, prudish. Living with my family— even with their problems—left me assured of their love, and that security freed me to test the waters of the exciting world of college. Being at home meant I never forgot where I came from, never got "too full of myself." I might have been enamored of the Ivory Tower, but never left the real world behind.

How unhappy was I because of my differentness due to Dad's strictness and my own complicity with the restrictions? Truthfully, I was not miserable, did not brood or think of rebelling. I was just not like that and can't pretend otherwise. Certainly, I've read about other Italian-American over-protected girls, who rebelled, sneaked around, met boys, took risks. Call me cowardly, a wimp, whatever, but I didn't have the protest gene. I just kept my future dream private, close to my heart. I truly believed that "my time would come."

In late 2015, the West Virginia University Board of Governors approved relocating Tech to the larger town of Beckley, about an hour's drive ⁹away.¹⁰ Saddened by this change, I feel deeply the loss of this institution that gave me and others so much. Back in the day, this local college was a readily available and affordable option for ambitious youths from struggling and poor families; they could never have gone away to school or even commuted to a regional campus. Brought up to honor hard-working parents who had survived the depression, we all dreamed modestly: a meaningful education, a decent job, a stable income, a respectable life. Joining the middle class seemed a worthwhile goal, especially in our exploited, poverty-ridden locale.

Young people today continue to grow up with alienation, poverty, discrimination, and all manner of hardships, many much worse than my unique challenges. In fact, *lucky* best describes my life experience—the college miracle and magic being just one example. While the contemporary world can easily overwhelm with its complexity, especially the unknown but pervasive impact of mass and social media, today's young people continue to generate personal dreams and goals. Individual circumstances differ greatly and the world is not a fair place, but their quests persist for a meaningful identity and life. I wish them the joy that I found on my journey.

CHAPTER 14

Leaving Home: Stage One

By age eight I was planning to leave my hometown. My dad, I don't think he really imagined that any of us would ever leave. Although he told us to "get your education," he didn't see our actual departures in the cards.

An early June morning, 1957, sitting around the kitchen table with Mother, Dad, Betty, and Frank. I was telling them about the job offer from the Kanawha County Board of Education to teach at Cedar Grove Junior High School, ten miles from home.

"That's good. You should do that," my dad spoke up immediately.

Mother, jumped in, "That will be just perfect for you."

"Well, I don't know. I'm not sure how I will get back and forth." Living with my parents, teaching in the local area—that was not part of my plan. I was ready to leave my hometown. In fact, I had foolishly imagined getting a teaching job in a private girls' high school, in hopes of avoiding my anxiety about classroom discipline. Silly me, I had even searched the "Pronouncing Gazetteer" section of the dictionary to identify girls' schools in West Virginia and Virginia and sent off a couple of application letters. Of course, nothing came of that effort. Naïve and provincial beyond belief, I realized only much later that alumni of elite schools or private colleges got those teaching positions.

Then Frank spoke up, "You should apply in Peterstown and around that area. I bet you could get a job, live with us. You could help with the kids and save money."

And so I did. His suggestion seemed reasonable, although I hadn't thought of that option as my way of leaving. In fact, I never really had a specific plan, but if I were to live with my oldest brother, Dad could hardly object to this step toward my independence

The first year, I was hired by the junior high school in Narrows, Virginia (population 2,500), a town just six miles from the southeastern West Virginia border community of Peterstown, population 600, where Frank lived and was employed as the band director. This highly rural area was a whole new environment for me. Although Narrows offered typical small-town features, my time there was limited to the school where I taught. What I saw on the drive back and forth included fields of crops and teenage boys driving tractors pulling farm equipment. That rural locale was even more provincial than the town I had left behind.

Once there I arranged to commute with a Peterstown resident who taught in the Narrows elementary school. Mr. Webb personified the perfect elderly gentleman, and we got along well, never at a loss for easy conversation during our commute. He expanded my knowledge of the area and its local flora and fauna. In the spring as I began to comment on blooming trees and bushes, he would name them. He explained that the farmers relied on teenage sons for the family farm operations. We also talked about our classes and students but never much about personal life. He was beginning to think of retirement.

Frank and Betty lived in a nice, fairly new rented house in a small subdivision: oak hardwood floors throughout and a big picture window in the living room. With three bedrooms, I had my own, my three little nieces shared one, and Frank and Betty had the other one. This living situation worked out well—we all got along. I felt close to Betty and helped as needed with the children and household tasks. But in the privacy of my own room in the evenings, I could do school work, read, or continue to expand my learning in hopes of going to graduate school. Of course, I sent money to Mother, as we siblings all did at various times, to help the family back home.

When my teaching year ended, traveling on my first long train ride, I set off to spend the summer in Houston with Brother Gene, wife Peggy, and their ten-month old baby Eva Jo. My goal was to get a summer job, make some money. I got hired by Joske's Department Store to work in the credit department. Since Gene and Peggy lived in a small downtown apartment near Methodist Hospital (He was doing his internship in medicine and she worked part time as a nurse.), I got a ride to work each day with one of them.

The job was an eye opener: my role, along with others on the fifth floor, was answering phone calls from store clerks and fingering through paper credit files to report whether a shopper could charge a given purchase. For the first time in my life, the sting of monotony struck my core and left me feeling demeaned by this mechanical task. But I stayed with the job till the end of summer and gladly returned to live with Frank and Betty and to a new teaching position.

I had taken the job in Narrows since there had been no openings the year before in the Peterstown schools. But when I applied again, I was hired to teach English at Peterstown High School, where Frank directed the senior high school band. That change made sense, was more convenient, and once again I had a ready-made ride for getting to my job.

As the new school year got underway, my usual optimistic mood took over: I was glad to have this position without the former six-mile commute, and I liked my assignment, sophomore English, which seemed a move up from the junior high classes in Narrows. I got along with students and faculty and sensed I was doing a good job. My social life, however, was nearly nonexistent. Virginia Daughterty, an elementary school teacher who grew up in the area, befriended me, and we sometimes ventured in her car to Narrows to see a movie and lament the lack of single men in this rural environment. After my year in Narrows and one double blind date arranged by a young female teacher there, I never had another date while living in Peterstown. So not much change from my college years.

During this period I corresponded with one of my former college professors/mentors, of course much older than me, and kept that contact private by receiving his letters at my school address. I enjoyed exchanging thoughts and experiences with this man—my reactions to teaching and students, books I was reading, my goal for graduate school. His letters offered acceptance, praise, and, yes, probably some warm feelings of affection, but we were both appropriate in our sharing. As with my previous sheltered life in the theatre box office, he was a safe and distant admirer.

My current teaching career had hardly transformed to the exciting life I hoped for, instead the routine remaining much like what I had left behind. I had my "brain work," that is, taught my classes, did lesson plans. graded papers, and then rewarded myself with reading and certain projects that I thought would help my admission to graduate school. I started studying Latin on my own, having learned that this language was recommended for graduate majors in English.

The other part of my life was family, just as before. We all got along. I loved my little nieces and gladly babysat when Frank and Betty went out or did errands. Later that winter, on a Saturday afternoon, we were expecting a weekend visit from Brother Ed and his wife Pat. They were in Montgomery to see our parents and planned to drive to Peterstown and stay overnight with us for a family get-together.

We welcomed the break from our usual routine, and Betty and I prepared food for their arrival. A ham and a pie were baking in the oven, the potato salad ready in the refrigerator. We expected them to arrive in good time before dinner. When they failed to show up, worry set in, but we just kept waiting, puzzled at their delay. It must have been two or three hours before we got word. And I don't remember how we heard—whether Frank finally called our parents or they called us. Ed and Pat had been in an auto accident on the way, having hit black ice, and had to abort the trip. They were okay but had returned to Montgomery to deal with car repairs.

Somehow it was decided that I would go to see them. Frank drove me the forty miles to Hinton, West Virginia, to get the train to Montgomery. The one thing I remember vividly—when I got home I had only a dime with me, which prompted my dad to say so insightfully, "Some people can be so smart they are dumb." The next day, Sunday evening, I took the train back to Hinton, this time Dad making sure I had money in my pocket.

As my second year in Peterstown continued, Betty was pregnant and at six months learned that she was carrying twins. Frank's teaching colleagues and friends hosted a shower that provided much-needed items for two new babies.

She gave birth in February to identical twin boys, healthy and thriving at five pounds each. All seemed to be going well until Betty fell into serious depression and became unable to manage the added responsibilities.

Although her family physician attempted to treat the depression with medications, he recommended inpatient treatment in a private psychiatric hospital in Radford, Virginia, thirty miles away. I believe she was there after the school year ended. I remember going to visit her along with Frank and my parents. The grounds of the old red brick hospital were pleasant enough, landscaped with trees and plants, but inside, the walk down a dreary gray hallway darkened my mood. Seeing Betty in her room, we all gave her a kiss and hug. Then small talk, not much about her treatment. We wanted our visit to be upbeat for her. On the drive back, Frank explained to my parents.

"The doctors believe her problems come from her childhood."

"Damn shame about her family," my dad added. He wanted to say more, but didn't. We all knew that Betty was the twelfth child born to her parents and that her mother got a divorce shortly after giving birth and left the father and siblings to raise this infant.

"How will the doctors help her with her family history? What are they doing to help her get better?" I asked. But no one answered. The conversation ended: mental illness a mystery beyond our understanding. In later years as we met some of Betty's adult siblings, we learned that several of them also had serious mental health conditions.

Before the end of summer, Frank had to move his entire family back to the Montgomery area where our parents could help Betty care for the five children. For a year they lived in a tiny town about a mile away; then the whole crew moved into our parents' home.

The most striking memory during this period and later—we were all dumbfounded by Betty's condition. Frank seemed unable to get clear explanations from doctors about her condition or prognosis, and my parents and I remained uninformed about mental illness. It seemed the medical field was trying some experimental treatments, and I know Betty received some of these. Insulin shock therapy may have been administered at the Radford facility, but she definitely received this treatment after the move to Montgomery, when she was again an inpatient in a small psychiatric hospital in Charleston.

My recollection is that Betty got very little relief from treatment. She complained to me about being unable to concentrate, difficulty remembering, and feeling confused. One medication she was prescribed, Doriden, left her groggy. In that era, this medication and other narcotic type drugs were widely prescribed for a variety of mental disturbances.

Our whole family felt a sense of helplessness but talked very little about her condition. As was our pattern, everyone accepted the reality of her illness, adapted, and helped, each in their individual ways. And Betty always did her share of the housework: vacuuming, doing laundry, and helping with meals.

Much later when I shifted my career to the field of clinical social work, I learned about severe mental illness. Although treatment has evolved today and new psychotropic medications have brought relief for many persons, still 20% to 30% of depressed patients do not improve with these drugs, especially if they have other diagnoses as well. For those patients and their families, the sense of helplessness continues.

With Betty's severe depression and the family's return to Montgomery, life changed for everyone in our household. Frank took a job as manager of a local auto dealership and helped with the declining taxi business. Mother and Dad adapted to houseful of grandchildren, including one-year old twins. My parents slacked off the supervision of my three young brothers at home, struggling to navigate the role of grandparent caregivers while Frank and Betty still held major parental responsibility for their children. A complicated family structure and, no doubt, chaotic at times.

As for me, I needed a new teaching position. Having worked the previous summer in Houston doing a boring job, I applied with the Houston Independent School District, got hired, moved, and continued my pattern of living with an older brother, this time Gene and family. Once again that arrangement allowed me to minimize expenses, give financial support to the family back home, and make leaving home acceptable to my father.

Shifting from life in an isolated rural area to a huge city, I mostly took the changes in stride and looked forward to this new adventure. My teaching assignment was at Deady Junior High School in the middle of the city—back to young junior high students and classes in both social studies and language arts. I certainly benefited from the more diverse environment (there students of Mexican-American descent were called Latino). And extensive cultural events were available. The suburban neighborhood, Gene and Peggy's nice home, and having my own room meant that, once again, I had a comfortable living arrangement. They welcomed me to the family, and I made sure to do my share with the housework and childcare.

I arranged a ride with another teacher at my school who lived in the neighborhood. On the daily commute to our inner-city school, Mr. Fuller, also an English teacher, and I had far-reaching conversations. He came to regard me as somewhat of a confidante as he complained at times about his wife's unpredictable temperament, which he attributed to her being an artist. While this level of intimacy was new for me, I gradually became more comfortable talking about personal topics, even sharing selectively about myself. He was never flirtatious, and we both enjoyed discussing literature, cultural events, and the world.

In Houston, I began to have a bit of a social life. A group of younger teachers in the school included me for group activities—going to an ice-skating rink, having meals at someone's house, seeing movies. I also went to plays alone and seeing for the first time, theatre-in-the-round. At church, I joined the Young Catholics Group, went to a couple of parties, and to an arranged double-date. My date was a school band director, and the four of us drove to Galveston Bay for a Saturday afternoon, my first beach experience. Since I didn't feel attracted to him, I didn't go out with him again.

With this church group, I felt out of place: they were mostly nineteen and twenty and primarily devoted to partying and drinking. Strange that all my life, I had been too young for an interesting life, and now I felt too old, too mature for this crowd. I had one other date, a young man who was a newspaper reporter. He selected a Bridget Bardot movie for us, and I was clearly not sophisticated enough for that fare—another experience of not belonging. We left early and I never saw him again, which was fine with me. My Houston year was rewarding in many ways, mostly cultural, but I continued to wait for my love life to begin.

Although I hadn't planned it, thus far leaving my family had been an incremental process. Happenstance had dictated my choices, but the results turned out lucky for me. I needed a gradual departure, needed my two brothers' emotional support, and needed time to become comfortable with and competent in different environments, break out of my shell of wariness and naiveté about the world. I recall that the first time I heard the word "queer'" it came from a fierce seventh-grade boy on the playground when I was teaching in Houston. Living with my brothers and their families had allowed me to mostly escape homesickness. Then too I had always counted on transportation from family or commuting partners. The first time (only time?) that I drove Gene's car alone to Houston for an appointment, I got lost on a freeway and found my way back only by the grace of God or a guardian angel. Even today I remain spatially challenged with no instinctive sense of direction. Growing up highly over-protected in our isolated, provincial area with small town values left me with a steep climb toward independence, which I probably denied in my typical fashion.

During my first three years of partial leaving, my life had not changed dramatically. I accepted the reciprocal benefits from being surrounded by a ready-made family. Nothing new about that. Feeling a sense of security and belonging, I could not imagine or tune in to the loneliness, the sense of abandonment that my parents must have experienced when I exited their daily lives. I knew of their continuing problems and helped financially, but I mostly assumed that my siblings nearby would look after their welfare. My way of being in the world, often out of touch with my own difficult feelings, left me too rational, too cold-hearted, too self-focused, and mostly unaware of the painful feelings of others. Yet in those days none of us spoke such words as "I love you, I miss you."

CHAPTER 15

Leaving Home: Stage Two

AFTER THREE YEARS OF TEACHING, in three different public-school systems, the most exciting part of my dream became reality. I was admitted for graduate study—the Master of Arts Degree in English at West Virginia University—and given a teaching assistantship. At last, the life that I'd been waiting for. No more baby steps toward independence, no more living with brothers, this was the real deal. And in this place I met someone special!

Everything began to fall into place. After returning from Houston at the end of the school year, I enrolled in graduate classes in the summer session of 1960, and lived in a women's dorm. That was definitely a different experience, especially the often crazy, wild behavior of undergraduate women students. One girl named Gypsy, who lived in my four-person unit, spent time making out in the hall with a boyfriend. I was shocked when he later asked me to go out with him. Older than these typical undergraduates, once again I felt strangely out of place. But it was at the dorm that I met Kay, a fellow West Virginian from Beckley, also a graduate student in English and scheduled to be a teaching assistant. We became roommates starting in the fall semester, renting a third-floor apartment in an older home in Morgantown. Although Kay had a car, she did not want the hassle and cost of parking on campus, so together we made the forty-minute walk every day to and from campus—a healthy pattern years before it became fashionable.

Kay and I were like two peas in a pod. We were both easy going in temperament, frugal to a fault, and entranced with our graduate courses. Like a good sister, she tolerated my messy desk in our office area, which I cleared only at the end of each semester. There was only one bedroom and one double bed. Although I initially volunteered to take the sofa, Kay said no, that we could share the bed. And we did. It was strange for a while as I had always slept alone and had my own bedroom. But it worked out fine. No embarrassment sharing this space as neither of us had any romantic feelings for women or each other or any notions of experimenting. Straight-arrow girls from the 1950s!

We both quickly made friends with several other graduate assistants in English. We enjoyed sharing meals at our places and expanding our tastes— Greek, Iranian, and, of course, I offered Italian. For me these were intoxicating times and all without any alcohol; I don't remember even any beer or wine, but we may have had some. And our group never went out to bars or restaurants. Just a dedicated bunch of graduate students. One of the young men wrote a couple of romantic poems to me, but I was not interested in him. What can I say? I simply would not encourage a man that I was not attracted to. My prim and proper existence continued, and I remained terribly naïve about the world.

Graduate study delivered exactly what I expected. I loved every class, and even appreciated the eccentricities of the professors. There was so much to learn, and the twelve specialized courses that I took gave me the opportunity: Chaucer, Sixteenth Century Literature, Seventeenth Century Literature, Milton, Dramatic Art of Shakespeare, Literary Research, Tragedy, the Romantic Movement, Victorian Prose, two courses in the English novel, and Selected English Authors. Never bored or critical of the program, I just studied hard and earned straight A's. My teaching assignment was "Bonehead English," which included a lot of student athletes. I had to get used to some of their "come-ons" and gazing and thwart attempts to push instructor-student boundaries.

Although I was on my own and following my dream, I remained close to my family. I missed them without really realizing it. I was excited when Mother, traveling from a visit to Baltimore with Ed and Pat, came on the bus to visit me in Morgantown for a day. I made the meals for us and wanted her to see me as competent and happy in my own place. I also looked forward to her letters and hearing about the family life I was missing. And I continued to send money home although my income was very small.

Attending classes, studying, and teaching kept me busy; the year seemed to move on a fast track and I willingly went along for the ride. I took time for church every Sunday. And I dated a couple of nice young men in the fall semester, but without any strong attraction on my part, I did not continue to see them.

In the spring semester of 1961, I began planning for my life when I would receive the Master's Degree in August. I hoped to get a college teaching position at the instructor level and started the process of seeking a job. The primary clearinghouse for these positions was the College Composition and Communication Conference, which met that year in early February in Washington, DC. I decided to attend, got a room in the conference hotel, traveled alone by bus, and took a cab to the Mayflower Hotel, trying not to look overwhelmed at all the luxury. On the first day of meetings, after talking to a young man there also looking for a job, I had lunch with him, although he may have had more in mind, not necessarily honorable intentions. But not to worry, I was nothing if not adept at fending off men. After several interviews and attending sessions, I returned to Morgantown. The rest of the year lay ahead of me: finish the spring semester, enroll in my final summer session courses, and hope for a job offer.

In March, an unexpected turn of events—I did "fall in love" and started a serious relationship. Here's the story of how we met. Kay and I had our furnished third-floor apartment in an older home. Two or three other male students rented the second-floor apartment. One young man was a Hungarian refugee studying engineering at the University (Maybe I had said hello to them once, maybe not.) One day his friend, R. B., was visiting and saw Kay and me entering the house. A week or two later, this unknown man called me for a date assuring me that his Hungarian friend would vouch for him. I agreed. The day and time arrived, and when my blind date was forty minutes late, Kay commiserated with my pacing about and feeling miserable and foolish. Five minutes later, he was at the door, offering the excuse of car trouble for his lateness. I liked his looks and we took off.

"Falling in love" seems an apt description: my experience being more akin to the first love of an eighteen-year old girl than a twenty-three-year-old would-be woman. I was still extremely innocent about men and love. He was a handsome ex-marine, maybe five years older than me and much more worldly-wise; compared to my seriousness about life, his demeanor was casual, light-hearted.

We started dating regularly, weekends only. He didn't attempt to monopolize my time or wow me with frequent phone calls. Little by little we got to know each other better, both feeling an intense attraction and enjoying our time together. He took the lead for dates. We went to movies. We did not go out to dinner. We went to one University dance, Homecoming, I believe. Once or twice I met the roommate with whom he shared an apartment, an engineering student who had a wife and child living in Ohio. R. B. told me about his roommate's local girlfriend, clarifying that their relationship was purely sexual. Although shocked by this arrangement, I probably said nothing.

As we became closer, we shared a little about ourselves, our families, our life goals. Still, I don't recall which field of engineering he was studying, although we talked about our degree programs, but not in depth. I must have told him about my large family since I was so close to them. I recall only that his father had been a coal miner in their small hometown in southcentral West Virginia and that R. B. criticized the coal industry. Was his father still alive, did he have a mother, brothers and sisters? I don't remember hearing of them.

After several months our relationship began to "jell." In love for the first time, I enjoyed the affection between us, my burgeoning sexual feelings, but remained wary as always, holding back against his desire. We began to think we might have a future together. We had barely talked about my Catholic faith and my accepting the Church's position on birth control, which he treated in a lighthearted, joking manner. Being in love seemed the only thing that mattered at the time. In August we were both scheduled to receive our University degrees.

One Saturday evening we were standing in line for a seven-p.m. movie. Even at this hour the midsummer sky was as clear a blue as R. B.'s oxford button-down shirt. I saw a young woman and her husband from my hometown walk by us heading toward the end of the line. From my home church parish, she was newly married and working in Morgantown while her husband was in medical school. Having them see me with my boyfriend filled me with pride. They likely remembered me as "Janie, who was never allowed to date." I said hello and introduced them to R. B. before they joined the end of the line. (A few years later my mother reported that this couple had divorced as soon as the husband had finished medical school and that he had physically abused his young wife.)

While the movie we saw that night has vanished from my memory bank, the rest of our date remains imprinted, stamped, sealed in my psyche. As we headed for the car under the darkened sky, the air still drifted warm in our faces. Arriving in front of my house, we sat close in the parked car, kissing, our bodies melding into embraces; we seemed about ready to say a reluctant goodnight as usual. Then he broke my near trance, moving his body away, his back leaning against the driver's seat door and said, "We should talk." Eager to listen, I wondered at the sudden change: a tightness in his face and his blue eyes darting, blinking.

"I need to tell you something. It's important for you to know," he started, then stopped. Waiting for his next words that didn't come, I remembered an early reaction to him, thinking that this man would fit with my family. I didn't mind that he smoked, my dad and brothers had also been smokers, though several had quit. I had grown used to the smoky odor of his breath masked by spearmint gum.

Then, his head down, not looking at me, "I have to tell you I was married before, but I can explain." My silent shock and disbelief must have been so obvious that he quickly reached for my hand, saying, "Just listen for a minute." As the rest came out in bits and pieces, I first felt my face burning, then my body shiver as if draped in an icy blanket.

"I was stationed in Florida and occasionally dating this woman. It was not serious. But she said I got her pregnant." I kept listening: his face a blur yet I was not crying. He continued before I could even think of saying anything. At that moment I sensed he needed to keep talking, not get sidetracked by my response.

"Here's how it was. I wasn't sure I was the one, but I did the honorable thing, said I would marry her. She was concerned about her reputation. She understood it wouldn't be permanent." Now thoughts flooded my brain but found no way to my voice. This was all wrong, not the way to look at marriage. How could he have been part of that charade? My dad had been right to protect me from all this.

"You see, we didn't really live like a married couple and several months after the baby was born, I was certain we needed to get on with the divorce. That's what we did. It made sense. I was being transferred anyway to a new base." I felt my thinking getting more and more logical and my emotions calming. I would not confront or lay blame on him. But what about the baby left behind? I would not judge him openly but my mind kept churning. Then at that moment a decision came to me, though left unspoken. He was not the man for me to marry; more truthfully, I could not tell my parents that this is the man I would marry.

"I was younger then, didn't know what I was doing. The whole thing was a big mistake," he continued. I knew my decision would not change, but awful feelings screamed for release. Hours ago, I had been happy. Now I felt betrayed. I still loved him but remained confused about his conduct that led to this mistake. In my naïve way of thinking, love and marriage should happen before sex. That was all I had ever heard or imagined.

Our relationship ended somewhat slowly. I cared about him and tried not to speak words that would hurt him. But I was clear on who I was: my decision was the only one possible for me. I attempted to explain, honestly talking about my parents, their Italian values, my place in my family, and that I was still the daughter that needed my parents' approval. He couldn't understand any of this. Who could?

I never told anyone in my family about him. I didn't have Kay to talk to; she had finished her degree in June and moved to Florida. So as usual I carried on without understanding and support from others. I focused on the here and now of my life. I had papers to write for my last two courses and waited anxiously for a call about a teaching position. Finally, it came, a job offer, a two-year appointment as an instructor in the Department of Communications at Western Michigan University in Kalamazoo. I accepted immediately.

R. B. and I had only a couple more weeks in Morgantown before we moved on—he to an engineering position in Texas, me to my new instructor's post in Michigan. We continued to see each other, and he kept trying to keep our options open, asking me several times to go to Texas with him. But I had made my decision. After I accepted the job offer, he teased me saying that I would need a fur-lined girdle to live in Michigan snow country. Graduation came and we went our separate ways; there was no commencement to attend, unless we wanted to return the following June.

It seems we made a clean break. I don't recall talk about keeping in touch; we were both moving, had no addresses or phone numbers to exchange, and made no plan for future contacts. Although I sometimes fantasized talking to him on the phone or writing him a letter, we never had further contact. That whole experience shed light on the kind of person I was. I sensed but could not admit that I was emotionally enmeshed with my family, bound to my parents' standards, and not my own person, despite having tried to leave home for the past four years.

I am not sure exactly when I began applying rational analysis and hindsight to deconstruct our relationship. We probably did have other differences besides in temperament, but they paled in comparison to his prior marriage and divorce. We disagreed about the Catholic Church's position on birth control, which I supported at the time (although I had private misgivings myself about the Church). Then another unspoken concern: he had criticized one of his professors, complaining that students who went in for conferences got the good grades. Later I was taken aback by this attitude since he knew I was, after all, planning to become a college professor. Then too, as our relationship had intensified, he let me know he was "burning his bridges behind him." This meant ending involvement with a local willing female sexual partner who was not a serious love interest. Just like his roommate, I thought! Prudish and naïve, I was shocked by the notion of casual sex. What can I say?

I must have felt that I had achieved a major part of my life dream and thought that my year of living on my own at West Virginia University meant that I could handle an independent life. Although anxious at times, I did what I needed to do, relying on my practical, stick-to-it attitude. After all I had survived being in a love relationship and then ending it. I was still confident and excited about life, yet unbelievably innocent and ignorant about the world, especially about men and love.

My next step was to get to Michigan and start my new life. For the move, Dad and oldest brother Frank went along to help me get settled. Frank had given me an old, barely running Plymouth, so our interstate caravan consisted of two autos driven by the men, me riding with my father. I think we started very early in the morning so they could return after delivering me. I remember getting fast food hamburgers along the way, still a novelty to me, and eating in the car while driving.

Once there, they carried my few boxes to the furnished apartment that I had arranged to rent in a remodeled older home close to the campus. But as we were unloading the car, my father noticed with dismay the two young men entering the other apartment in the house. Frank and Dad didn't linger, needing to get back on the road right away, no stopping for a motel. Saying goodbye with hugs and kisses, I still see my father's face downcast with worry and fear, almost tearful. What risks and dangers awaited his only daughter! Same old Dad. I couldn't empathize with his love and sense of loss in letting me go.

I settled into the rest of my dream: new job, new home, new people. Thrilled to be on the faculty at this university, I was impressed by the size of the campus, the many buildings, and the student enrollment of about 10, 000. My teaching of "communication" courses brought challenges as the stimulus materials for freshman composition were all new to me: communication theories, feedback systems, the Beat writers and poets. I had as much to learn as my students, so I soaked it up, trying not to display my ignorance to colleagues and students.

The faculty in the department were friendly, and social invitations came my way. A group of three or four of us instructors became friends, occasionally meeting at our homes for dinner (my lasagna was a hit). On a few days when a big snow kept me from driving, I even hitchhiked to the campus, a common practice in that time and place. I also participated in the regular routine of going to lunch at the Student Center with faculty colleagues. I felt accepted yet intimidated by my lack of familiarity with the department's teaching materials and philosophy.

While I was impressed by the mostly red brick buildings across campus, one senior faculty colleague labeled the architecture "prison modern." I was also surprised when a linguistics specialist in the department said in a friendly way that my West Virginia accent was among the easiest to detect. And I was not even aware of having the accent! I think my colleagues likely judged me as smart, doing a decent enough job, but also terribly naïve. Nothing new with that assessment. So much to learn.

Within a month or two some unexpected changes took place, causing me to realize that I was on my own, in charge of my life. I answered an ad in the newspaper and moved. The change allowed me to share a small unfurnished apartment with an elementary school teacher. The new place, on the second floor in a large older home closer to campus, reduced my rent substantially. I purchased a cheap brown fabric fold out couch (not a sleeper sofa) for the living room, which would double as my bedroom. Some built-in shelving and small cupboards in that room held my few personal items, and a hallway closet served for hanging my clothes. My roommate's bedroom likewise had little furniture. She was engaged to be married in the following year, so I became acquainted with her fiancé and his family.

The next thing that happened—my car died. Fortunately, the brother of my roommate's fiancé helped me shop for another car. I settled on an old two-toned green Ford, thankfully much smaller than the defunct Plymouth. I took on the new expense of owning and paying for a car, one more step toward independence.

The city seemed perfect for me; with a population of about 100,000, I felt comfortable and able to manage driving without being overwhelmed. I wanted a taste of everything offered. There was an art museum, a civic theatre, a ballet, a symphony, and I went to performances by myself. I also attended university lectures of interest. I even tried an evening of playing basketball with a few other young women faculty, only to quickly learn that I was out of shape and out of my league. I attended the St. Thomas More Catholic Student

Chapel on campus, where I developed a slight crush on a faculty member active in the parish; he ignored me and soon thereafter became engaged to an undergraduate woman involved in the church.

I even had the beginnings of a social life—that is dates. One blind double date, arranged by a young female faculty member in another department, set the four of us driving to a popular steakhouse fifty miles north. The young man was an engineer and nice enough, and I went out with him again, but he couldn't understand my later refusals for dinner together, "Why not? You have to eat anyway," he said. On another occasion I went to dinner with a man in the University's Business College, but didn't care to see him again. Then I had one date with a local newspaper reporter I met while we both served as judges for the ice sculptures in the campus winter festival.

These brief encounters didn't alter my dating pattern: if I wasn't interested in a man, I would not continue to see him. Now I know that I had three equally important standards for being in a dating relationship, First, I had to like the man as a person with qualities and values that I admired. Second, I had to feel attracted to him for an intimate, romantic, love relationship (chemistry). Third, he had to be someone my parents would find acceptable as my husband. This last standard had become clear to me during the breakup with my West Virginia University boyfriend.

After settling into my life in Michigan, I believed I had at last left home and become an independent woman. My teaching duties and other activities kept me busy and well beyond feeling homesick, yet I remained deeply connected with my family. Aware of their financial need, I continued to send checks home, exchanged letters with Mother, and made occasional phone calls. But I didn't really think about their feelings. Were they missing me? I didn't know, didn't ask, and we didn't talk about it. After all they had lots of people in their household, including my younger brothers and Frank and Betty and their children.

Yet at one point I was so impressed with my new city that I had a fantasy that my parents and brothers (not including Frank's family) should move to Kalamazoo, be with me, become one big happy family. I even spent one Saturday afternoon looking at houses! Who wouldn't want to live in such a nice city? Was I missing them or just wanting to rescue them, fix them? I may even have mentioned this crackpot idea to my mother (Her response would have been "No way.") No end to my naiveté! How could I even imagine that my parents, who had spent a lifetime in our hometown, would ever think of moving? I must have thought they should be like me—wanting a new start in life, an adventure.

Now I recognize this fantasy as emotional enmeshment with family of origin. Although I had left and was thriving on my own, I hadn't really disengaged from the deep entanglements with my family. Unconsciously, I was stuck, probably still wanting to elevate their social status.

I would remain closely involved with my family until I wasn't. Fast forward six months into my new life: I met a man, someone I liked, a lot. I wanted to keep seeing him, spend time with him, get to know him. And so I did, and my life with that person is another story, not told here except for a brief synopsis.

His story: How Robert Henley Woody and I met. In early fall 1961, a small photo of me appeared in the *Kalamazoo Gazette* as part of a press release on new faculty hires at Western Michigan University. Bob cut out the picture and, at a lunch several weeks later with his cousin Chuck, showed him the clipping, and said, "I will be dating her by the end of the year." Six months later, as a graduate student at Western in the school psychology program, he spotted me in the Student Center at lunch with my colleagues. After that he was somehow able to get my home phone number and address. One Saturday evening intentionally driving by my house, he spotted me in the upstairs front living room window, sitting on my sofa, looking "forlornly" out into the street. At that point he drove to the University Student Center and called me saying, "You don't know me but you should." He invited me for coffee the next day.

My story: I said yes.

Our dating began and continued in a "whirlwind" manner, especially as we discovered our many shared values: hard work, ambition, and education. In the summer we both enrolled for graduate courses at Michigan State

University and continued to get to know each other. In the fall I resumed my second year of teaching duties at Western, while he became Director of Special Education for St. Joseph County, thirty miles south of Kalamazoo. Early on as we openly talked of our lives, personal histories, and dreams, I told him what I had never told anyone else: my previous love relationship and breakup at West Virginia University.

By the next summer of 1963, when my two-year teaching appointment as instructor had ended, we applied for and were accepted for doctoral programs, his in Counseling Psychology and mine in English, at the University of Michigan and Michigan State University. We chose the latter since we both received teaching assistantships there.

Near the beginning of the fall term, we became engaged and started planning a future together. I lived in a boarding house for women students directly across from the campus, and Bob rented an apartment in East Lansing. We constantly shared with each other about our families and current lives, our teaching responsibilities, and our academic programs and professors. We put in long days working and studying but found time at the end of most days for unwinding at student hang-outs. I read and edited his term papers and became fascinated with his field of psychology; at the same time we talked endlessly about the literature I was studying. From reading one of his textbooks, I wrote a paper applying Freudian analysis to Thomas Hardy's character, Sue Bridehead, in *Jude the Obscure*. We were a couple of nerds in paradise. We exchanged ideas and felt attuned to the world. In November, together we grieved the death of President Kennedy.

Our doctoral studies went smoothly and we moved toward completing requirements. I assisted Bob in learning enough French to pass a written exam since a foreign language was required for his degree; two were required for mine. He completed the PhD in August, 1964, and accepted a position as assistant professor at the State University of New York at Buffalo and moved there. I remained at MSU for my final required coursework and a one-term instructor's appointment in the Department of American Thought and Language. We planned to be married in January, 1965, when I would join him in Buffalo.

I invited Bob to West Virginia to meet my family only after we were officially engaged. At some point my parents may have conveyed concern about our long engagement, but asked no direct questions. Were they worried about his intentions being honorable? Could be. By this time I think they knew I was intent on making my own decisions. I had made my commitment to him, and chose not to share details with my parents until I was sure he would agree to our marriage under the auspices of the Catholic Church.

Bob and I were adults, so we planned and funded our wedding, which would be in East Lansing. Invitations went out in the name of my parents, but only my immediate family would be able to attend. They arrived in good time for the rehearsal dinner on Friday. Brother Frank must have arranged for a large auto from his dealership to drive to Michigan; it had to hold ten people: himself and Betty (my matron of honor and only attendant), Mother and Dad, my twelve-year old brother Richard, who would serve as altar boy, and my nieces Beverly, Cheryl, and Janie, and six-year old twin nephews Fran and Jimmy. I'm sure the ride was crowded, but nothing new for a DiVita crew. I had reserved two rooms for them at the Howard Johnson Hotel, where the rehearsal dinner and wedding reception would take place.

Saturday, January 9, 1965, my wedding day, we were both twenty-eight (the same age as Dad when he wed my sixteen-year old mother.). I was in the St. John's Catholic Student Center next to the University campus, getting ready in the dressing room with Betty and my mother, for our eleven-a.m. ceremony, not a mass. The department store was to deliver my gown directly to the church. It arrived at ten. But it was not my dress! Not even close in style and way too big. A sign? From where? Panic set in but phone calls were made. The right dress would be sent. Then the waiting. Guests—only about fifty—were getting restless. But I didn't fall apart. Then the delivery truck arrived, this time bringing my dress. With my mother's help, I quickly slipped it on, and Dad, in his black tuxedo, and I walked down the aisle at eleven-fifteen.

After the delayed start the celebration went smoothly: the photos, the luncheon reception, the good wishes from family and friends. We opened gifts and then packed them up quickly for our departure, driving non-stop to

Buffalo. After inspection of our trunkful of gifts at the Canadian border, we arrived around midnight at 34 Delsan Court, Bob's apartment. A couple of days later we drove south for a wedding trip through Virginia and on to West Virginia for a party with my DiVita family relatives. The following week Bob went back to teaching at SUNY at Buffalo, and I started my new position as assistant professor of English at Canisius College in the city. Colleague Maria Kisiel and I became the first two women faculty hired at this newly co-educational Jesuit college.

When I first moved to Michigan and started my college teaching job, I thought that I had achieved my childhood dream. And I had accomplished a lot: I had left home and gained the degrees allowing me a career and an independent life in a place I liked. But I had still been waiting for the love and marriage part, the "happily ever after" segment of the dream. And then that part happened too.

Since then I have learned a lot about dreams and, in writing this memoir, much more about my family and myself. Having a childhood dream is only a beginning, an early step that worked out well for me. But living as an adult requires a succession of dreams, continually renewing, revising, and creating completely new hopes and aspirations. Things change, the unexpected happens. Both my parents could have told me that. Like them, I learned that the marriage dream is the most complicated of all.

If I had bypassed my parents' feelings of loss and sadness after I left home, my thoughts and feelings about them began to shift even further after marriage. Just as my mother before me, I began transferring my loyalty and love to my husband and to blending our dreams. Much of that would be normal, supposed to happen. But I wonder if I failed my parents in some way, became too distant, and should have found a better balance. Despite our numerous visits to West Virginia, my typical reticence left me willing to share only certain aspects of my new life with my family of origin.

My husband's career goals became primary but he always honored mine as well. With my marriage, I did a lot more leaving than I bargained for. But for me, leaving a place never caused me sadness or regret, and moving to a new place promised adventure not a burden. I was lucky in feeling at home wherever we landed—much more so than my husband. I chalk up this attitude to learning early on in my family to accept change and get on with whatever daily life required. Maybe leaving and adapting is part of my DNA: my parents and their parents before them left familiar places and found meaning in new homes.

Just a few highlights will suggest the trajectory of our new life course. After Buffalo, we lived a year in London, England, two years in the Washington, DC area, one year in Pittsburgh, two years in Grand Rapids, Michigan, two years in Athens, Ohio. By 1970, when I received the PhD in English from MSU, we also had two children. Two more moves would take place, and I would earn another degree, Master of Social Work, change careers and have a third child, all before we settled down in Omaha in 1975. With every change I was fortunate to find and enjoy enriching experiences I had never imagined.

My life became unbelievably busy and demanding but also exciting. From a "whirlwind" romance and courtship, we moved into a "whirlwind" life. Determined to do everything, we faced roadblocks and bumps along the way. But as we both had learned from our families, we stayed on task, adapted, and worked through difficulties.

But there can be a downside from too much adaptation. Like my mother, I had always been skilled in adjusting and accepting. From writing this memoir and taking an in-depth look at myself, I overused this entrenched character pattern—in my marriage and with my own children. I realize now that I remained too ready to ignore my own feelings, censor my opinions, avoid conflict, and keep the peace, all qualities I absorbed from my mother. As I have become more aware of this archaic lifelong blueprint for relationships, I consciously try now to block the knee-jerk response and choose how and when to express my honest feelings and needs and trust that others will listen and care and not reject me.

CHAPTER 16

My Mother, Myself

MY MOTHER HAS SPOKEN IN her diaries in ways that she never did as I was growing up with her. What should I think of this new mother? Unlike me, she didn't delay writing about her life. Instead, she began at age sixty and continued recording her activities and thoughts for the next two decades. The first time I read her diaries, I didn't detect her full persona. Although I compiled, typed, and printed copies of her writings, giving the title "Memoirs of Josephine Mary Maruca DiVita," I often missed or denied the meaning of her messages, especially when she wrote about me. My first reading found me in my typical professional mode, seeing her scribbled notes as a project to organize, design, and complete. I nearly forgot that here in front of me was my mother, not just papers, speaking from the grave, addressing her children— not to be taken lightly. The project took me four years to complete.

Re-reading her memoirs I bring my curiosity, heart, and mind to uncover the layers of meaning in her words. Those are the same qualities that she dared to express in her writings, revealing her authentic self more openly than she ever did in life with her family. Now I parse her words, try to uncover the meaning of everything she says. Can I be more like her—thoughtful, honest with feelings, insightful? Who knows what I can learn from breaking with my usual pattern of denying feelings, withholding opinions, and overzealously guarding my privacy?

Mother's first diary entry appeared in 1965, a typed train schedule for traveling alone May 10-11, to Houston to visit her son Gene and his family. The station master at the Montgomery depot prepared the itinerary when Brother

Bob explained his mother's fear of traveling, as she said, "simply scared out of my understanding" (p. 21). She subsequently made ongoing entries starting in February, 1970. At the end of that year, Mother and Dad took their first flight, initially visiting Bob and Arlene and me and my family in Grand Rapids, Michigan, and then continuing to Houston to spend Christmas with Gene and Peggy.

It was after Dad's death on January 26, 1973, that Mother began to voice her painful emotions and thoughts. From that date on and until four months later, apparently overwhelmed with grief, she wrote nothing in her diaries, nothing about his death or funeral. She also never wrote about other agonizing events: the divorces of her two oldest sons or her daughter-in-law Betty's death. After Frank's and Gene's remarriages, her writings reflected her contacts with and acceptance of their new wives.

Four months after her husband's death, Mother began to note in several entries her crying or choking back tears on leaving from a visit with one of her adult children. At one point she recounted a long dream in which she felt great anger that surprised her. Since this dream came the night before she was to work the voting polls, she speculated on the meaning: "Perhaps it was that your father still doesn't want me to work at the polls." Finally, she began to express feeling lonely, abandoned, and annoyed with her children's lack of concern for her.

On May 4, 1973, she recorded worry about money and finances and gratitude for the long-awaited arrival of her widow's Black Lung benefit check and noted that her son Gene had sent $100. She continued:

No matter how I cut corners. It seemed like I never had enough money to do me. Philip was paying on my drugstore account, which helped out a lot. But I would not ask anyone else for money to help me out. I felt like they had sense enough, and should realize I wassn't [sic] getting any income at all. Sometime I wonder about children. Oh! I know some of you would say. Well why didn't you ask me. I would have helped. I know the ones that could help and the ones that couldn't. (p. 45)

I had missed the meaning of her thoughts and feelings in this entry when I worked on her Memoirs. She was talking about me here and I didn't realize it. After Dad's death, I didn't think to ask her about money or even about the funeral expenses. Where was my heart and mind back then? Certainly, not with my mother. Was I really that insensitive, uncaring about her new reality? Yes, after the funeral I simply went back to my life and job and family in Athens, Ohio. There was no excuse for my behavior.

The entry continued with even stronger emotions: anger and disgust for her children's heartlessness and abandoning her. The numerous writing errors below reflect her anger and disappointment.

> I know when I was rearing you children. I never once failed to feed clothe and take chare of you. That's how it should have been with you children. Especially for the ones who could afford it. But. . .. .? was afraid o giving me one dollar more than the other one. I never thought there would ever be greed or jealousy among my children towards each other. But there is & not only now. Since your father passed away. But before. But thank God I wont need to ask any more now. And also I don't want to be a burden on none of my children. (p. 45)

I had never registered her disgust in this message or wondered if it referred only to me or to others. I still rack my brain for whether I ever said anything about which brothers were helping her financially or how much. I admit now that I didn't think about her financial need. I admit that I selfishly focused on my life and left her overall welfare to my brothers who lived near her. I was similarly unthinking, insensitive when she directly mentioned finances in the next entry, May 15, 1971: "I went up to the bank to pay on the note. We had borrowed the money to pay the funeral expenses" (p. 46). Although I had typed this information when I worked on her diaries, I never realized that money was borrowed, never considered that I could have and should have asked about, and contributed to, my father's funeral expenses. Again, no excuse for my self-centered behavior.

Throughout her diaries, Mother always expressed heartfelt thanks for cards and gifts from her children, but for several years after Dad's death, when she felt most abandoned, she couldn't help but add: ". . . So my children, while I do appreciate all these gifts, you have given me, how much more meaningful it would be to give me your gift of love and concern and care for me every week or even a phone call every day, from the ones that are close to me . . . " (p. 78). She was right about me on this thought written in December, 1975. By this point, my phone calls to her had probably become limited to holidays and birthdays, possibly even mechanical, obligatory.

Mother became adept at revealing both her happy and difficult life situations, changes in her mood, growing insight into herself, continued learning, and her relationship to God. But in my re-reading, I began to seek out the comments naming me.

Those entries are enlightening. Most are positive—her visits with me and my family, enjoying the activities we did together, and her challenging experience of babysitting four-year old Matthew a couple of times when I was teaching. I am most struck, however, by her off-the-cuff perspectives of my life. I force myself to uncover her deeper meaning and even imagine my defense, something that never happened, never could happen.

Here's one subtle complaint about my life being so busy, maybe self-focused. She had visited with me and my family three months after Matthew was born (one month premature), staying about one week and then traveling on to Texas to visit Gene and his family. From there she went to California, spending time with Ed and his family, and returning to Grand Rapids to visit with me again and with Bob and Arlene who lived there.

At that point on Sunday, February 16, 1975, she wrote that she wasn't feeling to well: "So they [Bob and Arlene] took me back to Jane. This I think should be shared by Jane also, to come and get me, as I came here really to help her. But they haven't mentioned it. And I did not ask them, as they are always so busy" (p. 60). On re-reading this, I must say that this remark hurt my feelings. It's true that my husband and I were busy—we were setting up a small clinical practice during this period, to make a living, while he was on an unpaid sabbatical leave; in addition, he was ill at the time, and I was also caring for six-month-old Matthew and Bobby in first grade and Jennifer in third. Even earlier I had felt that Mother had not shown much concern when I phoned with news of our baby's premature birth and my husband's surgery around the same time.

So with my feelings already raw way back then but unexpressed as always, only now can I admit my hurt. Mother was right, however, that we had a lot of irons in the fire. I doubt now my right to complain even in imagination. When I had a chance in real life, I had never shared with her about my "busy" life, never sought her understanding.

Mother offered a similar comment later that year after we had left Grand Rapids in July and moved for Bob to take a position as Dean for Graduate Studies at the University of Nebraska at Omaha: "My daughter Jane and her family have moved to Omaha, Nebraska. I was hoping they would be coming back to Athens [Ohio]. Perhaps someday they will stop searching for what??" (p. 66). Again, she was on target—we had moved frequently—to wonder what we were searching for. She wouldn't have known much about my married life because I had never explained to her that Bob initiated all our moves to promote his career. If Mother and I could have talked about this, I might have suggested that both she and I had simply followed our husband's plans for life. But having to imagine such a conversation with her simply reveals the strength of my typical pattern of denying feelings and guarding my privacy. As an adult and a professional psychotherapist back then, I should have known better, yet I remained that same child and youth who had been unable to share deep feelings with my mother or anyone else.

Mother and I had never talked further about religion since I had told her and Dad one year after my marriage that Bob and I were going to try the Episcopal Church; however, in her diaries, she subtly conveyed her on-going disappointment about my leaving the Catholic Church. She described in glowing terms her experience going to church together as a family with one of her sons, compared to visits with me, when I dropped her off at the Catholic Church in my neighborhood. With Ed and family in California: "Then off to church we all went. We have all been so happy here. And to go to church together. When we all believe in the same way. And accept the same religious facts" (p. 33). And on a later occasion: "It was so good to go and worship, and to have my Son, and all his family with me, meant so much to me" (p. 53). But a different story with me in Omaha: "I've been most happy to go here, but it isn't at all like home. I doubt if I ever could have the same feeling here. That we all have at home. I pray one day we can all be together in one church and worship our only God in His way of love faith and His way of life" (p. 117).

Why didn't I talk with Mother, during her visits, about my views on religion when she was alive and right in front of me? Probably because I couldn't reveal that my own confused thoughts and feelings about religion involved my marriage. I was disappointed that my husband and I didn't see organized religion the same way and avoided serious discussion of our differences. He criticized the couple of Protestant churches that we tried whereas I was satisfied. We quit attending, and I didn't assert or follow through on my preferences. I was likely so intent on keeping peace in the family that I didn't allow my opinions to reach my conscious mind.

So once again I saw my mother offering a subtle critique of me in her Memoirs. She had moved past the reticence she often displayed as I was growing up. But even as an adult and a psychotherapist who helped clients speak their feelings, when I should have shared more of myself with her, I remained stuck: withholding feelings, avoiding conflict, and maintaining an excessive sense of privacy.

If I could tell her my views today on religion and spirituality, I would honestly say I believe in God, believe in Christianity as embodying larger truths of the universe beyond our knowledge, and believe myself connected spiritually with God's intentions for humanity. In other words, I could respectfully let her know I am a good person without the Catholic Church.

My mother's Memoirs contain so much more than the few items highlighted here. Her amazing legacy reflects a whole person, an authentic person, a woman of substance, courage, and compassion. Her story captured her love for and pride in her husband, children, and grandchildren, even as she occasionally chided them for their shortcomings. Once she got past the initial shock of her husband's death, she wrote as eloquently as any memoirist in describing her loneliness.

> Mothers Day, May 13, 1973 "I have had many precious Mother Days year in and year out. But this is the first one, I had to spend alone. How I miss not sharing my day with my husband who made it possible for me to be a mother of all our fine children. Every card I have received this year, I have cried over it. (p. 46)
>
> Dec. 19, 1975 . . . I want anything around me, to remind me of him. As I miss him so much. My heart still aches for him more so since the Thanksgiving Holidays started. As any holiday was a big thing for him. Of course there were times when I didn't go along with the way he would celebrate [drinking too much]. But that was his way. And I knew I couldn't do anything about it. . . . So I cry for a while. And then choke back the tears, and pray for the courage I will need for the future and to live alone. (p. 70)

Mother's final entries in her diaries reflected her strong faith in God and her courage as she faced increasing health problems. For entries in 1990, 1991, and 1992, she used a cloth covered *Daily Prayer Journal: Promises, Prayers, Praises.* Most of the pages were blank, but when she did make an entry, she filled in the year and the date and offered thoughts for the bold-printed headings: "January 1 Monday 1990: **Praise.** God for the gift of life this day. **Prayers.** Heavenly Father I thank you, for letting me awaken to a new day this morning in the first day, of the New Year- Bless all my children and their families Amen" (p.132). The next two years of entries were similar, praising God and giving thanks for the friends, children, and grandchildren who came to visit her. In the final entry, May 2, 1993, she described with love and appreciation the fun and success of the eighty-first birthday party given by her West Virginia sons, along with details of friends, family, and food served: "That was a day of joy peace & laughter from all us" (p. 136).

In the following year, 1994, she suffered two strokes, the second one leaving her in a wheelchair, living in the nursing home in Montgomery. I came after the first mild stroke and stayed with her about one week, and came again when she was living in the nursing home. She had lost the ability for expressive speech, her words coming out garbled, while her mental capacity and understanding remained intact. Still, when I was with her, she was able to say clearly to every caregiver providing a service: "Thank you, honey." She died from another stroke on Good Friday, April 1, 1994, one month before her eighty-second birthday.

The mother who wrote her diaries was a much different person from the mother I experienced as a child and youth. Being a widow and keeping her writing secret from family until after her death freed her to speak true thoughts and feelings that she had often censored—to keep peace in the family. I understand that, as I too have spent a lifetime barricading my personal concerns and feelings to avoid conflict with others. Maybe I am not so different from her after all. Now in my own memoir I am trying to tell the truth of my history and openly speak my discoveries. I am trying to be more like her: feel my heart stir and struggle and yet admit the fear pounding against my ribs. Can I, who grew up cool, rational, ever doing mental gymnastics, claim my emotional life and not flee?

I want to feel my mother living in me. She who became a whole person as she secretly left messages for her children to find after her death. I want to feel her living in me. Not just in some theoretical way of having influenced development of my personality and character. She will live in me if, as I struggle between speaking my truth and stifling my soul, I dare to declare myself and trust that I will not hurt or destroy anyone or be hurt or destroyed.

I could start by talking with my husband and my adult children about religion and spirituality or other personal topics. She is living in me as I write and share my memoir now, not after my death. She is living in me as I risk changing every day: trying to express feelings of love and appreciation for others, share worrisome news with family who need to know, and let others into my previously highly protected private world.

Many entries in my mother's Memoirs capture the inevitable struggle and pain that follow when adult children move into their independent lives and, in some ways, leave parents behind. She herself left her family in Adrian to marry my father and gradually accepted the sadness at being so removed from them and unable to visit. She came to realize that her married life, her husband's business, her large family, her endless responsibilities did not allow for regular contacts. Yet she and her sisters exchanged letters, and her siblings and their adult children occasionally visited our family, and at least once she had her father come for an extended visit. She did the best she could to stay connected.

My parents probably didn't recognize that their children had, in fact, stayed close for extra years, because of attending college in our hometown. Three sons, Richard, Phil, and Frank remained permanently living in nearby West Virginia communities. Yet, even these close connections did not remove the sense of loss when others of us moved to distant states—Gene, Ed, Bob, and myself.

It's true that my mother's feelings of abandonment peaked after Dad's death and decreased in later years. In most entries her complaints referred to all her children, not typically naming names. But on closer reading, I recognize that my own distance and insensitivity deserved her anger and puzzlement.

Highlighting here my mother's few expressions of painful, difficult feelings in her diaries must not overshadow the other 95% of her entries that are overwhelming in their variety. She rendered honest, interesting accounts of her daily activities, describing with equal care and enthusiasm, travel, home-making tasks, meals, gatherings, conversations, and parties. She conveyed deep feelings of love and caring for her extended family members, friends, and neighbors. She constantly expressed gratitude for the blessings in her life, considered her heart and mind, and admitted her own faults and shortcomings—even asked her children's forgiveness for any mistakes she made as a mother. She presented for all to see a woman with spirit whose zest for life endured despite ongoing hardships and serious health problems. And always, every page brimmed with her sincere faith in God.

Most families probably muddle through the stage of life when adult children depart. Both generations likely experience some hurt feelings, but eventually find a decent balance. The younger generation establishes the right sense of boundaries between new families of creation and the aging parents who reared them, love them, and want to share in their lives.

Yet some of us struggle with finding the balance. My personality accentuated my sense of loyalty to my husband and my preoccupation with the demands of my career. Still, I don't think I totally failed my parents, but my periods of insensitivity and distancing happened. Now as I have faced that same struggle with my own adult children in their independent lives, I know the sense of loss and loneliness and longing for more closeness. I am learning from my mother to share, in the here and now, with my children more of myself, my current life, my feelings. My new openness seems to bring the closeness that I cherish.

Writing my story and re-reading Mother's diaries have helped me see my parents as real people. They had their faults and fears, but they were still good people, better than just good—amazing in strength and perseverance. I know them more fully and feel them alive in me now more than I ever did when I was growing up. And I recognize that I am just like them, a human being with my share of flaws and failures.

But what about my father? He remains somewhat a mystery. During my teenage years, our relationship was often about avoidance and silence. Never understanding him, his drinking, or his strictness, yet even then I sensed that his deep love for me was behind all his worry and protection. If only he could have shared more of his life with us when he was alive. If only I could have asked for this. As it turned out, and I feel this to be my truth: his unique way of taking care of me made me a lucky girl.

He left no diaries, no writings to explain more about what made him tick. Still, wondering and speculating, I wish that I could hear his voice again. My ever-practical rational self says that is just a fantasy. But at least in my writing here I have thought about him, had dreams about him, and allowed him into my consciousness, my heart, and my soul. So I have done that much.

CHAPTER 17

Hello, Daughter

HELLO, DAUGHTER. ONLY DAUGHTER, THAT is. As they say on earth, a rose among thorns (six brothers, but not thorns at all). Maybe you'll get this, maybe not. Nothing is assured. We don't know and don't ask how things work here. Sometimes, a human thought or moment of consciousness springs up out there, a kind of ping, and sometimes it touches a soul (for want of a better word) here (and don't ask me what "here" is).

For an infinitesimal moment your human need converged. And from my being, there seemed to flow a capacity to connect. How long this capacity lasts I don't know, but I don't think time is a concern here. Neither is language for that matter or language for communicating between our different universes. Here we don't attempt to explain, leaving that preoccupation to human beings on earth. But it does tickle me that I, an immigrant child who came to America from Sicily, can somehow speak from the grave (but not really there) in the highly educated English that you use.

A very human impulse on your part, wanting to know me, your human father, on a deeper level. A wish tinged with so many mixed emotions, and always that human fascination with explaining things. You ended up with a big dose of that, especially drawn to theories of human behavior, motivation, character, and personality. None of which I knew about when I was on earth, having only my fifth-grade education from Sicily. But for this moment and whatever reason, I can retrieve who I was and how I lived my time on earth, not that there is really any need for these insights now. In fact, there are no needs here—just perfect harmony and unity. How about that language!

220

I will try to keep this brief but who I was and became goes back quite away. As you know, my father first traveled to America in April, 1910, ending up in West Virginia to work in the coal mines. Then he returned to Sicily in 1912, and back to America that same year. During that visit back home, he arranged for our family to immigrate the following year.

Maybe telling you about our trip will help you know a little more about me. We traveled with my mother Filippa, age thirty-four—me, Liborio, the oldest at thirteen, and the younger children, Tony, Joe, and Mary. We left from Palermo on December 5, 1913, on the SS America, the middle of winter, and arrived in the port of New York on December 19.

Of course, we traveled in steerage. What an experience! I saw things not fit for my young boy's eyes or my mother's. The ship workers regarded all of us as the scum of the earth, hardly human. At sea for two weeks, I constantly watched over my mother, yet men, scoundrels, approached trying to lure her to take a walk with them. I could only huddle close, my arms surrounding her and the little ones, yelling in Italian to get out, leave. After a few days, they stopped coming.

We knew we were decent people, a family with a father waiting, but the trip left me with a great sense of inferiority and fear of facing a continuing hostile world. When we landed in America we stayed for several weeks in a boarding house in Brooklyn where our father had lived briefly, with Italian friends, the Savitierres, before he moved on to settle in West Virginia. There for several months I saw lots of turmoil, trouble, danger for immigrants, just like on the ship. Though I was frightened, I tried to protect our family. I took on these worries but kept up hope for a good life in my new home.

You wonder why I was so overprotective with our kids and especially you. That trip was the beginning. I saw the world as a threat to my family. And I must have felt that I had to prove myself as I went on to become a man and father. After working in the coal mines for a while as a teenager, then as an adult I got a job on road construction, met and married your mother, and later started the taxi business. Your mother and I, we were full of hopes and dreams when we joined our lives. We were happy as our babies came along. I was proud that I could support my family.

Then came the terrible tragedies—losing not one but two of our innocent little boys, within a period of five years, the second one just a five-month old infant. You were only three years old then. It felt like our lives and all our dreams died with them. Your mother would take care of you kids, get you fed and bedded down, but still many months later, when I got home she would break into tears. So we just held each other until we felt strong enough to face the next day.

A terrible fear consumed me: losing another one of our children. I was determined not to let that happen and tried to keep anything dangerous away from all of you kids. Maybe as an adult you figured out this was the reason for no bikes, no swimming, no venturing too far from home. And for you, my beautiful daughter, I had to protect you from the worse dangers that girls faced. I couldn't forget the men making indecent overtures toward my dear mother. Then day in, day out, at the taxi stand, what I heard about people! All the bad stuff, who was having affairs, the way they joked about women and girls, the names they called them. It was awful. You recall when I said once, half joking, but dead serious, "Men are no damn good!"

So, yes, I was very over-protective and strict with you. You didn't understand at the time and still wonder why. And maybe I did go overboard a bit. I wish I could have explained more to you. But back then parents and children didn't have "heart-to-heart" talks. And I had too much male pride to think I should have to explain to you, a mere child.

Maybe we could have talked more honestly if we both could have broken free of our prideful privacy shrouds. Except that I lost much of my "better self" as I moved into a period of really failing my family. That is, my alcoholism.

That too you wonder about and want answers. Like humans I can muster up a bunch of reasons. Excuses really. I can say that drinking was something I saw all my life in my family and our small town. I should have seen from my father, when he was drinking, how he raged and berated and hurt his family. But drinking then was just what men did, not women, a way to enjoy visits and good times with family and friends. I should have learned a lesson when I was in that terrible cab accident and nearly died. But I didn't and can't explain why. I just thank God that I was never angry or mean to my family when I was under the influence.

Later my drinking was not social. I gradually lost my usual good sense. Maybe the liquor drowned out some of my sadness at losing our children, kept me from feeling weak and helpless. I think I had always thought it was okay to take a drink or two while I put in the long hours at the taxi business. I had to be there all the time or the drivers would steal the fares.

Then something happened that I didn't count on: the business was declining. After the war, fewer people needed cabs once they could buy a car on credit. With that turn of events, it was an easy step to drink to forget that my income was dwindling, that I was failing my family. I gave up my good sense to alcohol and took a coward's way out. Never wanting to show any weakness as a man, I succumbed to another weakness: allowed alcohol to consume my life. Only much later, forced by illness, did I gain occasional control of my addiction.

There I've said it. But with your knowledge of human behavior, you probably were close to figuring this out for yourself. I wish I could have been smart enough, like you, to figure out what was happening to me back then. Or to have actually listened to and talked with your mother about my drinking. But lacking good sense and full of pride, I couldn't make that happen.

Later you and I did have some good and sober times together, but not nearly enough, after you married and had your young family. Your mother and I came and spent several months at a time with you in two different locations. We enjoyed being a part of your family—helping and playing with the kids while you worked on your dissertation, having meals together, building the grill for your backyard, talking about our country's struggles in the sixties, and playing cards in the evenings for fun. I felt close to you then and believed I had a part in helping you reach your educational goals and achieve a good life.

From then until now (there's that time thing again), you probably have experienced even more the turmoil that comes with life on earth. We do the best we can but it is never enough. It saddens me to know that that one of your children has also suffered from addiction. So many human ways to fail, no escape from the pain of living, but I wouldn't trade it for the world.

I took a chance to connect with you, to respond to your wish for deeper understanding of your father. It is ironic (to use one of your literary words) that I should be part of this phenomenon. You will remember that in the old days when the talk turned to death and the hereafter, I used to say, jokingly, "Well, no one ever came back to tell us." But a smarter man, a genius really, has offered hope: "There are more things in heaven and earth, Horatio, than are dreamt of in your philosophy." Will you open your heart to infinite possibility? A dream? A vision? A momentary surrender of human consciousness? To know and feel that my love is eternal!

NOTES

1. https://www.thoughtco.com/geologic-maps-of-the-united-states-4122863
2. http://www.wvencyclopedia.org/articles/924
3. http://www.coalage.com/features/2284-100-years-with-coal-age.html?showall=&start=2
4. https://en.wikipedia.org/wiki/Nylon_riots
5. http://www.midlandtrail.com/MidlandTrail/media/Midland-Media/Documents/5h-montgomery-gauley-bridge-1.pdf
6. https://en.wikipedia.org/wiki/Hawks_Nest_Tunnel_disaster
7. https://en.wikipedia.org/wiki/1950s_American_automobile_culture
8. http://www.voyagesphotosmanu.com/economic_problems_west_virginia.htm
9. https://en.wikipedia.org/wiki/Montgomery,_West_Virginia
10. http://wvutoday.wvu.edu/n/2015/09/01/wvu-beckley-will-become-home-to-wvu-tech-in-2017-wvu-board-decides

Made in the USA
Lexington, KY
04 January 2018